Christine Lötscher, Petra Schrackmann,
Ingrid Tomkowiak, Aleta-Amirée von Holzen (Eds.)

Transitions and Dissolving Boundaries
in the Fantastic

Fantastikforschung
Research in the Fantastic

Band/Volume 2

Transitions and Dissolving Boundaries in the Fantastic

edited by

Christine Lötscher, Petra Schrackmann,
Ingrid Tomkowiak, Aleta-Amirée von Holzen

LIT

Cover Illustration: Silvan Luzzi

Supported by Swiss National Science Foundation
and University of Zurich

This book is printed on acid-free paper.

Bibliographic information published by the Deutsche Nationalbibliothek
The Deutsche Nationalbibliothek lists this publication in the Deutsche
Nationalbibliografie; detailed bibliographic data are available in the Internet at
http://dnb.d-nb.de.

ISBN 978-3-643-80185-2

A catalogue record for this book is available from the British Library

©LIT VERLAG GmbH & Co. KG Wien, LIT VERLAG Dr. W. Hopf
Zweigniederlassung Zürich 2014   Berlin 2014
Klosbachstr. 107   Fresnostr. 2
CH-8032 Zürich   D-48159 Münster
Tel. +41 (0) 44-251 75 05   Tel. +49 (0) 2 51-62 03 20
Fax +41 (0) 44-251 75 06   Fax +49 (0) 2 51-23 19 72
E-Mail: zuerich@lit-verlag.ch   E-Mail: lit@lit-verlag.de
http://www.lit-verlag.ch   http://www.lit-verlag.de

Distribution:

In the UK: Global Book Marketing, e-mail: mo@centralbooks.com
In North America: International Specialized Book Services, e-mail: orders@isbs.com
In Germany: LIT Verlag Fresnostr. 2, D-48159 Münster
Tel. +49 (0) 2 51-620 32 22, Fax +49 (0) 2 51-922 60 99, E-mail: vertrieb@lit-verlag.de

In Austria: Medienlogistik Pichler-ÖBZ, e-mail: mlo@medien-logistik.at
e-books are available at www.litwebshop.de

Contents

Preface ... 1

TRANSITION

Leonardo da Vinci and Fantastic Animals: Free Assembly of Shapes ... 5
Sara Taglialagamba

The Threshold. An Iconological Analysis ... 19
Amos Bianchi and Gabriela Galati

Charles Nodier's Fantastic World in *Inès de Las Sierras* ... 29
Graciela Boruszko

The Alchemical Imaginary of Homunculi in *Fullmetal Alchemist* ... 41
Minwen Huang

Metaphorical and Metonymical Meaning in *The Lord of the Rings* ... 53
Thomas Kullmann

The Zone: Ontological or Epistemological Operator? ... 63
Maria-Ana Tupan

TRANSGRESSION

Hybridity as the Source of the Monstrous in Three Short Stories by H. P. Lovecraft ... 77
Alesya Raskuratova

Grotesque Desire: The Early Horror Films of David Cronenberg and the Limits of Morality ... 89
Daniel Illger

Modern-Day Superheroes: Transgressions of Genre and Morality in *Misfits* ... 99
Dana Frei and Lars Schmeink

"Love is a Psychopath": The Postmodern *Doppelgänger* in Steven
Moffat's *Jekyll* 125
Inken Frost

TRANSFORMING NARRATIVE

Good Fences Make Good Neighbours? On the Dialectics of Genre
Formation and Hybridization in Contemporary Fantasy Fiction 141
Dieter Petzold

Parody Upon Parody Upon Parody: Narrative Myth and Mythic Narration
in the American Metafiction of the 1960s 155
Michael Heitkemper-Yates

Deconstructing Dracula: The Vampire as Semiotic Body in Stephenie
Meyer's *Twilight* 167
Nils Jablonski

Life Writing Projects in Posthuman Science Fiction 179
Sarah Herbe

The Omega Legend: Or, How the Cyberpunk Discourse Infested the
Zombie Genre 191
Alexander Knorr

Contributors 201

Preface

Transitions and the dissolving of boundaries are crucial to the fantastic in all media manifestations. Fantastic texts include, among other things, crossings into other worlds, time travel, metamorphoses, hybrid creatures as well as a variety of transitions and transgressions. Hybrid genres, genre reconfigurations and various forms of intertextuality featured in fantastic literature(s) are based on transitions between texts and the dissolving of boundaries between topics and motifs of diverse origin.

The fantastic raises a number of significant questions about cultural and social developments and challenges existing boundaries. By creating hybrid zones of autonomy, the fantastic provides alternatives to conventional understandings of, for example, world, knowledge or identity. Fantastic elements serve to unveil social discourses and to articulate complex physical and psychological processes as well as abstract figures of thoughts.

Transitions pervade the fantastic and are manifest in numerous forms, such as in the shape of inter-media adaptations, transpositions into new media, as well as in various forms of crossover as exemplified in the increasing trend of generation-spanning all-age literature.

The present volume consists of contributions (in English) to the Third Annual Conference of the Gesellschaft für Fantastikforschung (GFF) [i.e. Association for Research in the Fantastic] which took place at the University of Zurich from 13th to 16th September 2012, in collaboration with the Institute of Popular Culture Studies (IPK) at the University of Zurich and the Swiss Institute for Children's and Youth Media SIKJM, Associated Institute of the University of Zurich, and within the framework of the Swiss National Science Foundation (SNF) research project "Transitions and Dissolving Boundaries. World, Knowledge and Identity in Fantastic (Children's and Youth) Literature and Media". Further contributions (in German) are collected in the volume *Übergänge und Entgrenzungen in der Fantastik* (2014).

With regard to transitions and the crossing of boundaries, the focus of the articles lies on objects, norms, knowledge, ascribed meanings and potential spectrums of interpretation associated with the fantastic. Representations of worlds and subjects, reality and fiction are being analysed. Arranged in chapters on TRANSITION, TRANSGRESSION and TRANSFORMING NARRATIVE, the volume is meant to contribute to a further assessment of the cultural significance of the fantastic – in its contemporary, historical, social and medial dimensions.

It is our pleasant duty to acknowledge the help and support of various individuals and financial institutions to the conference and the publication of the present volume. First and foremost, we are grateful to the University of Zurich, the Swiss National Science Foundation (SNF), the Hochschulstiftung Zurich, the canton Zurich, the township of Zurich, and the Swiss Institute for Children's and Youth Media SIKJM.

Second, we'd like to thank Manuela Bossart, Silvan Luzzi and Beatrice Schwitter. Special thanks go to Tamara Werner and Judith Schubiger for all their help and the outstanding organisation of the conference bureau.

Christine Lötscher,
Petra Schrackmann,
Ingrid Tomkowiak and
Aleta-Amirée von Holzen

TRANSITION

Leonardo da Vinci and Fantastic Animals: Free Assembly of Shapes

Sara Taglialagamba

Hovering between scientific attitude and recreational assimilation, Leonardo da Vinci's fantastic animals spring on sheets through a free assembly of shapes according to selection criteria. Fantastic animals represent a way to display the grotesque, a term that, in Leonardo's view, is equal to creative fantasy. At first sight, these drawings seem to be different from the other studies of Leonardo[1], but in greater depth they are interesting for their particular way of visualization and modality of creation. Although Leonardo seems to approach this session only in a simple recreational way, two fundamental elements move the representation of the fantastic animals: the mechanism of selection of the parts and the interest to arouse emotions. In fact, fantastic animals are a free creation of Leonardo's mind based on the non-restrictive assembly of shapes that seems to paraphrase inversely the procedure of selection by Zeuxis, the ancient Greek painter, who flourished during the 5th century BC and selected the best features from five models to create a composite image of ideal beauty to resemble the statue of Helen for the city statue of Croton. In contrast, Leonardo selects the most grotesque and fantastic characteristics in order to create a monstrous creature.

Giorgo Vasari stated the true love Leonardo felt for animals and nature and the great fascination he had for grotesque and fantastic creatures: "He delighted much in horses and in all other animals, often when passing by the places where they sold birds he would take them out of their cages and paying the price that was asked for them, would let them fly away into the air, restoring to them their lost liberty" (371). When he was a child, he built the ingenious *rotella* – a fearsome shield built by assembling different species of animals (lizards, grasshoppers, snakes, butterflies, bats) that scared his father:

---

[1] Up to this date, few scholars dedicated themselves to studying fantastic animals sketched by Leonardo. Among these unusual contributions, see: De Toni 55-88, 111–128, 177–185; Fumagalli 383–385; Taglialagamba 58–63.

"Then having prepared it for painting, he began to think what he could paint upon it that would frighten every one that saw it, having the effect of the head of the Medusa. So for this purpose he brought to his room, which no one entered, but himself, lizards, grasshoppers, serpents, butterflies, locusts, bats, and other strange animals of the kind, and from them all he produced a great animal so horrible and fearful that it seemed to poison the air with its fiery breath. This he represented coming out of some dark broken rocks, with venom issuing from its open jaws, fire from its eyes, and smoke from its nostrils, a monstrous and horrible thing indeed. And he suffered much in doing it, for the smell in the room of these dead animals was very bad, though Leonardo did not feel it from the love he bore of art." (Vasari 372)

In addition, we can add the story about the strange lizard that he invented in Rome:

"The vinedresser of the Belvedere having found a very strange lizard, Leonardo made some wings of the scales of other lizards and fastened them on its back with a mixture silver alloy, so that they trembled when it walked; and having made for it eyes, horns, and a beard, he tamed it and kept it in a box, but all his friends to whom he showed it used to run away from fear." (Vasari 387–388)

The aptitude for the commission of different species is the sign of that passion for the animals that will bring him to their scientific study and to comparative anatomy. These creations rise from the same process – selection and assembly of parts – in order to arouse emotions and feelings such as awe, gaze, wonder, amazement, and fear.

Moreover, a note of 1504 – stated in the folios 2v and 3r of the Codex Madrid II – testifies that Leonardo had a library of over 150 books and manuscripts. Among these, there were manuals about zoology and botany: ancient texts such as the *Naturalis Historia* by Pliny the Elder, the *Fables* by Aesop; some medieval *bestiaries* such as the moral anthology *Fior di Virtù*, the scientific poem with a popular base *L'Acerba* by Cecco d'Ascoli, the scientific poem with religious interpretation *Quadrerigio* by Federigo Frezzi, and also coeval works like the *Apologhi* by Leon Battista Alberti and the *Facetie* by Poggio Bracciolini.

As we well know, in 1466, at the age of fourteen, Leonardo was apprenticed to Verrocchio whose workshop was one of the finest in Florence. Much of the production of Verrocchio's workshop was done by his pupils. There is no surprise for us to learn that Leonardo may have taken part in the creation of the marble font in Sacrestia Vecchia in San Lorenzo. Realistic and fantastic elements seem to cohabit and interweave, in metamorphic fusion, in the font. Reality and fantasy pool together in a paradoxical agreement between natural and demonic details which works like the free assembly of the parts used by Leonardo in the representation of fantastic animals. As a matter of fact, the amazing naturalistic profusion and the meticulously described presence of fantastic elements could be a demonstration of the participation of Leonardo as apprentice, as confirmed by several scholars. In fact, the font seems to inspire the profile of a warrior in helmet (London, British Museum, Inv. n. 1895,0915.474) thanks to the presence of some details in common, such as the screaming lion's head and hooked bat wings. Leonardo mentions dragons, unicorns, and other mythological animals in his writings (fables, prophecies, tales, and notes). In his stories, nature is presented like a benevolent mother who is free to arrange her laws, while animals symbolize virtues. Respecting the laws of Nature, we can discover the secrets of living. Let's take a look at the fable of the butterfly written in the folio 692r [257r-b] of the Codex Atlanticus: "Butterfly – 'O accursed light! I thought that in you I had found my happiness! Vainly do I lament my mad desire, and by my ruin I have come to know your rapacious and destructive nature.' Light- 'Thus do I treat whoever does not know how to use me aright.' And a sit sunk immediately its life came to an end."[2] The butterfly, attracted by the brightness of the candle flame, gets too near and dies. Nature reproaches the butterfly for its stupidity, enclosing the whole Leonardesque thought.

How Leonardo's Invention Works in Order to Create A Fantastic Animal

Let's start examining how the assembly works in the mind of Leonardo by analysing a couple of drawings kept in Windsor that represent some animals: cats, lionesses, dragons and horses. It is a heterogeneous block, made of domestic animals (cats and horses), fierce animals represented in attack positions (lioness), and fantastic animals (dragons, similar to monstrous reptiles).

In the folio RL 12363, kept at Windsor, Leonardo studies the numerous positions that a cat can assume. On the right we can find a cat that sleeps rolled up. In a rapid sequence we can find a cat that observes, a cat that licks itself and a frightened cat with raised hairs similar to a porcupine. In some cases, the cat is represented in more dynamic situations as we can observe in the case of the fights which seem more similar to lively scuffles between kittens. Thus, looking at the big feline in the centre of the sheet we can assume that the cat transforms itself from a domestic kitten to an aggressive feline ready to attack. Let's see the cat at the far right in a curious position with raised ears and the moving tail. In this figure, Leonardo seems to sketch an animal in action. Up to this point, Leonardo's sketches show cats in separate situations: the cat limits itself to observe without being active. Leonardo seems to accumulate lots of notes able to give a general description of the behaviour of the cat conveying the idea of an active, dynamic and intelligent animal, able to respond with extreme readiness to external *stimuli*.

---

[2] Pedretti 1977, 267.

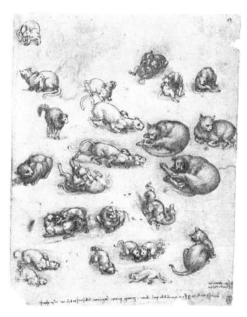

Image 1: Leonardo da Vinci, Cats, lions, and a dragon, c. 1513–1516. Pen and ink with wash over black chalk, 270 x 210 mm, Windsor, RL 12363

But this is not all: from the lively scuffles of kittens, this vivacity can be transformed into aggressiveness as the big, fierce feline can prove. It seems like the characteristics that the cat had in a benevolent shape are improved – or better – stretched to their extreme potential. In fact, the lioness seems to be caught in a crouching position ready to spring on its prey. What before was a playful violence is now transformed in a terrible power, able to arouse fear and awe.

Vitality, ferocity and action could not be represented in a better way: the feline has a powerful musculature and the face is contracted in a frightful roar. The passage is determined by the ferocity that becomes more marked in the wild animal. More curious is the presence of the little dragon that confirms the passage from real creatures to fantastic animals. Despite its small-sized dimensions (smaller than the cats around!), this little dragon is not short of amazement: the body is lengthened, emphasized by the long, lithe neck turned backwards, and the aggressive expression is made sharper by the open-wide maw. In other words, it seems that the dragon represents an ulterior variant of the feline aggressiveness: there is an indirect match between the little dragon and the other figures sketched on the sheet. Now, the twisted tail is an important detail: it is the element in common between the dragon and the cat. The dragon shares with the lioness the same characteristics but they seem to be more emphasized: the attack position, the nervous and tense body, the face contracted in a roar and the long, supple and twisted tail.

These considerations invite to conclude that the cat is the initial point of a process of transformation that works accentuating the feline characteristics. This process on a first level determines the passage from the cat to the lioness – from domestic to savage – and on a second level, it establishes the emergence of the dragon – passing from the savage beast to the fantastic animal. On the note in sheet RL 12363, Leonardo confirms that this transformation process starts due to the suppleness of joints. In fact, he wrote that these animals have in common "the contraction and the extension of their articulations". The passage from one animal to another is determined by the characteristic trait that remains quantitatively the same – the feral attitude that cat, lioness and dragon have in common –; on the contrary, the changes concern the intensity of the expression of this instinct. The feral attitude is absent in the cat (but still present), it is present in the fierce lioness and it is emphasized in the dragon.

In the folio 12331 of Windsor, a companion sheet of the RL 12363, the big feline is repeated: it could be defined as a key-figure because it is a common thread that links the two folios together and here it is the initial point for the transformation. It is interesting to notice that in the first sheet the lioness matched with the little dragon, while in this second sheet it is directly connected with the horse represented on the floor with broken neck. Let's notice the affinities between the two animals: the horse has the same willowy body of the feline (more dramatic for the extra-rotation of the neck that in turn seems to recall the same twisted position of the dragon). Also, the horse has the same squatting position of the lioness – with the same lifted tail! Thus, the horse is the element on which the transformation from feline to dragon can graft. On a next level, the transformation passes from the horse to the terrible dragon. In this folio, the dragon loses the little dimension sketched in the other sheet: it is represented as an invincible, wild beast in the fight with Saint George. The coils of this terrible snake are about to swallow the man and the horse, so the observer can anticipate how the fight could end. In the middle of the sheet, we can observe the dragon at the climax of its aggressiveness, when Saint George is ready to fling his spear.

In the folio RL 12331 the lioness became a common thread sketched in this sheet only for a pretext: the main creature is the dragon represented in a breaking out action and characterized by a vital, violent and terrible power. The dragon seems to be originated in both cases in a process of selection, which is the basis of all creations of the fantastic animals. Leonardo gives information about the process of "How you should make an imaginary animal look natural" in the paragraph 286 of the *Treatise on Painting* (1651). In this passage, Leonardo talks about the mixing of different parts of real animals in order to create a monstrous animal

Image 2: LEONARDO DA VINCI, *Horses, St George and the Dragon, and a lion*, c. 1517–1518. Pen and ink, 298 x 210 mm, Windsor, RL 12331

not really existing in life. This passage seems to give a description not only of the process observed in the previous drawing of Windsor, but also of the famous *rotella* and the green lizard of Belvedere.

So starting from the cat – an animal that Leonardo could observe daily – through different stages, Leonardo arrives at the representation of a dragon – a fantastic animal assembly starting from what is well known by himself and gradually accentuating its own features. The Leonardesque assembly of parts creates a monstrous hybrid that does not exist in nature, but it *could* paradoxically exist.

Dragons, Unicorns and an Elephantine Creature

We said that the other feature of the fantastic animals is their capacity to arouse emotions, just as man does: let's think about the studies of the *Madonna with the cat*; the *Sainte Anne* where the little Child plays with the lamb; the *Lady with an ermine* where the elegant, lively, little animal reflects the innocence and the purity that Cecilia Gallerani possesses. There is an emotional correspondence between the actions and the feelings. This connection reaches a climax in the lost painting of the *Battle of Anghiari*, commissioned to Leonardo in 1504 by gonfaloniere Piero Soderini in the Salone dei Cinquecento (Florence, Palazzo Vecchio). In this lost painting, as the several copies can confirm, horsemen and horses, in symbiosis and empathy, are involved in the fury of the fight. Men and animals feel the same impulses so much so that their bodies seem to merge together to grotesque hybrids. Animals are always characterized with an attempt and an effort of humanization such as, inversely, human is similar to the animal due to his innate instincts that can transform him from a rational being to a beast.

The dragon was one of Leonardo's favourite subjects both in drawings and in writings. He was interested in dragons since he was a little child: in fact they represent the hybrid creatures *par excellence*, through which his imagination could work and create. The fierce appearance reflects the dragon's dangerous nature when he wrote some fables about the dragon. He describes the attitude of the dragon at the folio 14v of the Manuscript H: "Cruelty. The basilisk is so utterly cruel that when it cannot kill animals by its baleful gaze, it turns upon herbs and plants, and fixing its gaze on them withers them up."[3]

The fight between dragons and horses is sketched in two other drawings: in the first one the dragon is succumbing to the blows of two horsemen, while in the other one it is the dragon that seems to have the victory.

Compared to the other drawings, an humanization attempt is present in the drawing sketched in the folio RL 12585r of Windsor that represents an elephantine, fantastic creature, probably a study for a carnival costume for a *homo selvatico*, one of the two made for the masquerades commissioned in Milan by Galeazzo Sanseverino in 1491 or in honour of Charles d'Amboise. Half human, half fantastic. The creature is a knight riding a horse and a musician who is playing some instruments. He has a wonderful elephantine head with a trumpet on the head and a flute instead of the hypothetic trunk, long wings on the prominent stomach and a curly tail. In this fascinating drawing, Leonardo seems to compete with Hieronymus Bosch's creatures depicted in *The Haywain Triptych* (Madrid, Prado Museum), maybe seen in Venice in 1500 by Leonardo himself. Emmanuel Winternitz compares it to a bagpipe costume and Carlo Pedretti underlines the similarities between the wind instrument and the cardio circulatory system. The assimilation is easy because – well – elephants trumpet.

A similar elephantine creature appears also in the *Physica Curiosa, Sive Mirabilia Naturæ et Artis Libris*, a compendium of abnormal births, strange animals and fabulous humanoid creatures thought to inhabit the far reaches of the

---

[3] Richter 317, § 1224.

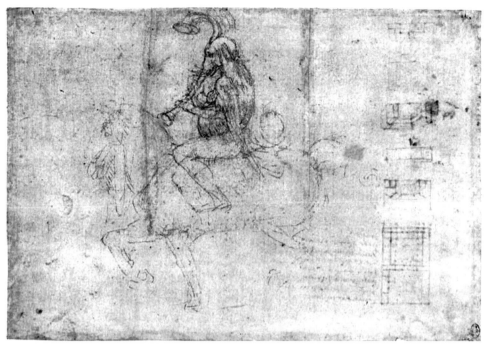

Image 3: LEONARDO DA VINCI, *A design for a musical elephant costume, c. 1507. Black chalk, 198 x 281 mm, Windsor, RL 12585r*

world written by the Jesuit Father Gaspar Schott[4] in 1667. The German scientist represents, on plate 9, an elephant-headed human and his companion, a rabbit-headed fellow with a long umbilical cord, both identified with these captions: *Fig. VIII – Puer capite elephantino* and *Fig. IX – Enfans cornutus ore patulo*. No doubt that, in the book, the ornate beauty is combined together with a distinct taste for the odd, macabre and irregular. They are connected in an indissoluble bond that creates a fanciful interplay between the beautiful and the monstrous, kept together thanks to a scientific – or even better – classifying attempt.

Modern viewers might associate this form of anthropomorphic trumpeting elephant with several animated films produced by the Walt Disney Productions, such as Robin Hood (1973), where the elephants are a part of the king's parade and their trunks serve as trumpets. At one point, one of the elephants that act as heralds for Prince John attempts to trumpet a warning but Lady Kluck, Maid Marian's lady-in-waiting, grabs the trunk, preventing the trumpeting and leaving the elephant flapping his ears ineffectually. The same joke was used in *The Jungle Book* (1967), with identical sound. Once again, modern viewers might be familiar

---

[4] For further information on Gaspar Schott (1608–1666): Heller 144; Sommervogel 903; Saint-Léger 36-49.

with this notion: *The Elephant Man* is a drama film directed by David Lynch in 1980 based on the true story of John Merrick, a deformed man found by surgeon Frederick Treves in a Victorian freak show in London. Due to this aspect, Merrick must wear a hood and cap when in public. The doctor brings him to the Hospital in order to examine the extraordinary and abnormal condition of the man in a lecture theatre, displaying him as a physiological curiosity. The urge to classify a deformity with a scientific attempt is an element in common between the fantastic elephantine creature described by Schott and the severely deformed man in 19th-century London. The scientific aptitude describes how the deformities disfigure both the human aspects. Analysing the grotesque with a scientific frame of reference, the results show abnormal creatures characterized by instance of real prodigious births, often elevated to mythic proportions. The fascination with the elephantine aspect inspired also Hans Rudolf Giger, a Swiss surrealist artist and set designer, who sketched a "Space Jockey" in a storyboard for a scene in *Alien*, directed by Ridley Scott in 1979. The name is referred to the Engineers, the oldest extra-terrestrial life, who were equipped with a bio suit that – as shown in the last scenes of *Prometheus* (2012), prequel of the *Alien* saga and directed by Scott – resembles a seven foot tall humanoid elephant and it is characterized by a trunk as the breathing apparatus.

A Fanciful Play: The Case of A Little Elephant and The Baby Unicorn

Conversely, in certain cases fantasy means the fanciful play working on the similarities with what Leonardo knows well, such as anatomy. Let's see the two drawings that represent a little, defenceless unicorn[5] (Oxford, Ashmolean Museum) and the cute, awkward elephant sketched on the background of the *Adoration of the Magi* (Florence, Uffizi). The common threads of both drawings are the elementary definition sketched with a childish attitude.

Another beloved animal is the unicorn. According to the *Bible* and ancient authors such as Pliny and Aristotle, for Leonardo the unicorn was able to purify water that had been poisoned by snakes with his horn. The fable, as a graphic *alter ego*, is illustrated by the drawing at the Ashmoleum Museum at Oxford where a young girl is pointing to a unicorn perfectly described from an anatomic point of view. Instead, the unicorn sketched in the folio kept at the Ashmolean Museum is characterized by the improbable position, far from the proportional sketches of

---

[5] Also the unicorn is described in the Manuscript H. In folio 11r we can read: "Incontinence. The unicorn, through its intemperance and not knowing how to control itself, for the love it bears to fair maidens forgets its ferocity and wildness; and laying aside all fear it will go up to a seated damsel and go to sleep in her lap, and thus the hunters take it." (Richter 320, § 1232.)

horses by Leonardo who considered them as the most similar animals to man. So for these reasons, the unicorn is still the legendary animal of the Middle Ages that resembles a white horse with a large, pointed, spiralling horn on its forehead, commonly described as an extremely wild, untamed woodland creature, symbol of purity and grace, which could only be captured by a virgin, as Leonardo's writings on Manuscript H can prove.

The little, exotic elephant on the background of the *Adoration of the Magi* doesn't own to the fabulous realm but seems to share an infantile vein sketched with a synthetic, graphic line, as if the author had made the figure without lifting up the pencil from the page. Among wild animals, the elephant has always held a leading place because it has aroused curiosity and wonderment, considering its great size and striking appearance.

During the Renaissance, we can count very few images of elephants. Luchino Belbello da Pavia painted a little elephant among the animals of Eden in the miniature of *The Creation of Eve* of the *Visconti Hours* (c. 1390, but completed after 1428) kept in Florence at the Biblioteca Nazionale Centrale (Ms. Landau Finaly 22, folio 46v). The fascinating border features both real animals and imaginary ones: the uncertain dimension and shape of the elephant introduce us to an exotic, uncommon animal similar to the domesticated leopard with the red collar and the winged griffin on the left, a cross between an eagle and a lion, both on the upper left. The roundish, unsteady shape, the same of the elephant sketched by Leonardo, could indicate that all they knew about elephants could only be read in bestiaries or accounts of travels to the East.

Undoubtedly exotic animals assert power and prestige to their owners. In Florence, there were lions held in captivity in the 'Serraglio' of Florence, which Leonardo had the opportunity of studying, and a giraffe, which the Sultan of Egypt sent in 1486 to Lorenzo the Magnificent in an attempt to win the support of the Medici.[6] The giraffe, who shortly after its arrival broke its neck and died, is depicted in several paintings like the *Gathering of Manna* (Washington, National Gallery, 1540) by Francesco Bachiacca, the *Adoration of the Magi* by Domenico Ghirlandaio in Tornabuoni Chapel (c. 1485–1490) in Santa Maria Novella, where the exotic animal is depicted descending a hill on the right-hand side. The famous giraffe is depicted also in the *Adoration of the Magi* attributed to Raffaello Botticini (Chicago, The Art Institute of Chicago, c. 1495) and on the ceiling of the Sala di Lorenzo il Magnifico in Palazzo Vecchio by Giorgio Vasari (1560–1570) in the frame of *Lorenzo receiving gifts from his ambassadors*.

A white Asian elephant called Hanno (in Italian Annone, c. 1510–1516) was given by King Manuel I of Portugal to Leo X in 1514 and quickly became the

---

[6] Joost-Gaugier 91-99; Belozerskaya 87-129.

Pope's favourite animal. The elephant is depicted in some drawings attributed to Raphael's pupils kept at the Ashmoleum Museum in Oxford and in the *Adoration of the Magi* painted by Vasari for his friend Vincenzo Borghini and known thanks to a preparatory drawing in the Uffizi and a small replica kept in Edinburgh at the Scottish National Gallery[7] (c. 1566–1567).

The little drawing in the background of the *Adoration of the Magi* that resembles the elephant might introduce us to another interesting connection between Leonardo and the Walt Disney Company: the baby elephant sketched by Leonardo seems to inspire the synthetic, roundish shapes of the elephants that saturate two films made around the same time: *Fantasia* (1940) and *Dumbo* (1941), both made by Hicks Lokey. The two most famous things the animator worked on at Disney were the *Dance of the Hours* segment in *Fantasia* (an out-of-control magic that includes one of the most iconic shots ever seen: the hippo ballerina crushing the crocodile) and the frightening *Pink Elephants on Parade* in *Dumbo* (the baby elephant falls asleep and dreams to blow a bubble that turns into a large pink elephant that, in turn, originates a sort of chaotic march composed by oneiric presences: elephants with musical instruments, big elephants stepping on smaller elephants, a pair of dancing elephants that leaps over a car hood).

Similar creatures will appear later in the animations of *Forbidden Planet*[8] (1956), directed by Fred M. Wilcox, one of the first science fiction films that, in fact, has some stunning animation courtesy of the Walt Disney animating staff and Metro-Goldwyn-Mayer's special effects. Despite the affinity with the hallucinating pink elephants and the other visionary presences that can also be connected with the fantastic elephantine creature (Windsor, RL 12585) I mentioned before, the little drawing sketched by Leonardo in the background of the *Adoration of the Magi* seems more similar to the little elephant that plays with Mowgli in a frame of *The Jungle Book* (1967) and to Heffalump, the fictional elephant in the *Winnie the Pooh* stories (1926-28) written by Alan Alexander Milne.

Despite the childish attitude of the shape, I cannot deny Leonardo shows us an outstanding element, result of a meticulous investigation: the man riding on the back of the elephant, called 'mahout'. Leonardo sketched with few lines, the man describing perfectly his realistic pose and the balance of weight. All of the sudden, considering the presence of the mahout who controls and drives the animal, the cute elephant becomes an enormous animal, domesticated by man and maybe used in triumph and parades.

---

[7] Winner 71-109; Boorsch 368-376; Bedini 80-143.
[8] For an interesting connection between the film and the theme of the fantastic, see: Battisti 60-61 and especially note 13; Pedretti 417-449.

Image 4: In a clockwise order: The Jungle Book (1967), Robin Hood (1973), Dumbo (1941). Fantasia (1940), Frames, Walt Disney Productions

Conclusion

It can be asserted that Leonardo seems to have played with the idea of fantastic animals throughout his entire life. As a child he scared his father with the ingenious *rotelli* – a fearsome shield built by assembling different species of animals like lizards, butterflies, grasshoppers, bats and snakes. A similar method was used in Rome in 1513 when he frightened his friends by showing them his tamed lizard with horns and wings. Therefore, as mentioned in the introduction, for Leonardo, fantastic animals hover between scientific attitude and recreational assimilation. Balancing these two attitudes, Leonardo creates fantastic animals that seem to be different from the popular tradition of prodigies and monsters thanks to their specific features: the mechanism of selection of the parts and the interest to arouse emotions.

This does not mean that Leonardo was not interested or fascinated with prodigies and monsters. Among his books were some medieval *bestiaries* and moral anthologies. Moreover, on the folio 17 r-c r-d 17 v-d v-c [58 ii v] of the Codex

Atlanticus he sketched the monster of Ravenna[9]. The recreational play is part of the scientific method used by Leonardo to investigate reality. In this case, it works for imperfection (*difetto*) and not for perfection (*electio*), in order to select, study and catalogue the world that is in a constant mutation.

Bibliography

Works Cited

Battisti, Eugenio. L'antirinascimento. Milano: Feltrinelli, 1962.
Bedini, Silvio A. The Pope's Elephant. Manchester: Carcanet, 1997.
Belozerskaya, Marina. The Medici Giraffe and Other Tales of Exotic Animals and Power. New York: Little Brown, 2006.
Boorsch, Suzanne. "'The Elephants' after Andrea Mantegna: an Engraving Drawn Over." Essays in Memory of Jacob Bean (1923-1992). Eds. Linda Wolk-Simon et al. New York: Master Drawings Association, 1993. 368–76.
Fumagalli, Giuseppina. "Gli animali favolosi del Vinci." Leonardo: rassegna bibliografica 10 (1938): 383–385.
Heller, Ágost. Geschichte der Physik von Aristoteles bis auf die Neueste Zeit. Vol. 2. Stuttgart: F. Enke, 1882.
Joost-Gaugier, Christiane L. "Lorenzo the Magnificent and the Giraffe as a Symbol of Power." Artibus et Historiae 8 (1987): 91-99.
I manoscritti dell'Institut de France. Vol. 12. Edizione facsimile con trascrizione di Augusto Marinoni. Firenze: Giunti, 1986–1990.
Il Codice Atlantico della Biblioteca Ambrosiana di Milano. Vol. 3. Edizione facsimile con trascrizione di Augusto Marinoni. Vol. 3. Firenze: Giunti, 2000.
Pedretti, Carlo. The Codex Atlanticus of Leonardo da Vinci: a Catalogue of its Newly Restored Sheets. New York: Johnson Reprint Corp., 1979.
– "La iella del mostro." Leonardo & io. Milano: Mondadori, 2008. 417–49.
– "Questo mostro non piacque a Leonard." La Nazione 28 luglio 1979: 3.
Pedretti, Carlo. The literary works of Leonardo da Vinci: a commentary to Jean Paul Richter's editions. Vol. 2. Oxford: Phaidon, 1977.
Richter, Jean Paul. The Notebooks of Leonardo da Vinci. Vol. 2. New York: Dover Publications Inc., 1970.

---

[9] In Italy, the first record of a 'prodigy of nature' was provided by Luca Landucci, a Florentine apothecary: in an entry of his diary written in March of 1512, he described a monster born in Ravenna as having a single horn upon its head, two bat-like wings, and markings upon its chest, a serpentine and hermaphroditic lower body, a single eye set in its knee and an eagle-like claw for a foot. While Landucci had only seen a painting of the marvel, the prodigious creature possibly did exist and was well known across Europe as dozens of woodcuts and engravings prove. The monster was also interpreted as a metaphor. The Ravenna monster is described also in the *Physica Curiosa* by Gaspar Schott at plate XVII, Fig. XXVII *Monstrum cornutum et alatum, cum pede rapacis avis*. See: Pedretti 1979: 307–317, plate 10; Pedretti 1979: 3; Pedretti 2008: 417-449. Indeed, the monster of Ravenna seems to have been an imaginary creature interpreted as a metaphor.

Saint-Léger, Bartholomeus Mercier de. Notice Raisonnee des Ouvrages de Gaspar Schott, Jesuite (1785). Paris: Kessinger, 2009.

Schott, Caspar. Physica curiosa sive Mirabilia naturae et artis, Würzburg: Nachdr. der Ausg., 1662.

Sommervogel, Carlos. Bibliothéque de la Compagnie de Jésus. Vol. 7. Paris: Alphonse Picard, 1896.

Taglialagamba, Sara. "Creature (im)possibili: gli animali fantastici di Leonardo." Art e Dossier 24 (2009): 58–63.

Toni, Giovanni Battista de. Le piante e gli animali in Leonardo da Vinci. Bologna: N. Zanichelli, 1922.

Vasari, Giorgio. Lives of the most imminent painters, sculptors, and architects. Trans. Jonathan Foster. London: Henry G. Bohn, 1851.

Winner Matthias. "Raffael malt einen Elefanten." Mitteilungen des Kunsthistorischen Institutes in Florenz 11 (1964): 71–109.

Films

Alien. Dir. Ridley Scott. Twentieth Century Fox, Brandywine Productions, USA 1979.

Dumbo. Dir. Ben Sharpsteen, Bill Roberts, Jack Kinney, Wilfred Jackson, Norman Ferguson, Samuel Armstrong. Walt Disney Productions, USA 1941.

Fantasia. Dir. Samuel Armstrong, Bill Roberts, Ford Beebe, Ben Sharpsteen, T. Hee, Norman Ferguson, James Algar, Hamilton Luske, Jim Handley, Paul Satterfield, Wilfred Jackson. Walt Disney Productions, USA 1940.

Forbidden Planet. Dir. Fred M. Wilcox. Metro-Goldwyn-Mayer (MGM), USA 1956.

Prometheus. Dir. Ridley Scott. Twentieth Century Fox, Dune Entertainment, Scott Free Productions, Brandywine Productions, USA 2012.

The Elephant Man. Dir. David Lynch. Brooksfilms, USA 1980.

The Jungle Book. Dir. Wolfgang Reitherman, Walt Disney Productions, USA 1967.

List of Illustrations

Ill. 1. Leonardo da Vinci: Cats, lions, and a dragon, c. 1513-1516, pen and ink with wash over black chalk, 270 x 210 mm, Windsor, RL 12363.

Ill. 2. Leonardo da Vinci, Horses, St George and the Dragon, and a lion, c. 1517-1518, pen and ink, 298 x 210 mm, Windsor, RL 12331.

Ill. 3. Leonardo da Vinci, A design for a musical elephant costume, c. 1507, black chalk, 198 x 281 mm, Windsor, RL 12585r.

Ill. 4. In a clockwise order: The Jungle Book (1967), Robin Hood (1973), Dumbo (1941), Fantasia (1940), Frames, Walt Disney Productions.

The Threshold. An Iconological Analysis

Amos Bianchi and Gabriela Galati

The aim of this paper is to demonstrate that the threshold has been linked to the status of representation and of language since the dawn of humankind, or better, since the moment in which the homo sapiens started visualizing her/his thoughts covering the walls of the Lascaux caves with pictures. Nonetheless, the urgency of an inquiry on the threshold in contemporary times has a different point of departure; namely, contemporary science fiction, and, more specifically, the novel *Burning Chrome*, written by a young Canadian writer, William Gibson, and published in 1981. The term matrix is used in this text for the very first time, according to the writer, the matrix designates the abstract representation of the connections among data sets. The term matrix itself has been very successful (the Wachowski Brothers' trilogy is the mainstream evidence of it), and it has also evolved later in a concept as powerful as the first one: the cyberspace. As sharply noticed by Antonio Caronia, "Gibson's new technological dropouts wind in this 'visualization of the whole field of electric forms' (counter to McLuhan), the new heroes or anti-heroes, neo-romantic (or 'neuromantics', as they have been defined by another sci-fi writer, Norman Spinrad), without neither project, nor future" (Caronia 26). In a subsequent passage, Caronia observes again:

"The cyberspace is deeply rooted in a kind of magic belief in the profane [...], in the existence of a world beyond the screen of the monitor: maybe in analogy with video, but perhaps according to the old fascination coming from the mirror, too. [...] So that, behind the artificial universes, the themes of holiness, reminiscences of transcendence, demiurgic functions reappear" (Caronia 26-27).

Matrix, cyperspace, neoromanticism, other worlds, holiness, transcendence are all terms related to different disciplines that this paper would like to unify on the same plane of immanence characterized by the threshold; a plane of immanence that radically faces the status of language and representation ab origine in order to give a partial answer to a set of questions: what is the element that opens to this other time-space? What is it that allows the transition from immanence to transcendence? The main question this work poses is if the threshold is a linguistic or an ontological problem; in other words, the problem is if language allows the existence of otherness, or if otherness exists before, or independently of language. In this way, the conceptualization of the threshold allows an original reading of the relationship between immanence and transcendence.

The Threshold and the Sublime

The first step backwards in this genealogic discourse about the threshold is to focus on some aesthetic themes developed in the period immediately before the Enlightenment. During the 18th century a new concept fiercely emerges in the aesthetic scene, a concept that would be a milestone for the following times: the sublime. In spite of the fact that the sublime was already present in previous poetics (the Lucretian reference on the spectacle offered by a sinking boat, for instance), Edmund Burke develops the concept in depth in the essay *A Philosophical Enquiry into the Origin of Our Ideas of the Sublime and Beautiful* (1757); and then Immanuel Kant considers it as a necessary step for the development on his text devoted to aesthetic issues, the *Critique of Judgment* (1790). As an antecedent of the understanding of the notion of the sublime that Romanticism would later completely fulfill, in the 18th Century all the basic features of this concept can already be recognized.

The reflection on the effect of the image upon the *I* substitutes the discourse about the truth of the image, based on mimesis. The ontological reflection on the status of the image changes. The platonic quest for pure aesthetic forms ends, even in the form of the neo-platonic quest that was born already polluted by the sense of the original sin of Christianity. Facing an idea of beauty that interrogates, perceives and theorizes the harmony among sensible forms, a new sentiment arises, the sublime, that disposes the failure of the platonic asceticism towards the pure forms and confines otherness to the absolute-other. This new sentiment is focused on pathos, in opposition to logos that was previously dominating the aesthetic scene, and that is now bankrupt. In a certain way, two different movements are intersecting each other: on the one hand, the passage from transcendence to the absolute-other; on the other hand, the passage from logos to pathos. As an intersection between these movements, the sentiment of the sublime assumes a both perceptive and poetic form. In its perceptive dimension, the sublime is codified as delightful horror, as Burke stated. In its poetic function, the sublime becomes a territory for the production of limitless representations, attesting the presence of an absolute-other whose traces could be perceived via pathos, and no more via logos. The Infinite, among the other concepts, breaks into the field of representation.

Which function is then assumed by a kind of image that, in the field of the sublime, loses any possibility to represent the existent? Two determinant apparatuses emerge under these circumstances, apparatuses that at first appear distinct, but which are deeply connected in a further analysis. On the one hand, the image recovers a pure phenomenological function: the image just represents itself, it is a pure factual sensible among other sensibles. On the other hand, this image that has lost all connection with transcendence and faces the absolute-other allows the possibility to envisage the light of nihilism: if there is anything beyond the image, it would go back to the dynamics of platonic or neo-platonic logos; but what is found behind this kind of image is just pure nothing. This approach to the status of the image was developed in Germany around 250 years ago, and it had a very long and influential tail in current deconstructionism, as Wunenburger (1997) keenly points out. Among all its consequences, the most interesting in the context of this discourse is the Deleuzian position.

The Dionysian Machine

In the *The Logic of Sense* ([1969] 1990), Deleuze deploys his army against the Platonic concept of image based upon the relationship original/copy by establishing the notion of simulacrum as main concept (a simulacrum that was terribly overthrown within the platonic foundation).[1] There is always, no doubt, a resemblance between resonating series, but this is not the problem. The problem is rather in the status and the position of this resemblance. Let us consider the two formulas: 'only that which resembles differs' and 'only differences can resemble each other.' There are two distinct readings of the world: one invites us to think difference from the standpoint of a previous similitude or identity, whereas the other invites us to think similitude and even identity as the product of a deep disparity. The first reading precisely defines the world of copies or representations; it posits the world as icon. The second, contrary to the first, defines the world of simulacra; it posits itself as phantasm: "[...] So 'to reverse Platonism' means to make the simulacra rise and to affirm their rights among icons and copies." (Deleuze 261-262) And moreover: "Resemblance subsists, but it is produced as the external effect of the simulacrum, inasmuch as it is built upon divergent series and makes them resonate. Identity subsists, but it is produced as the law which complicates all the series and makes them all return to each one in the course of the forced movement." (Deleuze 263).

---

[1] Deleuze already addresses these problems in *Différence et répétition* published the previous year, [1968 (1994); *Difference and Repetition*; London: The Athlone Press], but for the aims of the present work, we choose *The Logic of Sense* as reference.

Identity, the same and the similar dissolve each other in this new notion of simulacrum that would allow the coexistence of any kind of images on the same plane of immanence. The Platonic hierarchical order is rejected: original and copy, model and representation are excluded from the founding status of the image. A feasible Platonic stairway to the true being cannot be built up anymore.

This new way to order images, or better, to dis-order images, has a common ground with the phenomenological and nihilistic vision of the image explained above. Deleuze himself follows this path when he says:

"Simulation is the phantasm itself, that is, the effect of the functioning of the simulacrum as machinery, a Dionysian machine. It involves the false as power, Pseudos, in the sense in which Nietzsche speaks of the highest power of the false. By rising to the surface, the simulacrum makes the Same and the Similar, the model and the copy, fall under the power of the false (phantasm)." (Deleuze 263)

The path of Dionysus in opposition to Apollo, of the chaosmotic antagonism to order, of power against intellect emerges clearly in these passages. However, it follows then that even a platonic metaphysics is not as adequate to the understanding of the image as the simulacrum. Deleuze needs another strong conceptual step in order to insert the simulacrum into a new metaphysics. After having defined the simulacrum as a Dionysian machine, Deleuze puts on stage the notion of sign:

"That the Same and the Similar does not mean that they are appearances or illusions. Simulation designates the power of producing an effect. But this is not intended only in a causal sense, since causality would remain completely hypothetical and indeterminate without the intervention of other meanings. It is intended rather in the sense of a 'sign' issued from a process of signalization; it is in the sense of a 'costume', or rather a mask, expressing a process of disguising, where, behind each mask, there is yet another [...]" (Deleuze 263)

It follows that the Dionysian machine of the simulacrum can operate on a different territory that is outlined by Deleuze, here faithfully following Nietzsche, in the eternal return, "for it is in the eternal return that the reversal of the icons or the subversion of the world of representation is decided" (Deleuze 263). The existence of simulacra can be displayed just on the chaotic plane of the eternal return, the existence of this Dionysian machine that definitely has left the safe path traced by the order and the logos to embrace other dimensions: the power, or, as outlined in the previous chapter, the pathos. At the end: a non-logic of bodies instead of a logic of intellects.

Yet a step further must be taken, as something still remains unexpressed. Why the crisis of the image? Why the crisis of the platonic status of the image? There is an answer to these questions: The notion of image in the 18th century faces a deep crisis, since the ground upon which some theories of the image were built was perilous and fragile, a ground that was isomorphic to the relationship between transcendence and immanence, instable if considered from the point of view of reason. Christ is the figure to be investigated in order to understand this instability.

Christology as a Basis for the Western Image

In the construction of Western theory of the image, it is necessary to consider side by side the Christian and platonic paradigms. The Christian paradigm was developed both in Greek and Latin languages during the period from the death of Christ till the second Council of Nicea (787), which established the basic canon of the image in the Christian world, then to become the Catholic world.[2] In order to understand the conceptual evolution of the notion of image, it is necessary to face the lexical issue in which the Christian approach was rooted. The word image is directly derived from the Latin word imago, which originally designed the mask of wax that, in the pagan rite, was put upon the face of the corpse reproducing its features. The imago was not just the representation of an absence: the imago was the dead corpse, not just its representation; it was a living object, as Debray states: "a hyperbody, active, public and thinking." (Debray 31)

In this Latin background – ambiguous regarding the relationship presence – absence, and, consequently, identity and copy–, the Christological issue arises. In which sense is Christ God? Or better, where and how to place the corporeity, the physicality of Christ ("Verbum caro factum est, et habitavit in nobis, et vidimus gloriam eius", as it says in the prologue to the *Gospel of John*) compared to the absolute transcendence of God? Which is the sense of Incarnation? The term used by John in the Greek translation of the Gospel contains the root –th, that according to the Greek etymology has a strong sense of perception of the body.[3] John himself uses again a perilous lexicon when he affirms that the logos became sarx, meaning flesh. Two centuries and a half of theological debate about Christ resulted in the spreading out not only of a lot of heresies, but also in a canon, still valid, finally codified during the first Council of Nicea (325) that established the issue of the relationship between God and Christ – and it can be said, based on the concept of image.

However, the Christological issue is not just a matter of theology. The debate around Christ involves, in this moment, the notion of the world itself, and its value

---

[2] Orthodox Christianity and Lutheran Christianity will follow, starting from the two schisms of the 11th and 16th centuries, they followed different paths that cannot be compared to the Catholic approach to images. In the context of this work, the Catholic canon is the one taken into account, because of its pivotal influence on the general Western theory of images.

[3] The same root is present, for instance, in the word *theatron*, from which derives theater: the place of vision.

of being. If salvation resides in transcendence, but, at the same time, the plan of salvation resides in immanence: which is the economy of Salvation to be improved in the immanent world? The answer to the Christological issue is derived from the answer to the issue about Salvation, and vice versa. On the one hand, a sense of opacity and obscurity is perceived, perfectly synthesized in the statement by Paul: "Videmus nunc per speculum in aenigmate, tunc videbimus optime"; on the other hand, a rationalization of the relationship between immanence and transcendence is required.

In this context, the image establishes a double bind with these issues. The relationship between the incarnation of Christ and the Father, between the outer world and the inner world is read in the light of the concept of image, and, at the same time, the image acquires an ontological status determined by the relationship above. As Debray states, "theology of images is just a consequent Christology." (Debray 109)

Within the theology of the image, in order to solve these issues, the platonic paradigm – filtered by neo-Platonism and reinterpreted from the Christian point of view – is affirmed. The result of this process is a notion of image based on a prototype, on the dichotomy original/copy, according to the criteria of resemblance, whatever they are. In the horos, a dogmatic decision at the second Council of Nicea, held to face the contingent issue of iconoclasm that blew up in the Greek Christianity some decades before the Council, it is stated that the devotion given to the icon goes to the prototype; otherwise, the Incarnation itself would be denied.

The second Council of Nicea seems to fix a solid canon about the image. But history itself demonstrated how provisional this solution was: the orthodox schism of the 11th century would reach for a status of the image whose ontological value is higher, to begin with the liturgy, where the icon has the same ontological-objectual value of the Holy Bible; the Lutheran schism of the 16th century would deny any hypothesis of resemblance between image and prototype, as a result, the physical image as instrument for the rite was removed.

In order to complete this overview on the relationship between immanence, transcendence and image, and before introducing the theme of the threshold in the context of this discourse, one more step backward is needed. In the present work, the term image often has been used with a double sense: the concept of image and the concrete, manufactured image; the term image is somehow polysemic itself. Here a new question arises: why do manufactured images exist? The Platonic condemnation of the image would have never happened if the Greek world had not been rich with depicted or sculpted images, both bidimensional and tridimensional. In the Jewish-Christian world the problem of idolatry, from the well-known episode of the golden calf, is a recurring theme. The new question here, to which the next chapter tries to give a provisional answer, is the following: why does homo sapiens, unique among the living beings, fabricate images?

Caves

Possibly, the first threshold was to be found outside of the image, or, to be more accurate, outside of the space of representation, namely, in the Palaeolithic paintings of animals at the Lascaux caves in Dordogne, France. Where the desire of creating other worlds, of opening parallel spaces comes from is difficult to say, but it has obviously accompanied humankind from its origins. And it also preceded language, so the identification of a threshold which is beyond representation is related to a non linguistic element that has nonetheless a close relationship with what is called "imagination", as Vilèm Flusser explains:

"Images are significant surfaces. Images signify – mainly – something 'out there' in space and time that they have to make comprehensible to us as abstractions (as reductions of the four dimensions of space and time to the two surface dimensions). This specific ability to abstract surfaces out of space and time and to project them back into space and time is what is known as 'imagination'. It is the precondition for the production and decoding of images. In other words: the ability to encode phenomena into two-dimensional symbols and to read these symbols." (Flusser 8)

At the same time, this encoding of images presupposes the belief that there is someone "out there" to decode them, hence, it encompasses the assumption of the existence of someone or something "other" (Flusser 9). If the imaginary was born from the possibility of abstracting a four-dimensional world in the two-dimensional surface of the image, as Flusser proposes, the first record of a projection, or representation, of the imaginary are again the Lascaux caves.

What has this projection of the imaginary served for? Or in other words, why projecting the imaginary? The imaginary opened up the chance of projecting the desired, of "materializing" other worlds, other possibilities. This desire is obviously at the base of most representational artistic forms, from the immersive pictorial spaces of the Renaissance, such as the Sistine Chapel, to cinema, or virtual reality. All of these media hoped to immerse the viewer in a different reality, stimulating, for different reasons and with different aims, his/her emotions.

However, as Mitchell states in his book *Iconology: image, text, ideology* (1986), material images and the imaginary should be considered as having equal ontological status, or as belonging to "the same category": "Wittgenstein's way of attacking mental imagery is not, however, the direct strategy of denying the existence of such images. He freely concedes that we may have mental images associated with thought or speech, insisting only that these images should not be thought of as private, metaphysical, immaterial entities any more than real images are." (Mitchell 15)

Language is also another means of representation which constantly creates a parallel world, whether fictional or not, it is always in the place of something "other". Before the outset of (verbal) language, and more specifically, with the invention of linear writing, the circularity and the repetition of time and space invested images with magical power. This power came from the fact that "images mediate between men and the world" (Flusser 9); in the circular world of magic, there was an analogy between the level of reality and the "other" space represented, and one could act by analogy over the other. In a certain sense, the conception of the represented space as a "window" to another world by far precedes the invention of perspective and the limits of the frame. In this sense, the limits of the representation were a first, "outer" threshold: the first boundary between the physical/mental space and the projected/desired space of the image/magical world.

With the invention of linear writing approximately during the second millennium BC, the circular, magical world of images unfolds in the linear and chronological logic of history. In this process, humans move a level further away from the world: if until then the relationship between humans and the world was mediated by images, now there are also texts that explain those images, with the intention of stripping them of their magical force. Texts arise as a metacode of images, in the intention of making their meaning clearer (Flusser 9). This is when the second level of the threshold comes in: language opens the possibility to otherness inside the plane of representation.

As developed above, the threshold has been considered as a linguistic element that opens up to the appearance of otherness within a level of representation, therefore, the threshold not only conveys meaning, but also unfastens a significative dimension within the same plane of representation. As Flusser explains:

"The significance of the image as revealed in the process of scanning therefore represents a synthesis of two intentions: one manifested in the image and the other belonging to the observer. It follows that images are not 'denotative' (unambiguous) complexes of symbols (like numbers, for example) but 'connotative' (ambiguous) complexes of symbols: They provide space for interpretation." (Flusser 11)

In this regard, Charles S. Peirce's theory of signs may be useful to advance a semiotics of the threshold. According to Peirce, meaning is a triadic relation between a sign, an object, and an interpretant (CP 1.345). He describes a sign or representamen as anything which denotes an object, and he defines an object as anything which can be thought. He defines an interpretant as the mental effect of a sign and as the signification or interpretation of the sign (CP 8.184). Actually, for Peirce, every thought is a sign in itself, and signs a mediating between an external or material world of objects, and an internal world of concepts, or ideas. As is also well known, as part of his theory of signs, Peirce distinguishes three categories, or "modes of being", which give sense to all events and to all objects of thought, and he names them firstness, secondness, and thirdness. Firstness is defined as there being no regard for the other, secondness as correspondence to the/an other, for example, there is a reaction, and thirdness as the correlation between firstness and secondness: in thirdness there is mediation, or discourse. Firstness is the mode of being a possibility, but secondness is the mode of being a fact, and thirdness is the mode of being a sign or representation (CP 8.328).

If, as mentioned before, the threshold is a linguistic element conveying meaning, it is possible to think of a semiotics of the threshold assimilating the world to the realm of objects, and thus as part of a relationship of firstness: the imaginary, the mental quality of images, desire, as a sign and as part of a relationship of secondness, and the threshold as the boundary of a world of models, of simulacra, which works as the interpretant, and fully completing a relationship of thirdness.

At this point, it is possible to retrospectively consider the train of thought on the threshold in the light of the reflections advanced above following the list of questions introduced in the premise.

The sublime is the epiphenomenon of the crisis of the image, whose conceptual apparatus was built upon a platonic ground that positioned the image in a non-productive immanence, but that, in some ways, was participating in the transcendent sphere of the pure forms. Neo-Platonism and Christianity – starting from different foundations that later intersected –, solved the problem of participation by codifying the relationship between image and prototype, by which the "other", intrinsic to transcendence, is achievable by harsh paths. Until this moment, the threshold was the appearance of the division among different worlds, which, however, asked to be reunited by trespassing the threshold itself. Nonetheless, when the image returns to the subject during the 18th century, the theme of the absolute-other suddenly appears, a kind of otherness that can be reached only via pathos, not via logos anymore. Through this transition the threshold gains power: from being a trespassing tool, it becomes the boundary between two different worlds, the latter of which does not belong to the realm human finitude anymore.

When Nietzsche breaks into the philosophical scenario, the eternal return takes the position previously occupied by the platonic-christian world. Several decades afterwards, Deleuze situates the image into this new scenario through the notion of simulacrum. The simulacrum is image among images, out of the necessity of the Platonic hierarchy. The simulacrum unleashes the logic of the image from the logos, settling it into different conceptual universes: power, desire. In Flusser's analysis of the image, ab origine the threshold leaves the four-dimensional world to join the bidimensionality of the image. From that moment on, when it appears, the threshold becomes the sign of an otherness now internal to the set of images, outlining a moment of transition between divergent exteriorizations of the imaginary.

Given this scenario, the threshold moves away from the ontological discourse to be confined to a linguistic territory. It designates the boundary between divergent series of simulacra. The threshold does not lose the substantial connection with the human being – understood in its evolutionistic and biological sense; it is not confined to the pure abstract plane of language. The threshold, instead, remains alive as a spy revealing the process of intrinsic differentiation generated by the imaginary.

Bibliography

Burke, Edmund. A Philosophical Enquiry into the Origin of Our Ideas of the Sublime and Beautiful. (1757). Please name an actual book as source (place, publisher, year)
Ed. James T. Bouiton. South Bend: Notre Dame University Press, 1968.
Caronia, A. Virtuale. Milano: Mimesis, 2010.
Debray, Régis. Vie et mort de l'image. Paris: Gallimard, 1992.
Deleuze, Gilles. Logique du sens. Paris: Minuit, 1969. Translation: The Logic of Sense. London: The Athlone Press, 1990.
Flusser, Villem. Towards a Philosophy of Photography. London: Reaktion Books, 1983.
Gibson, W. Burning Chrome. (1981) New York: Harper Voyager, 2003.
Kant, Immanuel. Kritik der Urteilskraft. (1790). Trans. Bernard, J.H. Critique of Judgment. New York: Hafner Publishing, 1951.
McLuhan, Marshall. Understanding Media. The Extensions of Men. McGraw: New York, 1964.
Mitchell, W.J.T. Iconology: Image, Text, Ideology. Chicago: University of Chicago Press, 1986.
Nicée II. 787-1987, Douze siècles d'images religieuses, Actes du colloque international Nicée II. Ed. Boespflug, F., Lossky, N. Paris: Ed. Du Cerf, 1987.
Peirce, Charles Sanders. Collected Papers of Charles Sanders Peirce. Cambridge: Harvard University Press, 1960.
Wunenburger, Jean-Jacques. Philosophie des images. Paris: Press Universitaires de France, 1997. Trans. Arecco, S. Filosofia delle immagini. Torino: Einaudi, 1999.

Charles Nodier's Fantastic World in *Inès de Las Sierras*

Graciela Boruszko

> *C'est la parole qui a créé la civilisation;*
> *elle sait aujourd'hui qu'elle peut la détruire,*
> *et elle la détruira, parce qu'elle a été méconnue:*
> *vengeance criminelle et absurde,*
> *mais inévitable.*
>
> *Tout croire est d'un imbécile, Tout nier est d'un sot.*
>
> *De las cosas más seguras*
> *La más segura es dudar.*
> Charles Nodier, *Inès de Las Sierras* (23, 85, 85).

This article studies the literary work *Inès de Las Sierras* (1837) of Charles Nodier, who was a pioneer of the fantastic narrative in France, as he systematically transgresses the boundaries of history, literature and religion to access the uncanny fantastic world of his creation. This analysis explores the intersections of literary narrative, the transposition of biblical images and the results of inserting those modified images into a new network of meaning. This intertextuality favors the creation of a cosmogony that offers a new interpretation of the supernatural cosmos.

To leave traces of one's voyage, thus writing one's name in the literary fantastic world, is the equivalent of achieving immortality, and Nodier undoubtedly left his mark on the French literary fantastic world. The extent to which the fantastic story nodérienne acquires meaning by borrowing biblical images manifests itself not only through the co-occurrence of the images but also (and especially) through his plan to imbue the fantastic tale with the Bible. The effect is that the reading of the story becomes a fantastic double reading as long as the implicit or subtle references intertwine, engaging the reader in the multiple intellectual references in an activity of the imagination that establishes a dialogue between what is known and what is novel. By undertaking a comparative analysis of the biblical images in the fantasy world and the original biblical images, thus revealing the borrowing process (which includes modifications and adaptations of the image to insert it in the new context), we will discover the knowing eye of the writer.[1] Nodier links history to the literary fantastic story in such a way that the historical and literary events transcend themselves. Both 'stories' retain shared facts and images, initiating a dialogue in the form of a 'romanced history.' The mystery of history and the sacred history merge in the mystery of the fantastic story, composing a cosmogony of shadows in a playful esthetic mirage. A writer who adopts this writing process incorporates the reflection of the history of 'the other' into 'his' history, in this case, incorporating the history of Spain into the history of France. This strategy echoing the 'romanced history' fascinates both the writer and the reader.

In this esthetic expression, Nodier uncovers a prolific venue in which to express his personal stories and history through the history of 'the other.' He transgresses the limits of time and, in this way, inserts his work into human history. This intriguing process is marked by a fascination that emerges from an artistic literary source, where extraordinary images reflect two histories that are brought closer despite the distance between them. In this analysis of themes, images, and roles, I not only study the incorporation of the two histories into a literary story but also analyze the literary process that results from the multiple crossing of the fantastic boundaries. I also analyze the results of such an experience for the reader when those boundaries dissolve. The methodology is a comparative study of the literary fantastic, the role of history and the transposition of biblical images into the literary network of meaning.

In the letter inserted into the dedication section before the story is narrated, Charles Nodier introduces the literary work *Inès de Las Sierras* as "an outline written in leisure time"[2] rather than a formal literary work. The blurred boundary of the author's writing intentions creates the first uncanny sign in the story because the reader doubts the nature of the narrative and the intentions of the writer, who is introducing a literary work as a 'non-literary work'. This lack of literary seriousness seems to devalue the literary work that follows.

---

[1] "Laisser la trace de son passage, écrire son nom dans le monde littéraire fantastique, équivaut à atteindre l'éternité et Nodier est parvenu, sans aucun doute à laisser son empreinte dans le monde littéraire fantastique français. L'ampleur que l'histoire fantastique nodérienne acquiert, grâce aux emprunts des images bibliques, se manifeste non seulement à travers la coïncidence des images mais encore et surtout à travers son dessein d'imprégner le récit fantastique du biblique de telle manière que, la lecture de l'histoire fantastique devient donc une double lecture du moment que les références implicites ou subtiles s'entrelacent en engageant le lecteur dans une activité intellectuelle de références multiples et dans une activité de l'imagination qui établit un va-et-vient entre ce qui est connu et ce qui est nouveau. À travers l'analyse comparée des images bibliques dans le monde fantastique et les images bibliques d'origine et en dévoilant le processus d'emprunt qui comporte des modifications et des adaptations de l'image afin de l'insérer dans le contexte d'accueil nous allons découvrir le regard complice de l'écrivain." (Boruszko 199)

[2] "... plutôt ébauchée qu'écrite en quelques heures de loisir." (17)

This devaluation is true not only of the storyline but also of the fortune of a narrative that was left to obscurity and was considered a minor work of Nodier. In the dedication, which is presented as a letter to the editor, the writer continues to detach and distance himself from his own story, and he instead creates an uncertain emotional attachment to the editor. "The feeling that you attach to it (the story) could be the only way to give it some value."[3] The validation process, which is normally initiated by the writer who intentionally created the story, is now aborted by the author, who puts his own creation up for adoption with no concern for the future of the story. This lack of concern is indicated by the phrase "some value," which is not only dismissive of the dignity of the work but also creates doubt. The fantastic world is born in the doubt and ambiguity of the emotional topography of the literary work. The author gives the literary story a touch of emotional trauma that creates a dramatic 'baptism', or insertion, of the work into the literary and real realms. The story becomes a 'literary fantastic refuge' from another sphere that tries to find some sympathy in the real world. The situation is literarily aggravated when the 'one rejecting' it is the creator who called it into existence in the first place.

Nodier dedicates each of his books to his friends, indicating that these friendships are the only link between his works.[4] The next paragraph surprises the reader when the author speaks of this dedication as a tribute to the editor. The rejected work, which was introduced as a lesser work, is the object that the author uses to honor the editor. This strategy immediately raises suspicion, bringing opposite explanations to play against the doubt and ambiguity that creates the perfect atmosphere.[5] Is the writer being sincere about his doubts regarding the quality of his work, or, on the contrary, is he exhibiting a false modesty? Nodier, in an elegant but manipulative move, transfers the right of existence of each literary work to the editor and the publishing enterprise, stepping aside and abandoning his work of art.[6] In the following sentence, the writer affirms that the editor is the intermediary between the people who think (authors) and those who read.[7] Again, Nodier takes the stand not as a literary writer but as a philosopher who uses his words to diminish not the literary work but the reader, who is described as a mere consumerist. In

---

[3] "Le sentiment qui vous la donne peut seul y attacher quelque valeur." (17)

[4] "Je ne dédie mes livres qu'à mes amis, et j'ai mes raisons pour cela. Il n'y a pas un de ces volumes trop nombreux que je revisse aujourd'hui sans ennui et sans dégoût ; si je n'en avais lié le souvenir à celui d'une affection." (17)

[5] "Vous serez peut-être étonné si j'ajoute que je vous devais cet hommage. Rien n'est cependant plus vrai. N'êtes-vous pas l'éditeur accoutumé de mes frivoles compositions?" (17)

[6] "… n'est-ce pas votre industrie ingénieuse et libérale qui a fait de la publicité une ressource infaillible, pour la médiocrité comme pour le talent?" (17)

[7] "… n'êtes-vous pas, à peu de choses près, le seul intermédiaire possible des gens qui pensent avec ceux qui lisent encore?" (17)

this way, we could be led to think that Nodier is just discussing the reality of the publishing enterprise, denouncing their all-powerful take on the fortune of each printed work. From the beginning, he is nonetheless assuming a disdainful attitude towards his reader. The ambiguity of the literal and metaphorical senses is among the key elements that the writer uses in this story to maintain doubt and create the mysterious in a safe place outside the reach of any logical explanation, even in the second part of the story, when there is an apparent attempt to explain the fantastic story and individually uncover one by one the 'fantastic mysteries' of the first part of the story. Nodier continues to openly deny the fact that he is attempting to flatter the editor. His persona as a writer becomes increasingly shadowy and ambiguous as the reader, in the course of two paragraphs, is informed that the writer is not committed to his story, that he thinks of the reader as a consumerist and that the literary work was devalued as merchandise for the author to secure the affection of his friends.[8] In this systematic strategy, Nodier presents his literary methodology to construct the fantastic world. In the next sentence, we thus find the indication that he will explain himself.[9] A successful writer does not need to explain himself more than one time in the narration of each literary work. When another shadow is cast on the author, can we trust him in his *métier*? There is a nondisjunction of reality and fiction, of the performative and nonperformative aspects of language that undermines the comprehensibility that was systematically challenged in the course of the first page of the story, which is actually a letter. This leads us to study not what the text is but what the text does, as it becomes a self-agent and gives the impression that it disassociates itself from the author and the reader to claim an existence of its own. This modus operandi will be recycled in the second portion of the story, when the author claims to explain the supernatural events in a natural way. The undecided, the undetermined and the ambiguous resulting from blurring the borders between two opposite states opens the perfect topography where a ghost is displaced from the natural realm of existence into the real world. The dead body stays in the world; however, when ghosts come back, they do not belong here anymore. The borders between the natural and the supernatural become ambiguous, thus creating a solid, fantastic world based on ambiguity, doubt and fear. Opposites should not share the same space, so mystery transforms this space into a fantastic cosmos. Those who come back are not dead, but they are ghosts, which are more difficult to define. Hélène Cixous affirmed that "les contraires communiquent" (213) which means the contraries establish communication between them, and the uncanny is achieved when this happens.

---

[8] "Buloz, je vous proclame et je vous salue Mécène. | Vous accueillerez ce tribut d'estime avec confiance, car vous savez que je n'ai jamais flatté personne, pas même les directeurs des Revues." (17)

[9] "Je m'expliquerai maintenant:" (17)

The author's explanation continues in a more rhetoric tone as Nodier tries to justify his work as an author by bringing historical memory to the literary text. He first states the historical development of the human expression, encompassed in a trajectory that is ambiguous in the author's estimation, as he simultaneously affirms it to be a positive projection and casts a cloud of doubt on it.[10] The undetermined historical trajectory presented in a doubtful atmosphere brings down all of the scaffolding of the effort to elucidate the present, which is a product of a confusing past. Nodier thus immediately refers to the beginning of all times, the primordial times where he places the word, as performative in dispelling the chaos, thus making a clear reference to the book of Genesis in the Bible[11]:

"In the beginning God created the heavens and the earth. 2 Now the earth was formless and empty, darkness was over the surface of the deep, and the Spirit of God was hovering over the waters. 3 And God said, 'Let there be light', and there was light. 4 God saw that the light was good, and he separated the light from the darkness. 5 God called the light 'day', and the darkness he called 'night'. And there was evening, and there was morning—the first day." (Genesis 1:1–3)

Nodier, knowing the Bible, was himself a craftsman of the images that he consistently borrowed from the biblical accounts, reinserting them into his fantastic literary works. Since the beginning of times, man had the task of exploring his environment and ruling over it, thus taking possession of that space. At the same time, man was a complex individual; he looked into his own existence and explored his inner being. In this search, man tried to determine the boundaries between these two worlds and a cosmos that existed beyond these two realities, thus discovering his limits. An immediate desire to cross the boundaries marked the human experience at all levels. Nodier is, in this story, playfully working with the boundaries of history, literature, religion and the literary fantastic world. After the human experience approaches the boundaries, man faces conflicting forces that emerge from both worlds: the inner world that constitutes a personal fantastic cosmos, the conscience of the transcendental and the recognition of the forces that surround him or her. These parallel and sometimes conflicting worlds somehow relate to a supernatural mystery, creating enigmatic challenges that haunt him or her. The limits that each world exhibits unavoidably encourage the individual to transgress them. This tension thrusts the individual into an angst that will drive the

---

[10] "Les destinées de l'écrivain sont bien différentes dans nos jours de perfectionnement de ce qu'elles étaient dans les siècles de barbarie ; et ce qu'il y a d'étrange ; c'est que ce n'est pas en beau qu'elles ont changé ; on m'en apprendra peut-être la raison." (17–18)

[11] "Au commencement des sociétés ; la parole était vraiment la maîtresse du monde : C'est elle qui débrouillait le chaos." (18)

personal quest. In this way, Nodier, a writer of the 19th century faces this problem and tries to resolve it in a literary way.

In the literary cosmos, the writer takes the role of a god and creates a world according to his inspiration, using all of the elements that could serve that objective. The act of recreation, or re-creation, here using both meanings of the word, is present in each individual writing process. The literary world and any personal creative talents provide the author with a way to explore and experiment with a new creation in his or her own cosmogony, where he will enjoy freedom beyond the constraining boundaries and dissolve them. The fantastic world becomes the territory where this quest can take place, the territory where two completely different worlds meet. The transcendental, supernatural, intangible, outside-the-boundaries, mysterious and mystic world and the fantastic world that seems to emerge from the depths of the individual, thus projecting to the surface all of his inner anguishes and dissatisfactions, merge to create the essence of a work of art with an esthetic intent. When a human being discovers a world beyond the one that is known and personal, the individual starts to ask himself if he or she is part of a collective movement that transcends the personal experience. Does a supernatural reality exist beyond the personal experience and include a "we" or a "they" that could capture this individual interest with the same passion? Research, analysis, rationalization and comparative study all contribute to responding to this inquiry. Beyond the individual quest, there is a collective journey that could end up in a literary writing that is accessible to all.

The fantastic imagination, being essentially figurative to create a self-referential 'new world', borrows elements that could be profitable in the creation of his unique world. The element that links the contextual world of origin of the borrowed image and the fantastic world is the connection that is established between the two worlds, which crosses and dissolves the boundaries of each world. This connection causes the borrowed image to create a nexus of meaning that, while carrying the original meaning to the fantastic world, subverts it by inserting it into a new network of meaning, thus creating the uncanny and mysterious. When a reader who is versed in both worlds finds the image manipulated, sculpted, and maybe subverted, he or she perceives an image that has transcended and belongs to the uncanny world of mysterious duality that brings the image to a certain state of folly.

In *Inès De Las Sierras*, chooses a great variety of Biblical images to populate his fantastic cosmogony. The literary value of those images is that in the transposition of those images, the author seeks to permeate his fantastic story with the sense of the transcendental, which is inherent to the original image in the original network of meaning. Nodier achieves this literary strategy with the artistry of an artisan, carefully crafting each image to introduce it into his own fantastic world.

Victor Hugo, in his preface to *Cromwell*, elaborates on the nexus between religion and literature:

"The day when Christianity said to man: 'You're two, you're composed of two beings, one perishable, the other immortal, one carnal, the other ethereal, one chained by desires, needs and passions, the other carried on the wings of enthusiasm and reverie, it finally always bent towards the earth, his mother, the former constantly reaches skyward, his country', that day the drama was created. (…) … the character of the drama is real, the real result of combining any two natural types, the sublime and the grotesque, which intersect in the drama as they meet in life and creation."[12]

Sanguinet-Matabos, in his work, *Les personnages fantastiques*, states that

"Maybe considered fantastic every human being or entity which is meeting on the sidelines of the common human experience, whose appearance violates established rules (…)."[13]

The writer, who is situated in his fantastic cosmogony, is in an environment where he can explore the "possible worlds" that inhabit the cosmos outside the limits of reality in any of its manifestations. Nodier, as a writer in the 19th century, shares the interest of the romantics, but as a pioneer of the fantastic world, however, he decided to explore the literary possibilities of the fantastic that blurred all borders. At the same time, the 19th century in France is an era when religiosity was practiced alongside spiritual and metaphysical preoccupations. Literature took the place of illustration, which could not provide resolution to religious dilemmas, thus offering the fantastic space as a space for reflection without entering more radical or controversial fields.

The author is now presenting himself as the author, the creator of the text, thereby contradicting his posture in the previous page as a writer detached from his literary work.[14] The *telos* of the biblical creation is to glorify the Creator, as shown in Colossians 1:16, "all things were created through him and for him," or later in Revelations 4:11, "(God) created all things, and for (his) pleasure they are and were created." We can see how Nodier presents himself with the same

---

[12] "Du jour où le christianisme a dit à l'homme: "Tu es double, tu es composé de deux êtres, l'un périssable, l'autre immortel, l'un charnel, l'autre éthéré, l'un enchaîné par les appétits, les besoins et les passions, l'autre emporté sur les ailes de l'enthousiasme et de la rêverie, celui-ci enfin toujours courbé vers la terre, sa mère, celui-là sans cesse élancé vers le ciel, sa patrie"; de ce jour le drame a été créé. (…) … le caractère du drame est le réel; le réel résulte de la combinaison toute naturelle de deux types, le sublime et le grotesque, qui se croisent dans le drame, comme ils se croisent dans la vie et dans la création." (24)

[13] "Peut être considéré comme fantastique tout être humain ou toute entité dont la rencontre se situe en marge de l'expérience humaine courante; dont l'apparition viole les règles préétablies (…)." (151)

[14] "Je m'expliquerai maintenant: Les destinées de l'écrivain (…)." (17)

ambiguity and uncanny duality that he used to craft his literary work: he is simultaneously the disengaged author and a replica of the all-powerful biblical Creator. In the biblical account of the Creation, there is a tension between rule and energy, order and exuberance, instantaneous creation and biological creation. God's performative word is aimed towards creating order out of the primal chaos. Many mythologies, including the Mesopotamian and Egyptian cosmologies, also refer to chaos as being hostile to the god creator, which contrasts the biblical account, possibly indicating that there is no opposition to the creative performative word. The rest of the Bible highlights the fact that God always controls the natural forces, as observed in the story when Jesus calms the tempest in Mark 4:35–41:

"^{35} That day when evening came, he said to his disciples, 'Let us go over to the other side.' ^{36} Leaving the crowd behind, they took him along, just as he was, in the boat. There were also other boats with him. ^{37} A furious squall came up, and the waves broke over the boat, so that it was nearly swamped. ^{38} Jesus was in the stern, sleeping on a cushion. The disciples woke him and said to him, 'Teacher, don't you care if we drown?'

^{39} He got up, rebuked the wind and said to the waves, 'Quiet! Be still!' Then the wind died down and it was completely calm.

^{40} He said to his disciples, 'Why are you so afraid? Do you still have no faith?'

^{41} They were terrified and asked each other, 'Who is this? Even the wind and the waves obey him!'"

In the case of Nodier, there is a hint of arduous work on the part of the writer.[15] This image of an engaged writer is nested in the section in which Nodier explains himself as a separate entity from the writer who is engaged with the editor and the publication process. Nodier inserts himself into a lineage of poets and writers of great talent who ruled alongside political rulers.[16] The author is now interested in delineating the intersection of political and literary history as a means to explain his current status as a writer. By joining two histories, here, the ancient and Nodier's present, the literary tradition and the literary practice of his time, Nodier tries to justify his status as a man of letters. Later, he mentions the support of the Church to the *métier* of a poet or writer.[17] In this short narrative trajectory, the author has touched on the religious, the historical, the political and the literary realms, joining them in a journey that eliminates the boundaries to create a

---

[15] "Quand les eaux du déluge des Grecs se sont retirées, qui vient recommencer la civilisation? C'est un poète." (18)

[16] "… la position de l'homme de génie resta très belle : Orphée ; Parménides, Empédocle, Pythagore, ne sont plus des dieux: ce sont des législateurs. Dans ces siècles si pauvres d'esprit, l'esprit fut roi. | Il s'assit longtemps avec autorité à côté du trône. Esope fut l'ami de Crésus, et Platon celui de Denis. Je cite deux exemples; j'en citerais cent." (18)

[17] "Eginhard et Alcuin n'étaient autre chose que des gens des lettres. | L'autorité pontificale surtout s'appuya constamment sur lui." (18)

synergetic force.[18] Nodier express his despair as a writer who is not heard by his contemporaries and as a librarian who is troubled by the lack of interest in creating new libraries. The past, which offered support to the writers and philosophers, contrasts the present, which seems to lean on the side of indifference towards literary work. The author here turns and lashes out against the publishing enterprise that created the cultural chaos. The practice of dedicating literary works to other members of society became a dangerous affair because the recipients of the dedication fear being associated with the writer and his ideas. Again, Nodier introduces a cloud of doubt and anxiety that emerges from the reality of his time. The writer is submerged in the uncanny circumstances of the reality of his life, which could validate the theme of his fantastic writings.[19] The craftsmanship of Nodier is explained in this letter of dedication.

"It is the word that created the civilization which acknowledges that the word can destroy it, because it has been ignored: criminal and absurd vengeance, but inevitable."[20]

The author believes that the word is the most powerful source for building a civilization. He therefore worked as a craftsman to sculpt his images and place them in his fantastic cosmogonies, which functioned as a place to take refuge from the implacable real world. In erasing the borders between the two universes, Nodier somehow tried to create a new Garden of Eden.[21] Nodier expressed that the word had a creative and destructive power, contrasting the Biblical account that introduces the image of redemption: "Now we look inside, and what we see is that anyone united with the Messiah gets a fresh start, is created new" (2 Corinthians 5:17). In this verse, God is restoring what was damaged in the biblical fall and giving it the shape of a new creation. Creation is the witness of a "new creation", which is described as redemption through the use of the image of the Messiah.

Nodier worked to create a new literary world that, as did the garden of Eden, symbolized a new beginning. Nodier thus gave so much importance to the word because it was the performative word that, according to the biblical account,

---

[18] "Je ne sais trop quelle idée une reine de notre temps se fait de cette espèce qu'on appelle auteur ; mais je n'imagine pas qu'il se retrouve jamais une Marguerite d'Ecosse ; qui donne un baiser sur la bouche à un Alain Chartier endormi. | Et qu'on ne pense point que cette espèce de culte se renfermât dans la classe élevée de la société d'alors." (19)

[19] "Un de mes amis eut dernièrement l'étrange caprice de dédier son ouvrage à un préfet ; non par calcul certainement ; car une dédicace n'est plus un calcul ; mais par un mouvement d'estime ou par une concession de politesse : Le préfet refusa l'hommage de peur de se compromettre. Une dédicace peut compromettre celui qui la reçoit." (21)

[20] "C'est la parole qui a créé la civilisation; elle sait aujourd'hui qu'elle peut la détruire, | et elle la détruira, parce qu'elle a été méconnue: vengeance criminelle et absurde, | mais inévitable." (23)

[21] "'La Fontaine disait : | Jadis l'Olympe et le Parnasse | Etaient frères et bons amis. ' | Cette alliance est rompue. Où est l'Olympe maintenant?" (23)

brought into existence all that was created *ex nihilo*. The writer is aware that he is in a re-creation process, so he follows a similar strategy. In the Bible, as God orders the elements, he utters commands that instantaneously produce objects. The verbs that are more common in this narrative are "made", "separated", and "placed". Except for "separated", the other two verbs could be applied to the narrative of *Inès de Las Sierras*. The fantastic literature, as an act of re-creation, needs to simultaneously compile, associate, and conceal its traces by eliminating the boundaries between the known world and the newly created world that is placed outside reality. The strategy to hide this process aims to create "uncertainty, doubt", so the uncanny can transform the reality into a created supernatural. In the Biblical account, the supernatural seems to appear in the real world to bring order, so clarity is of the essence. We thus find a clearly delineated order of the creative process. The common words used in the biblical narrative are "and God said", "let there be", "and it was so", "and God made", followed by the self-assessment of the creation that casts no doubts about the intentions and the authorship of the created world, "…it was very good." This is contrary to the strategy of Nodier, who chose to subvert this aspect, though using the biblical narrative as inspiration.[22] In the book of Psalms 104:24 and 31, we find the same description of this Creative act:

"[24] What a wildly wonderful world, God! You made it all, with Wisdom at your side, made earth overflow with your wonderful creations."

"[31] The glory of God—let it last forever!? Let God enjoy his creation!"

The biblical images of creation are correlative to the domestic routines. The result is the domestication of wonder, as God is presented as controlling the forces of nature without displaying an unordinary way of doing it; he uses an ordinary and effortless method instead to bring into reality what was not there before. Nodier, as the creator of the fantastic world, takes that approach but describes it as taking a great deal of effort because he recalled history and the many penuries that poets and writers had to endure to create their own cosmogonies. The boundaries between the literary creation and the biblical creation that seems to inspire Nodier are hazy due to the direction of the creative action that begins in reality and is projected to the supernatural; the biblical narrative describes the contrary direction. In Hebrews 11:3, the creation *ex nihilo* is explained, "By faith, we see the world called into existence by God's word, what we see created by what we don't see."

---

[22] "3 And God said, 'Let there be light,' and there was light. 4 God saw that the light was good, and he separated the light from the darkness. 5 God called the light 'day,' and the darkness he called 'night.' And there was evening, and there was morning—the first day. … 18 … And God saw that it was good." (The Bible, Genesis 1:3)

Charles Nodier introduces the story in a duality of domains and uses the biblical account as the primary source whence the literary fantastic would emerge:

"– And you said Anastase, would you tell us a tale of ghosts? ...
– Stick to me, I answered, as I witnessed the strangest apparition that had ever been spoken of since Samuel ... ".[23]

The narrator inserts the story into a series of stories because the request implies that other stories had been told before. The literary field is delineated by the trajectory that stories have taken in different times. In this way, Nodier inserts his fantastic story into the long trajectory of literary production during different ages, thus continuing the rhetoric of the *dédicace*.

Nodier, as a writer seeking to create his fantastic world, takes inspiration from Biblical images and narrative structure to successfully introduce the reader into the world of the uncanny, shaping doubt as he erases and transgresses the limits between history, literature and religion to craft a cosmogony of the supernatural.

Bibliography

Bible, Nt., English, Peterson. The Message: the New Testament in Contemporary English. Colorado Springs: NAV Press, 1993. Print.

Boruszko, Graciela S. "L'imaginaire Fantastique Chez Nodier Et L'inspiration Biblique." *Neohelicon* 38.1 (2011): 199–212. Print.

Cixous, Hélène. "La Fiction et ses fantômes: une lecture de l'Unheimliche de Freud." *Poétique* 10 (1972): 199–216. Print.

Eugene, H. P. *The Message: The Old Testament Books of Moses in Contemporary Language.* Colorado Springs, CO: Nav Press, 2001. Print.

Hugo, Victor. *Cromwell.* Paris: Garnier-Flammarion, 1985. Print

Sanguinet-Matabos. "Les personnages Fantastiques." Extrait de *Fiction* Number 147 (1966). Print.

Nodier, Charles, and Georges Zaragoza. *Inès De Las Sierras.* Ivry: Phénix éditions, 2000. Print.

---

[23] "– Et toi, dit Anastase, ne nous feras-tu pas aussi un conte de revenants? ... | – Il ne tiendrait qu'á moi, répondis-je; car j'ai été témoin de la plus étrange apparition dont il ait jamais été parlé depuis celle de Samuel ... " (25).

The Alchemical Imaginary of Homunculi in *Fullmetal Alchemist*

Minwen Huang

Homunculus, etymologically referring to "little person" in Latin (Harper), is an artificially created human who owes its mythological and legendary birth to the practices of alchemy. Alchemy with its capability of processing the material and spiritual transformations grounding both in the western and eastern traditions is the particular means not only to transmute lead into gold but also to achieve immortality through producing the elixir of life or the philosopher's stone. Owing to the fantastic essence of creating homunculi, i.e. the desire to create artificial humans based on the imagination of the unreal or the unknown, this literary motif of creating a homunculus through alchemical practices has displayed its refracted crystallizations in various representations in literature and arts from ancient times to the present day across cultures. Hiromu Arakawa's *Fullmetal Alchemist* (*FMA*), a popular Japanese manga series running from August 2001 to June 2010, is one contemporary example that illustrates a fictional universe where alchemy is one of the most advanced scientific techniques and where homunculi are created through alchemical practices.

Adopting the theory of literary imaginary proposed by Gaston Bachelard and that of visual narratives especially centering on Japanese manga, this article attempts to delve into the alchemical imaginary of homunculi embedded in the spatial-topological mechanism of *FMA* as a contemporary visual representation that relocates the western archaic alchemical imaginary of homunculi in a Japanese manga narrative context. The alchemical imaginary of homunculi in *FMA* will be examined from three perspectives: (1) Homunculus as alchemical opus, (2) Narrative world as alchemical opus, and (3) Manga as alchemical opus. While alchemical opus designates both the process leading to the creation of the great work and the great work itself, it is through the gradual examination firstly from the individual world of Homunculus as a character, to the narrative world of *FMA*, and lastly to the generic world of manga that the alchemical imaginary of homunculi in *FMA* to a certain extent represents or projects the wanting of the contemporary epoch for an alchemical return to a spiritual and material union as C. G. Jung proposed in *Modern Man in Search of a Soul*.

Alchemy & Fullmetal Alchemist

Alchemy, a pre-scientific mode of investigation of the natural world that brings about the birth of our modern sciences, is the particular scientific means highly developed in the story world of *FMA*. Set in an imaginary world, which is specifically fashioned after the post-Industrial Revolution England but anachronistically located within the 20th century, *FMA* tells of the adventures of the young Elric brothers. They are two alchemists on their way to search for the legendary philosopher's stone in order to restore their bodies lost during the failed attempt to bring their deceased mother back to life. It is during the journey that they encounter the homunculi, the main antagonists who determine to create the philosopher's stone through the sacrifice of human beings, and consequently get more involved in unraveling the truth behind the scenes.

Quite essentially, alchemy plays the vital role of triggering the "imaginary," i.e. "a function of unreality" in a human's mind to form "the *imagined images*" proposed by Gaston Bachelard (13), which leads to the naissance of *FMA*. Arakawa explained in one interview that she was at first interested in the idea of the philosopher's stone, but then was drawn deeply into the fervent research on alchemy: "I was more attracted to the philosophical aspects of it than the practical ones" (*FMA. Perfect Guide Book 3*: 165). Due to the strong attraction to alchemy, Arakawa renders alchemy the main source and catalyzer of the active imagination that determines the creation of *FMA* both thematically and structurally. That is to say, under the operation of the alchemical imaginary, i.e. "a function of unreality" based on the working of alchemy, the visual and graphic renderings of *FMA* are, thus, the authentic representations of the "*imagined images*" illustrated by Arakawa, which moreover display, to a certain extent, the intimate correlation among alchemy, imagination, and art as Paracelsus and Jung declared.

Among them, the motif of creating a homunculus, i.e. the process of creating an artificial human through alchemical practices, is considered to be the main focus of this article, for the creation of a homunculus is closely related to the transformation and forging of alchemical opus. Since alchemical opus refers both to the alchemical process of transmutation and to the work of creation itself, the creation of a homunculus could be viewed as an analogy of the creation of a particular character, i.e. Homunculus in *FMA*, that of the creation of an artistic work, namely *FMA* in this case, or that of the creation of the genre of Japanese manga in general. Within the visual renderings of alchemical imaginary in *FMA*, these three types of alchemical opus will be examined distinctively in the following sections.

Homunculus as Alchemical Opus – The Transformation of Homunculus

Although there are several homunculi depicted in *FMA*, the one that is going to be examined here is the original homunculus who denominates himself "Homunculus" (19: 44) and triggers the birth of the whole narrative world of *FMA*. Moreover, it is through examining the alchemical transformation of Homunculus, or the evolution of Homunculus, that the exertion of the alchemical imaginary of homunculi on shaping the visual representation of Homunculus as a character could be detected. The transformation of Homunculus could be demarcated into three stages, from being the little man in the flask, to the living philosopher's stone in human form, and to a god-like perfect being.

Homunculus: The Little Man in the Flask

When thinking about the creation of a homunculus in a laboratory setting, it is very likely to refer to Paracelsus' recipe. Philippus Aureolus Theophrastus Bombastus von Hohenheim (1493–1541), a Swiss Renaissance alchemist, also known as Paracelsus, offers a recipe for creating a homunculus in *De rerum naturae* (1537):

"If the sperma, enclosed in a hermetically sealed glass, is buried in horse manure for forty days, and properly magnetized, it begins to live and move. After such a time it bears the form and resemblance of a human being, but it will be transparent and without a body. If it is now artificially fed with the *Arcanum sanguinis hominis* [the "secret blood of man"] until it is about forty weeks old, and if allowed to remain during that time in horse manure in a continually equal temperature, it will grow into a human child, with all its members developed like any other child, such as could be born by a woman; only it will be much smaller. We call such a being a homunculus, and it may be raised and educated like any other child, until it grows older and obtains reason and intellect, and is able to take care of itself." (qtd. in Lachman)

This western renaissance concept of creating a homunculus further inspired Goethe's literary creation of the homunculus in the second part of *Faust* in 1832 and exerted its magical effects on shaping the Japanese manga creation of Homunculus in Arakawa's *FMA*.

Recounted in a dream narrative, the creation of Homunculus in *FMA* is closely tied in with the historical reality revealed both in the fictional world of *MFA* and in the magical world of Paracelsus' recipe. Similar to the description of Paracelsus' recipe, Homunculus, or "The Little Man in the Flask" as the title of one episode suggests in *MFA*, is born accidentally in a laboratory in Xerxes, an ancient and prosperous country, in the mid-16th century through feeding it the human blood of a slave who has no name but is called "Slave 23" (19: 39). The alchemical birth of Homunculus in *MFA*, though revealed in a dream narrative, is attested as a historical fact in *MFA* as the story unfolds itself. Moreover, it realizes Paracelsus' recipe in the physical location of its birth in a sealed glass through feeding human blood as an experiment and in the temporal location of its birth that vaguely echoes the publication year of Paracelsus' recipe in 1537.

The visual representation of Homunculus in this stage, originated and deviated from the western alchemical imaginary of homunculi in the Renaissance, is pictured as a round conglomerate of mysterious black matter with one eye and two rows of teeth (*FMA* 19: 44), rather than being endowed with a small human child form as depicted in Paracelsus' recipe. This ambiguous form of black matter resonates with the status of the primal material, "the *prima materia*, the chaos or *massa fonusa*" which is usually mentioned in the initial state of the alchemical transformation, i.e. the stage of the *nigredo* or blackening as Jung explicates in *Psychology and Alchemy* (230). Ironically, Homunculus in this black matter form enclosed in the flask is very human in terms of its personality and capability. It has a sense of humor and is capable of expressing various emotions. It is erudite, has the access of truth, and names Slave 23 "Van Hohenheim" (*FMA* 19: 41), a name that refers to the family name of Paracelsus. However, it is due to its human desire to be freed from the little space of the flask that brings about the second stage of its alchemical transformation.

Homunculus: Philosopher's Stone in Human Form

In the second stage of the transformation of Homunculus, the conglomerate of dark material enclosed in the test tube is metamorphosized into a philosopher's stone in human form. This alchemical transmutation takes place in Xerxes under the occasion that the king of Xerxes in his old age is afraid of approaching death. In disguise of fulfilling the king's wish of achieving immortality, Homunculus sets up a trick to activate a nationwide alchemical ritual, which transforms Homunculus, the conglomerate of black matter, and Van Hohenheim, a white man with blond hair in his middle age, into the philosopher's stones in identical human form – the double as the opposites (*FMA* 19: 70–71). The ritual costs a great amount of human sacrifice, i.e. all citizens in Xerxes, and the tragic destruction of the prosperous Xerxes overnight. After this event, Homunculus and Van Hohenheim, the human philosopher's stones carrying thousands of human souls of the Xerxes citizens within them, disperse to the west and the east respectively and become the legendary philosophers who bring alchemy to the world.

Although it is also said that the appearance of the philosopher's stone does not refer literally to the shape of stone as Zosimos declares that it is "a stone that is not a stone" (qtd. in Guiley 250), Homunculus, the human philosopher's stone, is endowed with the legendary magical power. Being the central symbol of the mystical system of alchemy, the philosopher's stone, a.k.a "*lapis philosopho-*

rum," is the legendary alchemical substance which is capable of transmuting base materials into gold or silver and is usually viewed as the ultimate goal of alchemy (Gauding 188). Its alchemical capability to "speed a natural process of evolution in which minerals and base metals evolve[d] to higher and purer state" (Guiley 250) is entwined with the power to prolong life and to create artificial life in *FMA* as its other name, the elixir of life, suggests.

Attributed with the art of creating artificial life, Homunculus as the Father founds the country of Amestris in the 16th century and produces from his body seven homunculi as his children. They are named after the seven deadly sins, i.e. Pride, Lust, Envy, Greed, Gluttony, Sloth, and Wrath. The alchemical imaginary of the seven homunculi is pictured with distinctive character designs in accordance with the genuine features attached to the essence of the seven deadly sins. However, all of them share one tattoo placed in different parts of their bodies – the symbol of the Ouroboros (*FMA* 1: 97-98). Being an ancient archetypal image depicting a serpent or dragon eating its own tail, the Ouroboros symbolizes the immortality and the One as Jung suggests in *Mysterium Coniunctionis* (365). While the homunculi tattooed with the symbol of Ouroboros in *FMA* are portrayed as immortal, their separation from the body of the Father Homunculus ironically testifies their imperfection and the perfection of their Father. Homunculus' getting rid of the seven capital vices or the seven strong human emotions helps him to be transformed into a more perfect being as the philosopher's stone also symbolizes perfection, i.e. a state of being less human in contrast to his present human form and to his previous life form – the conglomerate of black matter capable of expressing various emotions. Moreover, his alchemical attempt to achieve perfection further drives him to reach the third stage of transformation.

Homunculus: A Perfect Being, an Existence like God

In the third stage of transformation, Homunculus, the philosopher's stone in human form, is transmuted into an absolute perfect being, an existence like God. This alchemical transformation takes place in the central city of Amestris, the nation founded in the 16th century specifically for activating this alchemical ritual, on the day when a full solar eclipse occurs in the spring in 1915. Similar to what has happened in the second transformation, a nationwide transmutation circle is designed and more human sacrifices are prepared. Empowered by the great amount of human sacrifice and the particular alchemical setting, the effective scale of the alchemical ritual is enlarged from the microcosm of a human body to the macrocosm of the universe, which rejuvenates the human body of Homunculus and endows him with the mighty force to control solar and nuclear power as God.

Alchemically, the geographical location of the transmutation circle and the astrological phenomenon of the full solar eclipse are essential to activate the alchemical transformation of Homunculus. As an alchemical opus, Homunculus is placed in the center of the transmutation circle during a full solar eclipse, the astrological moment constructed by the movement of celestial bodies, i.e. when Sun and Moon align together with Earth and the light of the Sun is blocked. This astrological phenomenon of a solar eclipse is termed "chemical wedding" or "sacred marriage" in alchemy, for it illustrates physically and symbolically the mysterious conjunction of opposites, the Sun and the Moon, which unveils the darkness symbolized by *Sol niger* (the black sun) and reaches the ultimate state of a perfect union. Homunculus, being capable of exerting solar and nuclear power, is turned into an absolute perfect being, an existence like God, for the sun symbolizes gold and "is rightly named the first after God, and the father and begetter of all" (qtd. in Jung, *Mysterium Coniunctionis* 94).

The alchemical transformation of Homunculus in *FMA*, i.e. from being the little man in the flask to the living philosopher's stone in human form and to a godlike perfect being, illustrates both the visual and mystical metamorphoses of the alchemical imaginary of Homunculus as alchemical opus. However, Homunculus as the main antagonist is not able to maintain his mighty force due to the efforts of his opposites, i.e. Van Hohenheim, the Elric brothers and their friends. They succeed in diminishing Homunculus' power into his original state as a conglomerate of dark matter and in driving Homunculus back to the Gate of Truth, the source of his origin, where all knowledge and information are stored. Nevertheless, the failure of the alchemical transformation of Homunculus as an antagonist in *FMA* helps to complete the transformation of Homunculus as alchemical opus and leads to the success of the forging of the narrative world of *FMA*.

Narrative World as Alchemical Opus – Searching for the Truth

The graphic narrative world of *FMA*, being the alchemical opus, is the one that needs to be read and decoded as an enigmatic alchemical text in order to reach the truth that lies behind the encoded signs, i.e. activating the third alchemical transformation of Homunculus. Through the unfolding of the story pertaining to the text-time, i.e. "the sequence of events presented in the book" (Grellet 79), or to *Erzählzeit*, "the (psedudo-) time of the narrative" which centers on "the pseudo-temporal order of [the] arrangement [of events]" (Genette 35), various layers of text worlds have been revealed and added to the narrative world of *FMA* as a whole. This section is demarcated into three narrative units in accordance with the text-time, including (1) the graphic narrative of the present, concerning the events that happen as the story begins, (2) that of the past, regarding the events that happened before the story begins, and (3) that of the present continuous, relating to the events that happen after the story begins.

The graphic narrative of the present regarding the setting depicted as the story begins is the one that discloses the surface information of the narrative world of *FMA* as an alchemical text. As the story begins, the narrative is set in Amestris in 1914 regarding the Continental Calendar. Amestris is a Unitary State with a Parliamentary Republic government, centralized by the State Military and supported by the State Alchemists, the most prominent human weapons. Concerning the administrative regions, the whole nation is composed of five regions, i.e. South Area, West Area, North Area, East Area, and Central Area, whose territorial shape actually echoes the nationwide hexagon transmutation circle to be activated in the end of the story.

Before the Story Begins: The Past

The graphic narrative of the past regarding the setting depicted before the story begins is the one that works to build the breadth of the graphic geography and the depth of graphic temporality of the narrative world of *FMA* as an alchemical text. Concerning what happened before the story begins, four events of the past are illustrated through distinctive forms of narratives, including memory narrative, documentary narrative, fairy tale narrative, and dream narrative respectively. All of them are enclosed within black frames, in contrast to the normal white frames, to signify the temporal dislocation spatially. Furthermore, they have been testified as the historical truth in the end to solidify the narrative world of *FMA*, as the goal is to activate the nationwide transmutation circle designed for the alchemical transformation in the future.

The first graphic narrative of the past refers to the Ishval Civil War, which lasts from 1901 to 1908 in the southeast of Amestris. Disclosed through memory narrative, the historical events of Ishval Civil War are told from the perspectives of various narrators, i.e. the characters personally involved in the war. All these unreliable fragments of personal memories are pieced together into a historical narrative, which helps to achieve the understanding of the truth hidden behind the scenes – namely, that the war is the means to prepare human sacrifice for activating the coming alchemical ritual in 1915. The second graphic narrative of the past concerns the founding and expansion of the territory of Amestris, whose time span covers from the 16th century to the present, i.e. 1914. Recounted through documentary narrative, the process of founding and expanding Amestris has been recorded in state military documents as classified information. Along with the unveiling of the secrecy of the event, the historical truth is recovered, which explains that Amestris has kept attacking the neighboring countries in order to draw a nationwide transmutation circle.

The third graphic narrative of the past relates to the fairy tale narratives concerning the philosopher from the East and the philosopher from the West. The fairy tales have circulated both in Amestris and Xing, the nation located east of Amestris across a desert, about the legendary fairy tale figures, the great Philosophers or Alchemists, who brought alchemy to Amestris and Xing respectively in around the 16th century. With the unfolding of the story, the fairy tale narratives have gained their historical solidity as the two figures, i.e. Homunculus the Father and Van Hohenheim, reveal themselves in the present. The fourth graphic narrative of the past refers to both the creation of Homunculus and the destruction of Xerxes, which happened in the 16th century in Xerxes. The whole event is disclosed ambiguously through dream narrative either from the perspective of Homunculus the Father or from that of Van Hohenheim. However, the ambiguity of the dream perspective manifests the intimate relation shared between Homunculus and Van Hohenheim. That is to say, the dream narrative is transformed from an individual dream into a collective dream, which turns the myth of the alchemical creation of Homunculus into a historical fact.

Through transforming the four narratives of the past into historical truth, the graphic geography of the narrative world of *FMA* is extended from Amestris to Xing, and to the legendary nation of Xerxes, along with the expansion of the graphic temporality from the present in 1914 and back to the legendary past in the 16th century, which will be referred back again to the future in 1915 and further on with the unveiling of the graphic narrative of the present continuous.

After the Story Begins: The Present Continuous

The graphic narrative of the present continuous regarding the setting depicted after the story begins is the one that pulls all the graphic narratives together to unveil the mysterious alchemical designs for the third transformation of Homunculus and to complete the narrative world of *FMA* as alchemical opus. After the story begins, the narrative is set in Amestris from 1914 to the promised day in the spring in 1915 when the nationwide transmutation circle is to be activated. However, a reactionary force to fight against Homunculus, i.e. Van Hohenheim, the Elric brothers, and their friends as the opposite of Homunculus, has grown along with the unfolding of the graphic narrative of the present continuous. All of them help to activate the reverse nationwide transmutation circle in the end, to drive Homunculus back to his source – the Gate of Truth, and to restore the world balance alchemically.

Manga as Alchemical Opus – The Union of Opposites

This section on "manga as alchemical opus" attempts to delve into the generic world of Japanese manga to explore the alchemical procedure of synthesizing the pairs of opposites, i.e. the union of opposites, or *Mysterium Coniunctionis* (Latin:

"mysterious conjunction"), "the final alchemical synthesis that brings forth the philosopher's stone" (Chalquist). The pairs of opposites to be explored regarding manga include its generic naissance, its generic form, and its generic mechanism.

Generic Naissance: Japanese Traditional Folk Arts and Western Visual Arts

Manga, referring specifically to a particular form of comics created in Japan (Gravett 8), is a genre born out of the synthesizing or union of the Japanese traditional folk arts and the western visual arts. Japanese manga has its generic roots in the historical art traditions in Japanese culture, which could be traced back as far as to the caricatures of people and animals carved on the planks of the Horyuji Temple built originally in 607 AD (Ito, "Manga in Japanese History", 26). Other art traditions that have influenced the generic birth of manga include *Tobae*, a style of painting referring to "the animal scrolls" invented by Bishop Toba, a Buddhist monk, in the 12th century (Schodt, *Dreamland Japan* 33), *Otzue*, the simple Buddhist pictures as a form of talisman emerged near the city of Otzu in the mid-17th century (Ito, "A History of *Manga*" 458), and *Ukiyoe*, or "pictures of the floating world," a genre of popular folk pictures invented since the late 17th century (Ito, "A History of *Manga*" 459), to name but a few. With the publication of *Hokusai Manga* in 1814, Hokusai Katsuhika (1760–1849) was the first to coin the term "manga," whose Chinese characters literally mean "whimsical pictures or sketches" (Brenner 3). However, the modern Japanese manga, a genre that incorporates the Japanese traditional folk arts with the western visual arts, still has to wait for the union with its western opposite that launched in 1853 when the Japanese government was forced to open its ports to trade with the West (ibid.).

Due to the trade with the West, new western art and traditions were imported to Japan and influenced Japanese art immediately. The western visual arts incorporated to bring forth the birth of manga include *The Japan Punch* (1862–1887), a magazine started by Charles Wigman, an English cartoonist, through imitating London's famous cartoon magazine *Punch* Brenner 4), *Tobae* (1887–1889), a French-style humor magazine issued by George Bigot, a French cartoonist (Ito, "A History of *Manga*", 461), American comics, which became the mass medium following the success of Outcault's *The Yellow Kid* serialized between 1895 and 1898 (Weiner 1), Hollywood films since its founding in 1917, and Walt Disney animations since its establishment in 1923.

Through synthesizing the Japanese traditional arts and the western arts as opposites, the modern Japanese manga as a genuine genre was born around World War II, when Osamu Tezuka (1928–89), "the Father of Manga" or "the God of Comics" (Patten 198), began to publish his works. Examples are *New Treasure*

Island in 1947, *Metropolis* in 1949, *Astro Boy*, serialized between 1952 and 1968, and still many others. Incorporating western visual arts, i.e. Disney animations and American comics, into the artistic production of Japanese manga, Tezuka invented the "cinematic-style," which was widely adopted by later manga artists (Schodt, *Manga! Manga!* 160), and further brought along the golden age of manga in Japan.

Generic Form: Image/Word

Similar to the synthesizing process working in the generic birth of manga, the generic form of manga is basically composed of image and word, both of which function as a pair of opposites that brings the alchemical imaginary alive through alchemical conjunction. Due to the seemingly contradictory features between the two, there exists the everlasting debate on the superiority of image over word, or *vice versa*, in both literary and art history, as Mitchell refers the division between image and word to "the relation between the seeable and the sayable, display and discourse, showing and telling" (47). However, all these pairs of opposites regarding image and word are essential and indispensable in the formation of manga and comics, as Art Spiegelman, the author of *Maus*, defined comics as "a medium using words and pictures for reproduction" (qtd. in Chute and DeKoven 768).

Furthermore, being reluctant to get involved in the theoretical impasse to consider that "comics are essentially the site of a confrontation between the verbal and the iconic" (8), Groensteen proposes to explain their relation in terms of "a system," a more complicated and intense relation in contrast to the surface pure dichotomy one. The graphic narratives are articulated in the manga narration through the alchemical union of image and word, as McCloud says "The mixing of words and pictures is more *alchemy* than science" (161). They are no longer exclusive from each other, but mutual and reciprocal for each other.

Generic Mechanism: Visible/Invisible

Extended from the generic form of manga, the generic mechanism of manga depends largely on synthesizing the visible and the invisible, the *praesentia* and the *absentia*. The visual literacy of manga is based on reading the linearity of the panels, where panels are separated and linked by various forms of gutters, the gaps and voids between panels. Without the ability to fill out the gaps that link panels sequentially, it is impossible to comprehend the story. Therefore, what actually happens in the gutter or between the panels becomes the key question that leads to the core of the generic mechanism of manga.

In *Understanding Comics: The Invisible Art*, McCloud proposes the term "closure" to designate "the phenomenon of observing the parts but perceiving the whole" (63) and further explicates the way to fill out the gaps between panels through imagination: "Here in the *limbo* of the gutter, *human imagination* takes two separate images and *transforms* them into a single idea" (66, emphasis in original). Moreover, Groensteen also proposes a concept of "iconic solidarity" to illustrate the relationship established between interdependent images (17-18). It is the alchemical practices of incorporating the visible with the invisible that the opposites are interwoven together to bring out meaning or resonance in reading the various combinations of images.

Conclusion

Through examining the alchemical imaginary of homunculi in shaping the individual world of Homunculus as alchemical opus, the narrative world of *FMA* as alchemical opus, and the generic world of Japanese manga as alchemical opus, this article delves into the graphic mechanism of *FMA* as a contemporary visual representation that demonstrates the alchemical relation between art and imagination through relocating the archaic western alchemical imaginary of homunculi in a modern Japanese manga narrative context. *FMA*, being a 21st century visual representation, retrieves the archaic alchemical imaginary to the present world, a modern world that is usually criticized due to the over-emphasis on science and the wanting of the imagination, and a postmodern one that suffers from fragmentation and flattening of images. With the boom of the visual rhetoric in the latter half of the 20th century, Sonja Foss notifies "the pervasiveness of the visual symbols and its impact on contemporary culture" (303). In this case, it is through the alchemical reading of *FMA* that the imagination is brought back and the depth of images is restored, i.e. through the mutual work between the artist and the reader to fill out the gaps and holes prevalent in the visual narratives. Due to the heavy reliance on reader's imagination, a strong alchemical attachment between the artist and the reader has been built in reading manga and comics, which is also essential in reading our contemporary world. Therefore, let us face the voids and gaps widespread in our world, as McCloud says to the reader of his illustrated book: "All I ask of you is a little *faith* – and a *world* of *imagination*" (93, emphasis in original).

Bibliography

Arakawa, Hiromu. Fullmetal Alchemist. 27 vols. Taiwan ed. Taipei: Tong Li Comics, 2001–2010.
– Fullmetal Alchemist. Perfect Guide Book. Vol. 3. Taiwan ed. Taipei: Tong Li Comics, 2010.

Bachelard, Gaston. On Poetic Imagination and Reverie. Trans. Colette Gaudin. Putnam: Spring Publications, 2005.
Brenner, Robert E. Understanding Manga and Anime. Westport: Libraries Unlimited, 2007.
Chalquist, Craig. "Mysterium Coniunctionis." A Glossary of Jungian Terms. Chalquist.com, n.d. 20.08.12.
Chute, Hillary L. and Marianne DeKoven. "Introduction: Graphic Narrative." MFS Modern Fiction Studies 52.4 (2006): 767–82.
Foss, Sonja. "Framing the Study of Visual Rhetoric: Toward a Transformation of Rhetorical Theory." Defining Visual Rhetorics. Eds. Charles A. Hill and Marguerite Helmers. Mahwah: Lawrence Erlbaum, 2004.
Gauding, Madonna. The Signs and Symbols Bible: the Definitive Guide to Mysterious Markings. New York: Sterling, 2009.
Genette, Gérard. Narrative Discourse. An Essay in Method. Trans. Jane E. Lewin. New York: Cornell University Press, 1980.
Gravett, Paul. Manga: Sixty Years of Japanese Comics. New York: Harper Design, 2004.
Grellet, Françoise. A Handbook of Literary Terms. Paris: Hachette, 1996.
Groensteen, Thierry. The System of Comics. Trans. Bart Beaty and Nick Nguyen. Jackson: University Press of Mississippi, 2007.
Guiley, Rosemary. The Encyclopedia of Magic and Alchemy. New York: Infobase, 2006.
Harper, Douglas. "Homunculus." Online Etymology Dictionary. N.p. 2001. http://www.etymonline.com/index.php?allowed_in_frame=0&search=homunculus&searchmode=none, 20.08.12.
Ito, Kinko. "A History of Manga in the Context of Japanese Culture and Society." The Journal of Popular Culture 38.3 (2005): 456–75. EBSCOhost. 23.08.12.
– "Manga in Japanese History." Japanese Visual Culture: Explorations in the World of Manga and Anime. Ed. Mark W. MacWilliams. London: Sharpe, 2008. 26–47.
Jung, Carl Gustav. Modern Man in Search of a Soul. Abingdon: Routledge, 2005.
– Mysterium Coniunctionis: An Inquiry into the Separation and Synthesis of Psychic Opposites in Alchemy. 2nd ed. Princeton: Princeton University Press, 1989.
– Psychology and Alchemy. 2nd ed. Princeton: Princeton University Press, 1980.
Lachman, Gary. "Homunculi, Golems, and Artificial Life." Quest 94.1 (2006): 7–10. The Theosophical Society. 21.08.12.
McCloud, Scott. Comics: The Invisible Art. New York: HarperCollins, 1994.
Mitchell, W. J. T. "Word and Image." Critical Terms for Art History. Ed. Robert S. Nelson and Richard Schiff. Chicago: University of Chicago Press, 1996.
Patten, Fred. Watching Anime, Reading Manga: 25 Years of Essays and Reviews. Stone Bridge, 2004.
Schodt, Frederik L. Dreamland Japan: Writing on Modern Manga. Berkeley: Stone Bridge, 1996.
– Manga! Manga! The World of Japanese Comics. Tokyo: Kodansha, 1986.
Weiner, Stephen. Faster Than a Speeding Bullet: The Rise of the Graphic Novel. New York: NBM, 2003.

Metaphorical and Metonymical Meaning in *The Lord of the Rings*

Thomas Kullmann

One of the most common charges against fantasy fiction is that it is supposed to provide a means of escape from the real world, that it makes us forget real life and its problems.[1] Consequently, we are told to read books which engage with our own everyday affairs, in order to learn to cope with things as they are and perhaps to change the world to make it better. Some people even suppose that fantasy fiction makes us unfit for real life as it presents a non-existent world as real. One of the first critics who held such a view, still quite common in German pedagogics, was the English lecturer Q. D. Leavis who in her book on *Fiction and the Reading Public* (1932) declared that "a habit of fantasying will lead to maladjustment in actual life" (54) and that "fantasy-fiction is the typical reading of people whose normal impulses are starved of the means of expression" (209).

I would like to suggest that this attitude is based on two misconceptions. One is that not just fantasy fiction but any kind of fictional text provides escape from one's personal problems, or rather demands this escape. When reading or listening to a fictional story you are obliged to leave off thinking about your problems for a while, otherwise you will be unable to imaginatively follow the plot; this applies to Shakespeare, to Dickens, to Virginia Woolf and even to David Lodge just as much as to a fairy-tale like *Little Red Riding Hood* or Tolkien's *The Lord of the Rings*.

The other misconception lies in the idea that so-called 'realistic' fiction is connected to 'real life' more closely than is what we call fantasy.[2] My contention is

---

[1] See, e. g., Neuhaus 49, who, however, excepts "literary fairytales" from the charge of being "escapist literature allowing the reader to forget his/her problems for a few hours". Cf. Tolkien's own ideas about the charge of escapism: "In using Escape in this way the critics have chosen the wrong word, and, what is more, they are confusing, not always by sincere error, the Escape of the Prisoner with the Flight of the Deserter" ("On Fairy-Stories" 148).

[2] This misconception can even be found in critical studies which clumsily, and apologetically, attempt to demonstrate that Tolkien in his works of fiction did, after all, respond to his own time: Verlyn Flieger, for example, contends that Tolkien's "own desire to pass through the door

that whenever we choose to read or listen to a fictional story we do so because what we read or hear in some way corresponds to previous experiences of ours; otherwise what we read or hear would not make sense and we would not be interested; in other words, we would not finish reading any text if it did not in some way or another refer to real life (cf. Petzold 63). It is true, however, that the relationship between a text and the readers' real lives is a different one in cases like *Oliver Twist*, *Mrs. Dalloway* or *Small World* on the one hand and fairy tales or *The Lord of the Rings* on the other.

It is here that I would like to make use of the terms of metaphor and metonymy. Metaphor in rhetorics denotes a relationship of similarity. If a person is referred to as a 'lion,' or a 'flower,' some similarity of person and lion is implied, such as strength, or, as in the case of the flower, beauty and impermanence. Person and flower are very different from one another but they are similar in certain particulars. Metonymy, on the other hand, does not denote similarity but contiguity. Saying that 'something goes against my heart,' I refer to the heart as the traditional seat of feelings, so the heart is not similar but contiguous to these feelings.

Roman Jakobson, in his famous essay on aphasic disturbances of 1956, used the two rhetorical terms to characterise two kinds of text production:

"The development of a discourse may take place along two different semantic lines: one topic may lead to another either through their similarity or through their contiguity. The metaphoric way would be the most appropriate term for the first case and the metonymic way for the second, since they find their most condensed expression in metaphor and metonymy respectively." (254)

According to Jakobson, Romantic poetry and realistic fiction can serve as examples of the two ways a discourse may be developed:

"The primacy of the metaphoric process in the literary schools of romanticism and symbolism has been repeatedly acknowledged, but it is still insufficiently realized that it is the predominance of metonymy which underlies and actually predetermines the so-called "realistic" trend [...]. Following the path of contiguous relationships, the realist author metonymically digresses from the plot to the atmosphere and from the characters to the setting in space and time. He is fond of synecdochic details." (255)

As I tentatively suggested in my introductory study on *Englische Kinder- und Jugendliteratur* (21–23)[3], I would like to go one step further and use the two

---

into Other Time, and thus to stand outside his own time and perhaps outside Time itself, led him to the creation of his own world of Faërie, Middle-earth" (Flieger 2), and that his reaction to his own time was "a nostalgic longing for a return to a lost past coupled with the knowledge that this was impossible save in the realm of the imagination" (3).

[3] Cf. also my article: "Intertextual Patterns in J.R.R. Tolkien's *The Hobbit* and *The Lord of the Rings*", 50.

rhetorical terms to characterise the relationship between the fictional world of the text and the real world of the intended reader.

My main thesis is that fantastic texts regularly take a grasp on the world of our experience by means of metaphor, i. e. through relationships of similarity, as opposed to 'realistic' fiction which is related to the world we know by means of metonymy, i. e. through relationships of contiguity. Queens who ask a mirror, as in the fairy tale of *Snow White*: "Oh, mirror, mirror on the wall,/ Who is the fairest of us all?" (Brothers Grimm 255) do not live round the corner, but their predicament can be similar to our own as we may also be familiar with the emotions of vanity and jealousy.[4] A crime writer who invents a murder committed in New York, or Cologne, or Zurich, does not create a world similar but contiguous to our own. We need not discuss the question whether the fairy-tale or the crime story is related to 'real life' more closely, but we should acknowledge the fact that the appeal of both kinds of story does, in fact, depend on their connectedness to 'real life'.

To illustrate my thesis I propose to analyse J. R. R. Tolkien's *The Lord of the Rings,* as this work subtly combines fantasy and realism, i. e. a 'metaphoric' and a 'metonymic' mode of referring to the readers' lives. The plot of *The Lord of the Rings* is 'fantastic', with creatures we know from old legends and fairy tales, such as dwarves and elves, or which were invented by Tolkien, but combine old motifs, such as hobbits and orcs. Frodo's quest could not be undertaken by any of our friends and neighbours, but it is certainly in many ways similar to ambitions, enterprises or tasks we may have set ourselves and which have resulted, or may result, in success or failure.

A typical motif from the area of fantasy is, of course, the Ring, whose properties and history Gandalf expounds in a conversation with Frodo:

" 'When did I first begin to guess?' he mused, searching back in memory. 'Let me see – it was in the year that the White Council drove the dark power from Mirkwood, just before the Battle of Five Armies, that Bilbo found his ring. A shadow fell on my heart then, though I did not know yet what I feared. I wondered often how Gollum came by a Great Ring, as plainly it was – that at least was clear from the first. Then I heard Bilbo's strange story of how he had 'won' it, and I could not believe it. When I at last got the truth out of him, I saw at once that he had been trying to put his claim to the ring beyond doubt. Much like Gollum with his 'birthday present'. The lies were too much alike for my comfort. Clearly the ring had an unwholesome power that set to work on its keeper at once. That was the first real warning I had that all was not well. I told Bilbo often that such rings were better left unused; but he resented it, and soon got angry. There was little else that I could do. I could not take it from him without doing greater harm; and I had

---

[4] Cf. Tolkien's interpretation of "The Frog King": "[...] the point of the story lies not in thinking frogs possible mates, but in the necessity of keeping promises (even those with intolerable consequences) that, together with observing prohibitions, runs through all Fairyland" ("On Fairy Stories" 152–153).

no right to do so anyway. I could only watch and wait. I might perhaps have consulted Saruman the White, but something always held me back."' (46–47)

Gandalf alludes to several stories characteristic of fantasy: the antagonism of a "White Council" and a "dark power", Bilbo's story (told in *The Hobbit*) of the riddling game with Gollum, the story of Gollum who killed his brother to obtain the ring and then claimed it was his birthday present, Gandalf's suspicions with regard to the magic power of the ring and finally his hesitation to consult another wizard. None of these stories are part of 'real life' or are connected with features of 'realistic' narrative such as circumstantial detail, social background etc.

All of them, however, clearly partake of metaphor: Metaphors in the rhetorical sense are found in the opposition of 'white' and 'dark' which obviously stand for 'good' and 'evil' and provide a visual externalisation of the moral opposites.[5] A metaphor taken from light effects is then used to describe Gandalf's feelings: "A shadow fell on my heart then". The abstract entities described by means of metaphor: good, evil, fear, also exist in real life, though not usually in a pure, unmixed form. I should like to suggest that the antagonism of the good wizards of the "White Council" and the "dark power" can be interpreted as a metaphor for choices we make or which are made for us in real life. Fantasy fiction and the metaphoric mode of storytelling allow the storyteller to discuss ethics in an abstract, or basic way. In realistic fiction, on the other hand, this cannot be done easily. No crime writer who writes realistically will depict his murderer as completely evil, as there will always have been social or psychological circumstances which made the murderer what he is. Although pure good or pure evil cannot be found in the real world, we do make moral judgements and so proceed from the assumption that good and evil exist. Their literary representation, however, requires a metaphoric mode.

The story of Gollum/Sméagol killing his brother can be taken as a metaphorical visualisation of feelings of greed, envy and rivalry. The two stories told by the possessors of the ring obviously function as visualisations, or metaphors, of a more complex moral failing: the tendency, quite common in real life, of embellishing past events for the purpose of justifying a privilege. The ring's magical power, of course, serves as a metaphor for the temptations offered by certain privileges, or by power itself. Gandalf's hesitation with regard to consulting Saruman (which will turn out to be justified) obviously stands for many fears we entertain of friends abusing our trust.

This metaphorical discourse, however, is juxtaposed to a metonymical one: Gandalf's revelations about the ring are preceded by a description of the environ-

---

[5] Concerning 'externalisation' cf. my book *Englische Kinder- und Jugendliteratur* 163–164.

ment which may well resemble the reader's, or remind him or her of an idyllic scenery:

"Next morning after a late breakfast, the wizard was sitting with Frodo by the open window of the study. A bright fire was on the hearth, but the sun was warm, and the wind was in the South. Everything looked fresh, and the new green of Spring was shimmering in the fields and on the tips of the trees' fingers." (45)

As in a 19th century novel, the open window and the fire metonymically suggest fresh air and warmth, just as the "new green" suggests the time of year. The reader's gaze is directed to what is contiguous to the characters, first in the room and then outside of it. Following another convention of realist novels, the season of spring provides the association of a certain period in the past:

"Gandalf was thinking about a spring, nearly eighty years before, when Bilbo had run out of Bag End without a handkerchief. His hair was perhaps whiter than it had been then, and his beard and eyebrows were perhaps longer, and his face more lined with care and wisdom; but his eyes were as bright as ever, and he smoked and blew smoke-rings with the same vigour and delight." (45)

In a realist novel, the visitor's appearance would metonymically inform the reader about his state of health, his habits and his social background. This basically also applies to the present passage; it is only the number of years mentioned ("nearly eighty years before") which reminds the reader that the scene is actually set in a non-existent, fantastic world.

Frodo's quest to have the ring destroyed in the "Cracks of Doom in the depths of Orodruin, the Fire-mountain" (59–60) is, of course, a basic metaphoric motif of fantasy narratives. When Frodo and his companions set out on their journey, however, they pass through landscapes with which the reader might be familiar:

"They turned down the Ferry lane, which was straight and well-kept and edged with large white-washed stones. In a hundred yards or so it brought them to the river-bank, where there was a broad wooden landing-stage. A large flat ferry-boat was moored beside it. The white bollards near the water's edge glimmered in the light of two lamps on high posts. Behind them the mists in the flat fields were now above the hedges; but the water before them was dark, with only a few curling wisps like steam among the reeds by the bank. There seemed to be less fog on the further side." (96)

The mass of circumstantial detail, the white-washed stones, the bollards, the lamp posts, the curling wisps, the reeds, may make the reader feel at home, as places like the one described can certainly be found in the English midlands, or, perhaps, East Anglia. *The Lord of the Rings* thus joins ranks with fictional celebrations of the English countryside current in the second half of the nineteenth and the first half of the twentieth century.

Tolkien's epic narrative actually abounds in descriptions of the characters' outward appearance, their habitations and the landscapes they pass through during their quest. In these respects, *The Lord of the Rings*, in spite of its fantasy plot, is indebted to the nineteenth-century realist novel. When reading about "The Shire" English readers will certainly be reminded of landscapes and rural places they have been to or passed through. These places are contiguous to the readers' lives; he or she may relate to them in a metonymic way.

When the travellers leave the Shire they find themselves in environments which are perhaps not quite as familiar to English readers but which may still be recognisable from experience, such as forests, swamps or mountains (cf. Kullmann, "Intertextual Patterns" 44–45). In passages describing these parts of the journey an intricate mixture of metaphoric and metonymic elements is prevalent. At one stage the travellers of the "Company" rush down the "Great River" (e.g. 371) by boats, trying to escape from Gollum, who is following them:

"The night passed without Gollum showing so much as a shadow again. After that the Company kept a sharp look-out, but they saw no more of Gollum while the voyage lasted. If he was still following, he was very wary and cunning. At Aragorn's bidding they paddled now for long spells, and the banks went swiftly by. But they saw little of the country, for they journeyed mostly by night and twilight, resting by day, and lying as hidden as the land allowed. In this way the time passed without event until the seventh day.

The weather was still grey and overcast, with wind from the East, but as evening drew into night the sky away westward cleared, and pools of faint light, yellow and pale green, opened under the grey shores of cloud. There the white rind of the new Moon could be seen glimmering in the remote lakes. Sam looked at it and puckered his brows.

The next day the country on either side began to change rapidly. The banks began to rise and grow stony. Soon they were passing through a hilly rocky land, and on both shores there were steep slopes buried in deep brakes of thorn and sloe, tangled with brambles and creepers. Behind them stood low crumbling cliffs, and chimneys of grey weathered stone dark with ivy; and beyond these again there rose high ridges crowned with wind-writhen firs. They were drawing near to the grey hill-country of the Emyn Muil, the southern march of Wilderland.

There were many birds about the cliffs and the rock-chimneys, and all day high in the air flocks of birds had been circling, black against the pale sky. As they lay in their camp that day Aragorn watched the flights doubtfully, wondering if Gollum had been doing some mischief and the news of their voyage was now moving in the wilderness. Later as the sun was setting, and the Company was stirring and getting ready to start again, he descried a dark spot against the fading light: a great bird high and far off, now wheeling, now flying on softly southwards.

'What is that, Legolas?' he asked, pointing to the northern sky. 'Is it, as I think, an eagle?'

'Yes,' said Legolas. 'It is an eagle, a hunting eagle. I wonder what that forebodes. It is far from the mountains.'

'We will not start until it is fully dark,' said Aragorn." (375–376)

In the first paragraph of this passage, there is a remarkable absence of landscape description. The danger of being pursued by a malevolent creature is certainly a common motif in quest stories and lends itself to metaphorical interpretation. It is unusual in a quest story, however, that a motivation or excuse is given for the absence of description: "they saw little of the country". The second paragraph, by contrast, provides a 'metonymic' description of the evening sky – making use of the metaphors "pools" and "shores," which correspond to the real "remote lakes" which reflect the new moon. Metonymic realism is carried on in the third paragraph, which describes a rough landscape which, except for the big river, might be encountered in parts of Scotland.

The two paragraphs describing time of day, weather and landscape may remind us of nature descriptions found in novels such as Emily Brontë's *Wuthering Heights* or Thomas Hardy's *Tess of the d'Urbervilles*. These descriptions, while being 'realistic', are connected to the human plot in various ways which could be termed metaphorical: They might pinpoint narrative turns or personal crises, or depict the mental states of one or several of the protagonists (cf. my book *Vermenschlichte Natur*, esp. 468–469). In the passage quoted, the light effects of sunset and moonshine, unconventionally described, may indicate the strangeness of the situation and the suspense experienced by the travellers. The wilderness of the mountainous landscape in the third paragraph obviously provides a narrative image of the travellers' sense of being alone in the wilderness and may also function as indicating an imminent crisis.[6]

The same applies to the first sentence of the fourth paragraph, about the birds circling in the air. The ensuing sentence, however, should be taken as an example of the metaphoric diction of fantasy: It is not just up to the reader to interpret the birds as a narrative illustration of the human plot, but the birds might be taking part in this plot, e.g. by conveying messages. The eagle is not just a narrative sign by which the author or narrator conveys a message to the reader, but is identified as an ominous sign by a protagonist, and makes the travellers modify their plans. It is thus part of the elements belonging to a quest story, which, as stated above, can metaphorically represent human tasks and enterprises of various kinds.

The crisis in question is initiated by the boats passing two gigantic statues of kings, which remind Aragorn of his kingship:

---

[6] This corresponds to what I called "Indexfunktion" (*Vermenschlichte Natur* 130-134, 469).

"Sheer rose the dreadful cliffs to unguessed heights on either side. Far off was the dim sky. The black waters roared and echoed, and a wind screamed over them. Frodo crouching over his knees heard Sam in front muttering and groaning: 'What a place! What a horrible place! Just let me get out of this boat, and I'll never wet my toes in a puddle again, let alone a river!'

'Fear not!' said a strange voice behind him. Frodo turned and saw Strider, and yet not Strider; for the weatherworn Ranger was no longer there. In the stern sat Aragorn son of Arathorn, proud and erect, guiding the boat with skilful strokes; his hood was cast back, and his dark hair was blowing in the wind, a light was in his eyes: a king returning from exile to his own land.

'Fear not!' he said. 'Long have I desired to look upon the likenesses of Isildur and Anárion, my sires of old. Under their shadow Elessar, the Elfstone son of Arathorn of the House of Valandil Isildur's son, heir of Elendil, has nought to dread!'

Then the light of his eyes faded, and he spoke to himself: 'Would that Gandalf were here! How my heart yearns for Minas Anor and the walls of my own city! But whither now shall I go?'

The chasm was long and dark, and filled with the noise of wind and rushing water and echoing stone. It bent somewhat towards the west so that at first all was dark ahead; but soon Frodo saw a tall gap of light before him, ever growing. Swiftly it drew near, and suddenly the boats shot through, out into a wide clear light." (383–384)

The size and shape of the cliffs accentuate the crisis in the manner of the 19th-century realist novel. The personifications of the water and wind as "roaring" and "screaming" amount to the phenomenon which John Ruskin, speaking of poetry, called "pathetic fallacy" (*Works*, 5: 201–219), i. e. the fallacious assumption of a lyric speaker that natural phenomena mirror, or react to his feelings. Sam's comments are of course concerned with the physical sense of hardship, and with his feelings of danger and terror; they relate to the reader's world in a metonymic way.

Sam's commonsensical exclamations are answered by the "strange voice" of Aragorn, whose stilted, archaic words convey the reader to the discourse of fantasy and myth.[7] From Frodo's point of view a metamorphosis has taken place: Strider, the efficient travelling companion, whose skills safeguarded the company in the wilderness, becomes a mythical king who will resume his power. In a way, metonymical Strider becomes metaphorical Aragorn. His question: "whither now shall I go?" reenacts the archetypal situation of having to choose between two

---

[7] Aragorn's "Fear not!" of course echoes *Luke*, 2.10, where the angel of the Lord admonishes the shepherds not to be afraid. It is in the Authorised Version of 1611 that this admonishment is rendered as "Fear not". These words were changed in the Revised Version of 1881, which reads "Be not afraid". On the variety of styles and discourses in *The Lord of the Rings* cf. Shippey 160-61, Rosebury 65-76 and Kullmann, "Intertextual Patterns" 47-49.

opposing options: to accompany Frodo to accomplish his quest or to turn to his capital to claim the rights of kingship; which in the geography of Middle-earth is rendered as a "choice between the east-way and the west" (385). This choice reflects the antithetical interests of Aragorn and Frodo: Aragorn wishes to resume power, Frodo wishes to get rid of it and to destroy the potential of any individual achieving absolute power. We know, of course, that Frodo's success will enable Aragorn to rule in peace, but for the moment, the discrepancy of their purposes is given metaphorical emphasis.

The obvious question to be raised here concerns the purpose of this juxtaposition of the metonymic and metaphoric mode in Tolkien's great novel. Perhaps the 'real' world of the English countryside serves to make the horrors of Middle-earth appear closer to our own world – but if so, does this intensify the horrors or does it make them more palatable?

There are various ways of answering this question. Concerning narrative technique we can certainly say that the realistic or metonymic elements facilitate the "willing suspension of disbelief for the moment," which according to Coleridge "constitutes poetic faith" (6), or, as Tolkien himself prefers to call it, "Secondary Belief" ("On Fairy-Stories" 132). The fantastic world is given a familiar colouring and thus drawn into our everyday imagination. The closeness of the world through which the questants travel, to the world we know from real life certainly intensifies our sympathetic response to their endeavour. The landscapes Frodo and the "fellowship" pass through resemble real English and Alpine landscapes and may remind readers of landscape experiences of their own; to the landscapes we could add depictions of rooms, clothes and other objects. These metonymic connections to our own experience certainly make it easier for us to imaginatively follow the plot.

The metaphoric mode (as typically found in fantasy), by contrast, allows an author to make general statements on character, ethical principles and world views in an abstract and philosophical way (cf. e. g. Petzold 99). Tolkien, it appears, is interested in both ways of literary communication. By subtly combining metaphor and metonymy he certainly widens linguistic and literary horizons, rendering literary language and discourse far more flexible than either realist fiction or fantasy proper. Perhaps it is this combination of the metaphoric and metonymic mode, and the wealth of language and meaning brought about by this combination, which has led to the enormous success of *The Lord of the Rings*.

Bibliography

The Bible: Authorized King James Version, ed. Robert Carroll and Stephen Prickett. Oxford: Oxford University Press, 1997.

The Holy Bible (Revised Version). Oxford: Oxford University Press, 1892.

Coleridge, Samuel Taylor. "Biographia Literaria." The Collected Works of Samuel Taylor Coleridge, vols. 7.1–2, ed. James Engell and W. Jackson Bate. Princeton, N. J.: Princeton University Press, 1983.

Flieger, Verlyn. A Question of Time: J. R. R. Tolkien's Road to Faërie. Kent, Ohio: Kent State University Press, 1997.

Grimm, The Brothers, Fairy Tales. London: Collins, 1954.

Jakobson, Roman. "Two Aspects of Language and Two Types of Aphasic Disturbances." Selected Writings, vol. 2: Word and Language. Den Haag, Paris: Mouton, 1971. 239–259.

Kullmann, Thomas. Englische Kinder- und Jugendliteratur: Eine Einführung. Berlin: Erich Schmidt, 2008.

– "Intertextual Patterns in J.R.R. Tolkien's The Hobbit and The Lord of the Rings", Nordic Journal of English Studies (NJES), 8.2 (2009). http://ojs.ub.gu.se/ojs/index.php/njes/article/view/338, 10 Apr. 2014.

– Vermenschlichte Natur: Zur Bedeutung von Landschaft und Wetter im englischen Roman von Ann Radcliffe bis Thomas Hardy. Tübingen: Niemeyer, 1995.

Leavis, Q. D. Fiction and the Reading Public. London: Chatto & Windus, 1965 (^{1}1932).

Neuhaus, Stefan. "The Politics of Fairytales: Oscar Wilde and the German Tradition." Intercultural Connections within German and Irish Children's Literature. Ed. Susan Tebbutt and Joachim Fischer. Trier: WVT, 2008. 47–59.

Petzold, Dieter, J. R. R. Tolkien: Fantasy Literatur als Wunscherfüllung und Weltdeutung. Heidelberg: Winter, 1980.

Rosebury, Brian. Tolkien: A Critical Assessment. Basingstoke: Palgrave Macmillan, 2002 (^{1}1992).

Ruskin, John, Works, ed. E. T. Cook and Alexander Wedderburn, 39 vols. London: George Allen, 1903–1912.

Shippey, Tom. The Road to Middle-earth. London: George Allen & Unwin, 1982.

Tolkien, J. R. R. "On Fairy-Stories." The Monsters and the Critics and Other Essays. Ed. Christopher Tolkien. London: George Allen & Unwin, 1983. 109–161.

– The Lord of the Rings. London: Harper Collins, 2002 (^{1}1954-55).

The Zone: Ontological or Epistemological Operator?

Maria-Ana Tupan

Peri phantastikos

The heart of the fantastic seems to be more resilient and elusive than any other province in the republic of letters, judging by the heated controversies it has generated among genre theorists and by the wildly divergent definitions of the entry in dictionaries of literary terms. The reason probably lies in the confusion of the semantic content and the generic meaning of the word. If fantasy and reality are set in polarity, the former will undergo revisions along time concomitantly with changes in the way the latter is defined by disciplinary and discourse communities. On the contrary, if the word is understood as indicative of genre, some core meaning and basic parameters (type of setting, plot, characters, motifs) will remain invariant indices of the respective corpus of texts. Moreover, the generic status will remain the same across changing regimes of knowledge. Whereas Jules Verne's contemporaries needed suspension of disbelief, we need suspension of belief in order to experience his characters' sense of wonder at "miracles" which have become commonplace gadgets. And yet we encounter no difficulty putting ourselves in their state of mind in the act of reading, since a literary work is a system of representations and conventions which condition reader response.

The "world of representations" is a phrase commonly attributed to Martin Heidegger ("Die Zeit des Weltbildes") or to Hans Vaihinger (*Die Welt des Als Ob*), but actually the split between an unfathomable reality and intuitions organized under concepts goes back to Immanuel Kant. The physical world is placed under erasure, while its reflection in the mind multiplies being relative to the perceiver and levels of consciousness (intuition, representation, object for cognition, apperception). In Plato, the thing and its representation obey the laws of modal logic: one can only exist in the absence of the other. The image of Cratylus cannot reproduce all of his qualities, for then there would be two Cratyluses. Representation subtracts or adds something to the referent. In Aristotle, physics and metaphysics are spheres apart, yet both are open to the human mind, which, unlike the divine *noesis noeseos*, can also take some other object for thought apart from itself. In contrast, the

Kantian mind thinks to itself, shutting out the physical world as an impenetrable "thing in itself". Aristotle's *hulê noêtê* mediates between matter and intelligible form, whereas Kant's schemata are pure forms of intuition. The German philosopher refutes on a scornful tone the existence, within matter, of anything coming near to something in the way of "Gestalt":

"Thus, all appearances are thoroughly inter-connected according to necessary laws, which means that they stand in a transcendental affinity, of which the empirical affinity is a mere consequence. It sounds very strange and absurd to say that Nature directs itself according to something subjective, namely the basis for our self-awareness, and that it depends on this for its lawfulness. But remember what this Nature intrinsically is: not a thing in itself, but merely a whole lot of appearances, a crowd of mental representations. Then you won't find it surprising that what enables Nature to have its special unity is something that lies at the base of all our knowledge, namely transcendental self-awareness." (Kant 68)

Born in the age of Immanuel Kant, fantastic fiction treats nature as a demonic other, excluded like Frankenstein's monster from the order of names, of language and intelligibility. Nature is the Enemy, seen from inside a self-conscious narrator fleeing in terror from its grotesque aping of human attributes. Qualities disengaged from things breed anxiety. The dematerialization of colours, for instance, exposed by Newton as nothing more than effects of perception, had a strong psychological impact, their specter-like forms haunting the Helvetic Alps. The Brocken Spectre is alluded to by S.T. Coleridge or James Hogg precisely in this sense of delusive outward shape of what is actually a projection of the traveller's own mind.

It was meanings breaking away from things, from the firm materiality of *hulê*, rather than the break with ordinary reality that fed as basic experience into stories labelled as "fantastic". By placing the referent within brackets, Immanuel Kant had released upon things the haunts of their ideal others. Major writers of the age broached the issue of this anxiety aroused by the existence of perfect copies, of doubles. Whether trying desperately to get rid of one's self perceived as other (E.A.Poe's William Wilson), whether being in the run from one's polar opposite cast in one's own image (George and Robert, in James Hogg's *The Private Memoirs and Confessions of a Justified Sinner*), or seeking one's genuine self in an outward projection before discovering it inside (*Peter Schlehmil*, by Adalbert von Chamisso), the post-Kantian stance of the medieval *psychomachia* (fight for the soul between God and Satan) removes the double's encounter from a metaphysical/theological or moral site to a haunted one, one on which one body is played against another of equal ontological dignity: being in itself and being reflected in consciousness Unlike Socrates's *daimon*, or the Platonic *eidos* (metaphysical fullness) versus thing (its earthly counterpart, negatively assessed as ontological lack), these modern doubles are sources of ontological uncertainty, of that kind we associate today with quantum physics notions of non-locality or superposition of states. As long as the real and the ideal are safely kept apart, as in classical physics and modal logic (the logic of identity), we enjoy a sense of ontological consistency and epistemological certainty over the notion of "reality". Any breach of that consistency or certainty takes us into the heart of the fantastic.

The crisis of the concept of matter (*hulê*) reported about 1900 was as consequential for ontology as Plato's exclusive attribution of existential fullness to the archetypes in the Godhead in comparison to which the earth looked like a dome of shadows or pale imitations. And yet the newly born particle world would be the perfect stuff for mainstream novels written by Flann O Brien, Thomas Pynchon, Jeanette Winterson, Angela Carter or Ian Mc Ewen, who could well claim that their mapping of space and time is more realistic than the realists'. It is not the notion of matter but the construction of reality that conditions the building of worlds with a fantastic chronotope. Immanuel Kant had struck the onto-epistemic key, when he had reduced nature/ being to nature as object for the mind's metaphysical sublimations of the "Ding an sich". Not only dematerializing processes but also the collapse of categorical distinctions blocking the operation of symbolic systems are likely to generate a sense of "unreality". Whatever escapes the cognitive map into rhizomatic sprawl, whatever opens an area of non-signification is experienced as violation of the normal order of things. Fantastic spacetime is a "sleepy hollow", a loop in time, a wormhole in-between worlds. Royalist allegiances in a new republic (as in William Austin's *Peter Rugg*) are likely to sweep the protagonist away from the historical scene and whirl him into a temporal void. Events of the order perceived as "fantastic" are of the "What Was That?" (FitzJames O'Brien) type. The "chronotope" of the fantastic is outopos/ ouchronos. Reality's Other.

The way reality is understood depends on the epistemai changing over time. What used to be perceived as modal contradiction may be explained by the quantum physicist in terms of superposition of states or interferences; apparently "supernatural and causeless" things, that baffle the understanding of Shakespeare's Lafew, may now be accounted for through simultaneous changes in non-contiguous yet correlated quantum systems, the dialectic of extrinsic and intrinsic order (David Bohm) turns reality inside out like a glove, etc. The fantastic is, therefore, an ontological and implicitly epistemological operator. It is the genre whose definition needs the most frequent revisions and whose history is retrieved through recourse to an archaeology of knowledge. As any text is a system of conventions in relation, the invalidation of the counterfactual status of events by later scientific theories will not modify its generic appurtenance (one more proof of the relevance of context, of the lived culture to the phenomenology of the art work), but they are no longer productive (they suffer a sort of entropy, can no longer be used in the building or simulation of fictional worlds).

A paradigm of reality's others is unfolded, for instance, in the *Zeitschrift für Fantastikforschung ZfF, 2/ 2011*: science fiction, chimeras, the miraculous, fairy tales, fantasy, monstrosity, mythology, the supernatural, ghostly-ness. Surrealism, magic realism and historiographic metafiction are also invoked by those who argue that the crisis of the notion of reality in classical physics in the last century displaced the generic identity of the fantastic from ontology to regimes of representation. We doubt, however, that the fantastic is an umbrella term for all the generic forms mentioned in the *ZfF*, limiting its extension to those texts in which a coherent symbolic order is displaced by the hyperreal (lack of distinction between the real and the imaginary) and epistemic uncertainty about what world one is in. Thinking in binaries does indeed give a sense of safety, but it is not fantastic:

"Even when we do not want to do it intentionally, it is very hard to us not to think in terms of true/false, objectivity/subjectivity, real/fake. And even when sciences and humanities have reached high theoretical levels in which this scheme of things has been brought into question, we still look at our world this way. Maybe it is because of the fact that this way of seeing draws neat borders to our frames of mind, and gives us a sense of safety." (Sifontes Greco 279)

We would, therefore, proceed to a severe cut of the items on the fantastic writer's "bill of fares", considering that science fictionists work with a scientific hypostasis, which scientists themselves usually do, surrealists erase the real/ unreal boundary, metafabulators cannot be blamed for ontological transgression, magic realists are not aware of it, etc. Out of Rich Cooper's "radical realms" of fantasy (Cooper 2011), actually classified through a temporal fourfold taxonomy, it is only paraxial spacetime that still serves the poetics of the genre as it is inscribed in its genealogy:

Antihistorical time, the "illo tempore" of mythology, is running on the other side of the historical world, without ever crossing an empirical period of history (which is time "kairos" of revelation).

Abhistorical time provides a 'point of exist' from which to comment on the real world (Cooper 2011, 44). Such is Rushdie's Hegira time in *Shame*, tangent on calendric time, diverging from it and fulfilling a metafictional function. It allegorizes the land as one steeped in medieval fundamentalism in which situations drawn from the real world can be modelled and used as ground for thought experiments.

Not being attributable to any place on any planet, *unhistorical* time, removed from actual time and place but having a modelling function in relation to them, is the equivalent of Bakhtin's chronotope. It is no longer a category of intuition but a genre-specific (epic, romance) parameter. By "unhistorical time", Cooper understands the time when metaphysical queries displace material interests – economic, political, ideological, sexual (Cooper 43).

Paraxial time, so called by analogy with paraxial rays, which are infinitesimally displaced from the optical axis of a system, is located by Cooper in the real, ordinary world, but constructed as subversive of established orders of society and thought. We take paraxial timespace to mean, not "violation of natural law" (Cooper 11), which implies the operation of some systematic principle of opposition, but simply absence of any law, non-linearity, non-meaning.

Binaries no longer work in the age of generally accredited theories about superposition of states, uncertainty, chaos or emergence. The plot is not spinning off "infinite possibilities" as an extension of dream life, because the wave function is a virtual matrix of a system's possible states; resolution to one or the other is the effect of measurement (collapse of the wave function).

With the disappearance of an entire set of topoi, as a consequence of their scientific "canonization", the "radical realm" of the fantastic has been drastically limited to fictional equivalents of Deleuze's rhizome and deterritorialization, or of Baudrillard's hyperreality. Metafiction is usually a point of exit from illusion, where the writer is promoting his poetics in his own person, or one out of several layers of fictionality, whose ontological continuity is not disrupted. Cognitive estrangement in postmodernism springs from theories cutting across disciplines about indeterminacy, delocalization, entropy, end of history, marginality … Demonic history and arcane politics, the paranoia of world conspiracies, the parsimonious exchange of information across the Iron Curtain, and universal mistrust contributed in various degrees to an epistemological crisis which was perceived as lack in being. It was epistemology's turn to backfire and instill existential uncertainty, particularly in the writings of the last mid-century with the Kafka-Borges-Pynchon trinity occupying center stage. *Terry Pratchett*'s Discworld, placed "right on the edge of reality", or "right on the very edge of unreality", is, for Cooper (75), the typical example of postmodernist "middle-world". Of indefinite status, it has transcended the real/ imaginary polarity which had provided the ground for the rise of the fantastic in modernity. Jean Baudrillard found words to articulate the unnamable "desert of the real itself":

"Perhaps only the allegory of the Empire remains. For it is with the same Imperialism that present-day simulators try to make the real, all the real, coincide with their simulation models. But it is no longer a question of either maps or territory. Something has disappeared: the sovereign difference between them that was the abstractions charm. For it is the difference which forms the poetry of the map and the charm of the territory, the magic of the concept and the charm of the real. This representational imaginary, which both culminates in and is engulfed by the cartographer's mad project of an ideal coextensivity between the map and the territory, disappears with simulation whose operation is nuclear and genetic, and no longer specular and discursive. With it goes all of metaphysics. No more mirror of being and appearances, of the real and its concept. No more imaginary coextensivity: rather, genetic miniaturisation is the dimension of simulation. The real is produced from miniaturised units, from matrices, memory banks and command models – and with these it can be reproduced an indefinite number of times. It no longer has to be rational, since it is no longer measured against some ideal or negative instance. It is nothing more than operational. In fact, since it is no longer enveloped by an imaginary, it is no longer real at all. It is a hyperreal, the product of an irradiating synthesis of combinatory models in a hyperspace without atmosphere. In this passage to a space whose curvature is no longer that of the real, nor of truth, the age of simulation thus begins with a liquidation of all referentials-worse: by their artificial resurrection in systems of signs, a more ductile material than meaning, in that it lends itself to all systems of equivalence, all binary oppositions and all combinatory algebra." (Baudrillard 2)

The Zone, or, the "Desert of the Real"

We might say that, whereas the science fiction of the classical world is either the utopia of science, whose progress is accelerated, or its dystopic version, where scientific progress has disastrous consequences for mankind, the fiction of the quantum world is always to some extent the space of an anxiety-ridden perception, because of the unfamiliarity of the world outlook which it is trying to impose. Niels Bohr is reputed to have said in 1927, that "anyone who is not shocked by quantum theory does not understand it" (Barad 254). What a plunge into principled agnosticism and essentially unstable whirls of gravity-free particles is any mental intrusion into the micro-universe, which, moreover, will not stand in place but send up, into our macro-universe, its agents of "entanglement and re(con)figuration" (Ibid.)! Books as heterogeneous as *The Garden of Forking Paths*, *Gravity's Rainbow* and *Roadside Picnic* look neither to the bright nor to the dark side of science, but to its potential for generating ontological uncertainty.

Thomas Pynchon's *Gravity's Rainbow* (1973) is a sort of fictional transposition of vector algebra, that is, another matrix created through equivalent actions. Pynchon's history is a reduction of the official one to invariants of a universal conspiracy, whose symbols are shared in common by several sets of representations. An episodic character in the novel is actually called Sammy Hilbert-Spaess. The episodes in the book are divided by rows of seven squares which may be an allusion to the orthogonal projection of a Hilbert space in a number which equates the days of the Genesis. The narrative has a paradigmatic (i.e. characters with symbolic function) rather than syntagmatic structure. There is no consistent and continuous plot line. Every set of symbols functions like a subset of a Hilbert space created through orthogonal projection. The complex vector space is generated by a function of two variables on V, presenting properties such as symmetry, additivity, linearity and conjugate or mirror correspondences.

The German bombs V1 and V2, to which the final launch of the atomic bomb is added at the end of the novel, are events along a trajectory whose finality is death, destruction, the same as the succession of symbols on the tarot cards. The imaginary creator of Imipolex G, Laszlo Jamf (the initial letters are symbolical: I and J are unit vectors in Hilbert space and interchangeable in Tarot symbolism, while Lemma is a theorem in vector space), conditions Slothrop, the protagonist, in a plot which fuses, on a symbolic plane, the German militaristic project, the exploits of Japanese Ensign Mori-turi (probably an allusion to the *morituri* saluting Caesar, as subjects of an emperor). Miss Grable (Death) will govern the battle-front till E-Day (victory in Europe). The German, Hungarian, Japanese alliance seems to be evoked here. At the end of the novel, another conspirer with the Italian sounding Blicero name is launching a young man, Gottfried, to his death, acting as a Bleacher: the light shot forth by the rocket is dazzlingly white, like the race of Aryan origin (Caucasian pallor). Slothrop, Siegfried and Gottfried can be reduced to the "vector" Fool, the first of the Tarot cards. The card relates to the letter Aleph and to ZERO. The four elements, and the union of man and beast suggest Creation. Aleph is the Mother letter, whose transliteration in Roman characters is ALP – Anna Livia Plurabelle, the mother of Being in James Joyce's *Finnegans Wake* (1939). Here, Slothrop stands for Everyman, the life symbolism being transposed into the conjugate of Death.

The letter-number-image structure of the Hebrew alphabet allows of the representation of both quantitative and qualitative features. The rocket transposes onto the plane of death the sexual and vital symbolism of a banana or of Slothrop's reputed virility. The death drive which is the falling trajectory, induced by gravity, of the rocket, reverses the uranic ascension to the spirit, the post-V bomb evacuation taking Londoners to a hell of quantum indifference: the dizzying imaginative loops straddle categorical boundaries between animate/ inanimate, and organic/ inorganic, a chaotic zone like that which opens Apolinaire's *Alcohols*. This is the physical undoing of the universe, which is the prelude to the collapse of cognitive and axiological patterns.

The Zone in *Gravity's Rainbow* is the spiritual desert spreading over postwar Europe, where the ruins of the former civilizations coexist with the ruins of concentration camps, geopolitical frontiers have burst open, and the rush of expatriates takes with it human lives uprooted from the narratives which had temporarily ascribed them identities and social roles. These are now empty representations in a cinema which projects pornographic movies. As pawns in a game whose rules they no longer understand, people feel entrapped along the corridors of labyrinthine history or metaphysics. The Zone has no coordinates. It is a belt, a meaningless trajectory outside the territories of identitarian cultural forms and corporate lives. The Tarot Magician has descended to a prentice, the eternal disciple who cannot succeed to his master's knowledge, that is, to the all-encompassing view of Mondaugen (both names appear in V as well). The capitalist system of productivity uses individuals as cogs in its machinery. They are not agents anymore but consumers or tourists in a world which allows no revelation but keeps going and going like the serpent eating its tale in the alchemist's bowl:

"On you roll, across a countryside whose light is forever changing—castles, heaps of rock, moons of different shapes and colors come and go. There are stops at odd hours of the mornings, for reasons that are not announced: you get out to stretch in lime-lit courtyards where the old men sit around the table under enormous eucalyptus trees you can smell in the night, shuffling the ancient decks oily and worn, throwing down swords and cups and trumps major in the tremor of light while behind them the bus is idling, waiting—will now reclaim seats and much as you'd like to stay, right here, learn the game, find your old age around this quiet table, it's no use: he is waiting beside the door of the bus in his pressed uniform, Lord of the Night he is checking your tickets, your ID and travel papers, and it's the wands of enterprise that dominate tonight, as he nods you by, you catch a glimpse of his face, his insane, committed eyes, and you remember then, for a terrible few heartbeats, that of course it will end for you all in blood, in shock, without dignity—but there is meanwhile this trip to be on … over your own seat, where there ought to be an advertising plaque, is instead a quote from Rilke: 'Once, only once …' One of Their favorite slogans. No return, no salvation, no Cycle— that's not what They, nor Their brilliant employee Kekulé, have taken the Serpent to mean. No: what the Serpent means is—how's this— that the six carbon atoms of benzene are in fact curled around into a closed ring, t like that snake with its tail in its mouth, GET IT?" (412)

Modern boredom in a senseless universe is contrasted with the moralized plot of ancient Greek drama: "Oh, I'd much rather bee/ In a Greek trage-dee,/ Than be a VICTIM IN A VACUUM to-nite!" (415). We see Gottfried, who is asked to accept self-sacrifice out of devotion to Blicero, disintegrating at the moment of the bomb's critical mass, the image being exactly that of the first Tarot Card:

"What is this death but a whitening, a carrying of whiteness to ultrawhite, what is it but bleaches, detergents, oxidizers, abrasives— Streckefuss he's been today to the boy's tormented muscles, but more appropriately is he Blicker, Bleicheröde, Bleacher, Blicero, extending, rarefying the Caucasian pallor to an abolition of pigment, of melanin, of spectrum, of separateness from shade to shade, it is white that CATCH the dog was a red setter, the last dog's head, the kind dog come to see him off 't remember what meant, the pigeon he chased was slateblue, but they're both white now beside the canal that night the smell of trees I didn'? to lose that night CATCH a wave between houses, across a street, both houses are ships, one's going off on a long, an important journey, and the waving is full of ease and affection CATCH last word from Blicero: 'The edge of evening … the long curve of people all wishing on the first star. … Always remember those men and women

along the thousands of miles of land and sea. The true moment of shadow is the moment in which you see the point of light in the sky. The single point, and the Shadow that has just gathered you in its sweep ...
Always remember.

The first star hangs between his feet.

Now —" (573)

The end of the novel is a virtuoso exercise of reduction through narrative vectors to a single point like the infinite at the North Pole of the Riemann sphere. The star is the image which shows at the end of the tarot querent's quest. When the card comes out upright from shuffling, it signifies hope, wishful thinking, confidence in the future. On the contrary, when the tarot star card is reversed, it symbolizes hopelessness, absence of meaning in one's life. The wishing people are on the first star, but Gottfried is hanging with his head down, like the Tarot Hanged Man. Moreover, the star is not above his head but between his legs. The sex pointer is in the Tarot a symbolic one, the very reverse of spiritual quest or enlightenment. The bleaching is not the Golden Dawn, the true self incarnated in the golden ring of personalities, missing the Yod and Qof incarnations of Aleph as 10s and 100s (existence and cosmic Aleph, timeless). The bomb is not the pentagram represented by five A letters, but five zeros: exponential nothingness.

In Joyce's *Finnegans Wake*, Anna Livia Plurabelle, living in real Dublin, is the first Mother Aleph as incarnated Air. At the end, through memory, she transcends to Mem, Water, flowing forth to infinity. In Pynchon's novel, only the Fire Water mother aleph is realized as a rainbow which shows up in the vapour enveloping the falling rocket.

In *Roadside Picnic* (1971), Arkady and Boris Strugatsky worked out a version of the Zone on the other side of the former Iron Curtain, which became internationally known due mainly to the fact that it served as source of Tarkovski's *Stalker* (1979). Whereas Slothrop experiences a Sartrean nausea towards his condition as an Empire citizen, the Russian zone, homonymous with the Gulag, is constructed as dead end and offside road, as a loop outside the wide vistas of civilization. The Zone is not of their making, but neither is it a coded space of some huge international conspiracy. It is simply an area spawn with the debris left behind by a party of aliens picnicking in it. Even for them it had only been the place of some holiday exploit. The Zone effects a similar levelling down of traditional values. Dr Valentine Pilman, the scientist (from the International Institute of Extraterrestrial Cultures and Canadian consultant to the UN Commission on Problems of the Visitation) is credited wih the invention of the Pilman radiant, but he says it had actually been invented by some schoolchild. Given the underlying alchemical symbolism of the text, his name may be an allusion to Valentin Andraee and his alchemical wedding. The Russian writers may also have had in mind the White Visitation in Pynchon's novel (The Zone episode). The Pilman radiant is a representation, a psychological reality matching a physical one (the Earth): "Imagine that you spin a huge globe", he tells a Harmont radio correspondent,

"and you start firing bullets into it. The bullet holes would lie on the surface in a smooth curve. The whole point of what you call my first serious discovery lies in the simple fact that all six Visitation Zones are situated on the surface of our planet as though someone had taken six shots at Earth from a pistol located some-where along the Earth-Deneb line. Deneb is the alpha star in Cygnus. The Point in the heavens from which, so to speak, the shots came is the Pilman Radiant." (Strugatsky 2)

Pynchon's cognitive metaphor for his fictional space is the Hilbert vectorial space, while the Strugatsky brothers have chosen a mythological correlative, for the Cygnus, which, as well as Ensign, stands both for the book's semiological space and for the Swan constellation in the Milky Way. Related images are Orpheus and his harp. The pattern of the stars being a cross, the Northern Cross, we may conclude that, similarly to *Gravity's Rainbow*, dominated by the Aleph imagery, there is overlap between the life generating symbolism of the Milky Way and the crucified condition of humanity.

In political terms, this crucifixion translates as spiritual death, as lack of education, economic backwardness, political terror, surveillance, reversion to a beastly state. Feeding on a plant brought over from the Zone, the protagonist's daughter and father revert to primitivism and even to the monkey condition:

"When you look at it, it looks like any other piece of land. The sun shines on it like on any other part of the earth. And it's as though nothing had particularly changed in it. Like everything was the way it was thirty years ago. Yellow ore piled up in cone-shaped mounds, blast furnaces gleaming in the sun, rails, rails, and more rails, a locomotive with flatcars on the rails. In other words, an industry town. Only there were no people. Neither living nor dead. You could see the garage, too: a long gray intestine, its doors wide open. The trucks were parked on the paved lot next to it. He was right about the trucks – his brains were functioning. God forbid you should stick your head between two trucks. You have to sidle around them. There's a crack in the asphalt, if it hasn't been overgrown with bramble yet. Forty yards. Where was he counting from? Oh, probably from the last pylon. He's right, it wouldn't be further than that from there. Those egg- head scientists were making progress. They've got the road hung all the way to the dump, and cleverly hung at that! There's that ditch where Slimy ended up, just two yards from their road. Knuckles had told Slimy: stay as far away from the ditches as you can, jerk, or there won't be anything to bury. When I looked down into the water, there was nothing. This is the way it is with the Zone: if you come back with swag – it's a miracle; if you come back alive – it's a success; if the patrol bullets miss you – it's a stroke of luck. And as for anything else – that's fate." (11-12)

The fabled golden sphere which grants any wish, the alchemist's gold, in search of which Redrick and Arthur are going like Childe Ronald to the Dark Tower, turns out to be a squalid brass ball, coming out of the steamy yellowish vapours, similar to all the other "empties" in the Zone: It had not been carefully placed here, it had been left behind, littering up the Zone like all the empties, bracelets, batteries, and other rubbish remaining after the Visitation. Young Arthur is rushing forward, looking much like the Fool of the Tarot Aleph, and crying out his wishes of freedom and happiness to the divinity looming behind an excavator bucket, like some other doomed but unwitting Gottfried: "Happiness for everybody! ... Free! ... As much as you want! ... Everybody come here! ... There's enough for everybody! Nobody will leave unsatisfied! ... Free! ... Happiness! ... Free!" (124) Twisted and looking like the Tarot Hanged Man, Arthur vanishes into the Meetgrinder, leaving Redrick in a state of horrible confusion, which only now, at the sight of the youth's sacrifice, clears up, and the truth about the psychological condition of living in the Zone is dawning on him. They were slaves, living outside the order of words and thought, along some metaphysical corridor that went round the Logos:

"He had stopped trying to think. He just repeated his litany over and over: 'I am an animal, you see that. I don't have the words, they didn't teach me the words. I don't know how to think, the bastards didn't let me learn how to think. But if you really are ... all-powerful ... all-knowing ... then you figure it out! Look into my heart. I know that everything you need is in there. It has to be. I never sold my soul to anyone! It's mine, it's human! You take from me what it is I want ... it just can't be that I would want something bad! Damn it all, I can't think of anything, except those words of his ... ' HAPPINESS FOR EVERYBODY, FREE, AND NO ONE WILL GO AWAY UNSATISFIED!'"

The amoral, uncertain, chaotic or quantum world serves Arkady and Boris Strugatsky and their western contemporary as imaginative correlative for their views of the World War II aftermath. The collapse of the axiological order, forms of totalitarianism, of militaristic threat or of spiritual paralysis suggested to them a Hobbist Leviathan world – Pynchon even quoting Hobbes somewhere. Searching for an appropriate figure in the narrative carpet, these postmodern Ishmails can only tell us: Call it THE ZONE.

Bibliography

Barad, Karen. Meeting the Universe Halfway: Quantum Physics and the Entanglement of Matter and Meaning. Durham: Duke University Press 2007.
Baudrillard, Jean. The Precession of Simulacra. Translated by Paul Foss, Paul Patton and Philip Beitchman. New York: Semiotext(e), Inc. Columbia University 1983.
Cooper, Rich. Radical Realms. A Materialist Theory of Fantasy Literature. Rouge, La.: Louisiana State University 2011.

Kant, Immanuel. *Critique of Pure Reason*. Edited by Jonathan Bennett, 2007. www.earlymoderntexts.com/pdfs/kant1781part1.pdf. 7 March 2013.

Plato. *Cratylus*. Translated with an introduction by Benjamin Jowett. http://ebooks.adelaide.edu.au/p/plato/p71cra/complete.html. 7 March 2013.

Pynchon, Thomas. *Gravity's Rainbow*. New York: Penguin, 2000.

Sifontes Greco, Lourdes C. *Science and Literature: the World(s) of Representations*. http://elea.unisa.it:8080/jspui/bitstream/10556/804/1/Sifontes%20Greco,%20L.C.%20Science%20and%20literature.%20The%20worlds%20of%20representations.pdf. 7 March 2013.

Strugatsky, Arkady & Boris Strugatsky. *Roadside Picnic*. Translated from Russian by Antonina W. Bouis. New York: MacMillan 2011.

TRANSGRESSION

Hybridity as the Source of the Monstrous in Three Short Stories by H. P. Lovecraft

Alesya Raskuratova

Fear of the Other – prehistoric, extra-terrestrial or simply non-human – is in the centre of H. P. Lovecraft's (1890–1937) fiction. In fact, Hans Richard Brittnacher argues, that paranoia over the invasion of the Other might be described as the aesthetic principle of the American author's writings (85, 87). Lovecraft's racism and xenophobia were noticed by many critics, such as Rottensteiner (118), Lévy (61), or Evans (109), to name only a few. Purity of race, on the other hand, guaranteed for Lovecraft the stability of the Western civilization. In his early years, Lovecraft expressed a certain fascination with the idea of a supreme Aryan race (Lovecraft 17), even though there were people of Jewish descent among his close friends, and even his wife, Sonia Greene, was a Jewish *émigré* from Eastern Europe. Lovecraft, who was very proud that his ancestry could be traced as far as to the early New England settlers, but failed despite his respectable background and relatively good education to find a job in New York. He blamed immigrants for 'stealing' career opportunities from white Anglo-Americans, and expressed support to the compensatory ideas of racism and anti-Semitism, both privately (as can be seen in the collection of his *Selected Letters*, pp. 333-334), and in his literary works. But while foreigners were simply annoying and undesirable for him, children of mixed marriages bore a more threatening meaning in Lovecraft's fiction.

The aim of this article is to show how hybridity is constructed as monstrous in Lovecraft's mythology. We will try to show how miscegenation is demonized, while children from mixed marriages are associated with a threat to humanity – quite different from foreigners, who are avoided and disliked, but seldom have any real power in Lovecraft's fiction.

Lovecraft's works draw considerably on the tradition of the late 19th century British Gothic novels, a kind of literature for which Patrick Brantlinger coined the term 'Imperial Gothic'. 'Imperial Gothic' is obsessed with three major themes: "individual regression or going native; an invasion of civilization by the forces of barbarism and demonism; and the diminution of opportunities for adventure in the modern world" (Bratlinger 230). It can be argued that at least the former two – individual regression and invasion by alien forces – are among Lovecraft's recurring motifs. Besides, Lovecraft follows the late 19th century patterns of representing mixed-race people, especially, the tradition of 'gothization' of half-breeds, as Malchow formulates it:

"The racial and sexual cross-boundary confusions implicit in the idea of 'half-breed', the problem of the secret identities betrayed by readable signs of difference, of fated, unstable natures torn between two worlds, of a violent contradictory combination of opposites – of villain and victim, masculine and feminine – makes the mixed race as constructed in nineteenth-century British popular culture an *essentially* Gothic type." (103)

For Lovecraft, the decline of Western civilization and 'going native' is invariably linked to hybridity; his "insistence on the readable signs of depravity and the demonic concealed physiognomy ... visible reminders of what came to be felt as a white fall from grace" (ibid.) is comparable to the tendencies observed by Malchow in the nineteenth-century discourse on miscegenation. We shall try to show how Lovecraft employs demonized images of hybrids and children from interracial marriages to create the sense of paranoia and imminent threat to humanity in his short stories.

My choice of short stories for analysis is not accidental – all three of them deal with hybrids and their threat to humanity, but on different levels. *Arthur Jermyn* investigates the decline of one particular family, *The Shadow Over Innsmouth* studies the problem on the level of community, of one particular town, and in *The Dunwich Horror* all humanity is threatened with extinction as the result of the union between a human being and a monster from another dimension.

Arthur Jermyn was published first in the *Wolverine* in March and June 1921 (Joshi, Schultz 89). *The Shadow Over Innsmouth* was written between November and December 1931, but was rejected by Farnsworth Wright, the editor of *Weird Tales,* a pulp magazine in which many of Lovecraft's stories appeared. The story was first published only five years later as a book by Visionary Publishing Co. (Joshi, Schultz 237). The third story, *The Dunwich Horror,* was written in 1928 and Lovecraft believed it to be "so fiendish that Wright may not dare to print it" (Lovecraft 240). However, it was successfully published in *Weird Tales* in April 1929.

Arthur Jermyn: The Horrors of Heredity

Arthur Jermyn (1920; also appeared under the titles *Facts Concerning the Late Arthur Jermyn and His Family* or *The White Ape*) is written in the tradition of the late Victorian Gothic and deals with the problem of degeneration and 'going native', the problem of hidden identities, of "how much ... can one lose – individually, socially, nationally – and still remain a man" as David Punter formulates it in his study of Gothic fiction (240). For Punter, one of the major fears of the late 19th century is the fear "about human status and dignity, generated by Darwin" (Punter 253). *Arthur Jermyn* bears similarity to such Gothic classics as Robert Louis Stevenson's *The Strange Case of Dr. Jekyll and Mr. Hyde* (1886) and Arthur Machen's *The Great God Pan* (1890), with the shared view that "[t]he human being may be the product of a primal miscegenation, a fundamentally unstable blending, which scientific or psychological accident may be able to part" (Punter 245).

Lovecraft deals with this problem as he develops the plot of *Arthur Jermyn*. The story begins with an account of the Jermyn family history, starting with the main hero's great-great-great-grandfather Sir Wade Jermyn who travelled to the Congo region to trade and study local customs. It seems that many generations of the Jermyn family after him bear some kind of curse – they have tastes and interests not befitting their title, marry below them, seem attracted to animals and violence, and often show early signs of madness.

The second part of the story is set around Arthur Jermyn's attempt to prove Sir Wade Jermyn's theories about a white African civilization. This brings him to the Congo region and later, he manages to acquire a ceremonial mummy from the temple in the heart of the jungle. The body belongs to a creature that looks like a very advanced primate, a white ape princess. To Arthur Jermyn's surprise the body has a locket with his family's coat of arms on it. Even worse, one look on the face and stature of the creature reveals a striking resemblance to the Jermyns. It turns out that Sir Wade married the white ape princess while he studied the Congolese civilization, and all Jermyns after him had the ape blood in them, which explains their interests and inclinations.

Lovecraft's major scholar, S. T. Joshi, remarks that "unlike the spectacular miscegenation affecting an entire clan or city (and potentially all civilization) as we find in 'The Lurking Fear' (1922) or 'The Shadow Over Innsmouth,' we appear here to be concerned only with corruption of a single family" (158). What is interesting about *Arthur Jermyn* for us is the role of hybridity in the degeneration and decline of the family. The Jermyns that succeed Sir Wade are hybrids in more than one sense: "[t]he white ape is itself a result of miscegenation", states Joshi (160), because, as Lovecraft remarks, it comes from the "things that might have sprung up after the great apes had overrun the dying city" (67). There is a clear parallel between what happened to the "prehistoric white Congolese civilization" and the Jermyn family, as both of them became 'polluted' by the blood of an inferior race – the former by the blood of apes and the latter – through the ape-like hybrid princess. Lovecraft indicates that the fall of the ancient civilization and the fall of the Jermyn family are both the result of miscegenation. Symptomatically, Sir Wade's descendants are described as more abominable and terrifying in their deeds than the Congolese savages Sir Wade and Arthur encounter on their journeys, because their hybridization happened in two steps: first, between the descendants of the white African civilization and apes, and then, between the humans and the human-ape hybrids. It is possible to suggest that for Lovecraft hybrids are more dangerous because they can hide their true identities, and thus spread their 'bad blood', 'infecting' more people around them (a parallel with another Victorian Gothic character comes to mind: the vampire). Interestingly, even the surname of the family – Jermyn – seems to remind us of 'germination'.

This part of our analysis can be best concluded by Simmons's observation concerning *Arthur Jermyn*: "[t]he story adroitly illustrates Lovecraft's ambiguous use of the abject as a means of representing personal fears about miscegenation, racial hybridisation and their deconstructive effects on Anglo-Saxon subjectivity" (127). In this short story, only one particular family goes into decline as a result of intermarriage. In the further examples, we shall see the threats of hybridization to a larger community and the importance of keeping the boundaries between races and species.

The Shadow Over Innsmouth: The Other from the Depths

The Shadow Over Innsmouth, written in 1931 and first published in 1936, is one of the most well known H. P. Lovecraft's short stories. It belongs to the mature period of the author's work and shows many characteristic features of his writing: interest in genealogy, the anxiety over an invasion of unknown and uncontrollable forces, but also fear of miscegenation and insecurity over one's identity. For Lovecraft, the identity is defined, even predestined by origin and heredity, and even a small portion of 'foreign' blood can be fateful to the line, as we have seen in *Arthur Jermyn*. But the tragedy in *The Shadow Over Innsmouth* is not limited to one family only – the whole city goes into decline because of 'mixing up with strangers'.

The story follows an unnamed narrator on his trip to the ill-famed seaport Innsmouth that is shunned and avoided by the people of neighbouring towns. The exact reason of this avoidance is not clear, but it definitely has something to do with the so-called 'Innsmouth look' – certain repulsive peculiarities in appearance shared by all inhabitants of the town. The narrator first observes them in the bus driver who takes him to the notorious place:

He had a narrow head, bulging, watery-blue eyes that seemed never to wink, a flat nose, a receding forehead and chin, and singularly undeveloped ears. His long thick lip and coarse-pored, greyish cheeks seemed almost beardless except for some sparse yellow hairs that straggled and curled in irregular patches; and in places the surface seemed queerly irregular, as if peeling from some cutaneous disease. (Lovecraft 395)

Other features of the Innsmouth look include a "shambling gait" and immense feet (ibid.). Lovett-Graff remarks that Innsmouth in the story "appears as a puzzle to be solved by the narrator, a puzzle whose solution lies in the mysterious sexual taboo that has been violated" and points out that "[r]acial migration, inbreeding, disease – each is a red herring meant to trap narrator and reader alike" (Lovett-Graff 175). There is a certain "moral 'sixth' sense" (ibid.) that makes the narrator and people he interviews perceive the inherent difference between 'normal' people and 'devious' inhabitants of the infamous town.

However, this does not stop the narrator who travels to Innsmouth and is forced to spend a night there, narrowly escaping the throng of locals enraged by his inquiries into the history of the town and the reasons of its decay. His report to the authorities causes "a vast series of raids and arrests … followed by the deliberate burning and dynamiting" (Lovecraft 382). It turns out that the inhabitants of the town have a pact with the sea creatures, the so-called Deep Ones, who bring schools of fish and rich exotic jewellery in exchange for human sacrifices and, later, the right to mate with people of Innsmouth. By the time of the events in the story, almost everyone in Innsmouth has blood of the Deep Ones in their veins.

Just as the horror seems to be over, the events take a typically Lovecraftian turn: the narrator learns that his own great-grandmother was from Innsmouth and possessed some of the peculiar jewellery brought by the Deep Ones. At first he is horrified and thinks of suicide, but later changes his mind, deciding to join his ancestors in the underwater city and live eternally as one of the Deep Ones, whereby his transition from one decision to another is constructed by Lovecraft as a descent into madness and degradation.

It is difficult to deny the fact that the story, even in the brief outline given above, is a warning against "the ill effects of miscegenation, or sexual union of different races, and as such can be considered a vast expansion and subtilization of the plot of 'Facts Concerning the Late Arthur Jermyn and His Family'", suggest Joshi and Shultz (239). The 'foreigners' in *The Shadow Over Innsmouth* remain content with the human sacrifice only for a while, and soon begin demanding the right to produce the mixed progeny that will have eternal life in the sea. But the ultimate goal of the Deep Ones is much more threatening. When the narrator interrogates Zadok Allen, the oldest person in Innsmouth, he reveals the secret plan of the Deep Ones:

"Yew want to know what the reel horror is, hey? Wal, it's this – it ain't what them fish devils *hez* done, but what they're a-goin' to do! They're a-bringing things up aout o' whar they come from into the taown ... Them houses north o' the river betwixt Water an' Main Street is full of them – them devils *an' what they brung* – an' when they git ready ... I say, *when they git ready* ... ever hear tell of a *shoggoth?*" (Lovecraft 428)

It is implied that the Deep Ones are preparing to overcome humanity using shoggoths – the creatures from Lovecraft's bestiary that had destroyed a pre-historic alien civilization described in the novella *At the Mountains of Madness*. Apparently, the Deep Ones were going to use them as a weapon of mass destruction against people. It is interesting, though, that before they could begin with this project, the Deep Ones needed to have a treatise that would allow them to infiltrate the human society and create hybrids – creatures described throughout the story as the main source of danger to the narrator personally and to humanity as a whole. Lévy discusses this peculiarity of Lovecraft's monsters stating that:

"[They] do not stray radically from the human form. They keep the general aspect, its silhouette, but are endowed at the same time with attributes that belong to a different animal species. They are characterized above all by their *hybridism* – a hybridism that is not the simple juxtaposition of disparate elements as in some monster of antiquity, but a result of a sort of contamination or collective pollution. " (56)

Hybrids in Lovecraft's stories are agents of evil; torn between two natures they ultimately succumb to the more primitive, animalistic or monstrous one. Delpech-Ramey, reading Lovecraft in terms of Deleuze and Guattari's notion of 'Becoming', notices that his "stereotypically 'male'" characters tend to be "paranoid about ... fragile identity" (10-11), while we can also notice that if the characters have a portion of foreign blood in them, it often comes from a female relative (as we have seen both in *Arthur Jermyn* and *The Shadow Over Innsmouth*). Even though the characters bear the name of their father – and here we almost fall into the Julia Kristeva's version of the Lacanian psychoanalysis – they cannot overcome their connection with the maternal, with the semiotic, the time-space of impulses and rhythms, and ultimately succumb to it. Not surprisingly, the narrator of *The Shadow Over Innsmouth* dreams of his grandmother and "that which had been her grandmother" living in the underwater city, whom he longs to join forever, symbolically returning to the origin, into the mother's womb represented by the sea depths.

Lovett-Graff remarks that "[T]he fundamental menace for Lovecraft was the proof the immigrants provided of the uncontrollable animal sexuality needed to make natural selection operate" (Lovett-Graff 175). Fear and disgust over sexuality and uncontrollable reproduction is characteristic of Lovecraft's dealing with any 'lower' race, especially when it comes in conflict with a more civilized, but also a more inhibited one. Susanne Smuda discusses various narrative strategies in H. P. Lovecraft's works, and dedicates one chapter of her study to the role of the disgusting in the construction of the terrible. She bases her enquiry on Aurel Kolnai's work on disgust, *Der Ekel* (1929), in which he sees disgust as existing on two levels: on one, it is always related to something organic, but is also found in the sphere of immoral (Smuda 147). Sexuality is one of the main sources of disgust and fear for Lovecraft, especially if it is an excessive or perverse sexuality. Smuda suggests that "für die Untersuchung der Ekeldarstellungen Lovecrafts erweisen sich die Aspekte des Überdrusses und der Vitalität am falschen Ort als gewinnbringend" (Smuda 173) – "the aspects of surfeit and vitality in the wrong place prove valuable for the study of Lovecraft's representations of the disgusting" (translation A. R.). She states that the two are represented either as incest or as human-animal-hybrids. It is an example of what Kolnai defines as "Sexualität am falschen Ort" – "sexuality in the wrong place", and Lovecraft's disgust "wird sich gegen die Unmoral [z. B. die ungeordnete Sexualität – *added by Smuda*] soweit richten, als sie als 'Beschmutzung', 'Besudelung' des Lebens und seiner Werte empfunden wird; weniger etwa gegen 'satanische' oder mechanisch-oberflächliche Sexualität" (Smuda 175) – "will direct itself against the immoral (for example, the disorderly sexuality), because it is felt as 'contamination', 'defilement' of life and its values; much less against 'the satanic' or mechanic and superficial sexuality" (translation A. R.). Lovecraft assumes the lexicon of repulsion to create the images of men-fish hybrids in *The Shadow Over Innsmouth* as they stand for sexuality that facilitates the spread of the 'bad' stock, the crossing of boundaries and violation of the categorical distinctions. And the desire to overcome the boundaries, "to violate the sexual taboo against interbreeding is cast as the sick desire of the alien Other" (Lovett-Graff 175).

One very inelegant and from today's point of view outright appalling remark made by Lovecraft in *The Shadow Over Innsmouth* is his nod towards the Nazi ideology as the way to hold the Other at bay. When Zadok Allen describes the destruction of the Kanaky's island by their neighbours who did not want to have the Deep Ones in their proximity, he mentions "little stones strewed about – like charms – with somethin' on 'em like what ye call a swastika naowadays" (Lovecraft 419). Given that the short story was written in 1931, Lovecraft must have been aware of the Nazi's use of the sign and applied it consciously against the intrusive outsiders who threaten to destroy human civilization by mixing up and making it degenerate.

However, the plan of the Deep Ones to destroy humanity fails at the end, and they have to wait on the sea bottom for the time when they are summoned again. Their tactics in conquering the world is reminiscent of another story of interbreeding – *The Dunwich Horror*. However, while the Deep Ones of Innsmouth are limited in their activity to one particular town, the hybrids of *The Dunwich*

Horror have a greater, more universal goal, and it takes only one generation to put humanity under the threat of extinction.

The Dunwich Horror: The Sons of God and an Apocalypse Reversed

The Dunwich Horror (1929) is one of Lovecraft's "most widely read" stories, claims Burleson (140), and it belongs to the cycle of works united into the Cthulhu mythos, as it contributes to the construction of Lovecraft's cosmology through the technique of *bricolage* (as remarked by Smuda 35-42 and Evans 127). It also constructs the image of a kind of Lovecraftian Antichrist (the author himself, being an atheist and a materialist, would have been appalled by this definition, but we can carefully apply this term here for our purposes).

The story begins in a rural area in Massachusetts, where an albino farm girl, Lavinia Whateley, gives birth to Wilbur Whateley, whose father remains unknown. The girl's father, who is notorious for his interest in magic and a collection of ancient grimoires, prophesizes a great future to his newly born grandson, and soon after begins to rebuild his old house and a barn. The child develops surprisingly fast, physically and intellectually, but his appearance remains utterly repulsive. After his grandfather and his mother die, Wilbur undertakes his first journey into the outside world, to the neighbouring Arkham, where he wants to borrow a precious copy of the *Necronomicon*, a grimoire invented by Lovecraft but ascribed to "the mad Arab Abdul Alhazred" (Lovecraft 116). After his request is refused, Wilbur attempts to steal the book, but is killed by the dog guarding the library. As the chief librarian, Henry Armitage, rushes into the room, he sees some details of Wilbur Whateley's peculiar anatomy:

"It was partly human, beyond a doubt, with very manlike hands and head, and the goatish, chinless face had a stamp of Whateleys upon it. But the torso and the lower parts of the body were teratologically fabulous, so that only generous clothing could ever have enabled it to walk on earth unchallenged and uneradicated. Above the waist it was semi-anthropomorphic; though its chest ... had the leathery, reticulated hide of a crocodile or alligator ... Below the waist, though, it was the worst; for here all human resemblance left off and sheer phantasy began. The skin was thickly covered with coarse black fur, and from the abdomen a score of long greenish-grey tentacles with red sucking mouths protruded limply." (Lovecraft 123)

But the story does not end with Wilbur's death. Soon Armitage, who is the main protagonist and the heroic figure of the story (even though this view is contested by Burleson and Airaksinen), receives news about a horror raging in Dunwich – an unseen force slaughtering cattle and people in a most terrible and mysterious manner. Together with a group of confidants, Armitage hurries into town to stop the unnameable force. Using a specially created powder they manage to make the invisible horror visible for a split second, and the group of observers from the Dunwich folk can view the creature with terror and disgust: "Bigger'n a barn ... all made o' squirmin' ropes ... hull thing sort o' shaped like a hen's egg ... nothin' solid about it – all like jelly, and made of sep'rit wrigglin' ropes pushed clost together" (ibid., 148). But it's not the outworldliness that startles the observers most – it is the face they see on the top of the creature through the spyglass: "that face with red eyes an' crinkly albino hair, an' no chin, like the Whateleys ... It was an octopus, centipede, spider kind o' thing, but they was a haff-shaped man's face on top of it, an' it looked like Wizard Whateley's" (ibid., 152) – Wizard Whateley mentioned here is Wilbur's grandfather. As it turns out, Wilbur Whateley was not the only child of Lavinia – on the same night she gave birth to his twin brother, a creature more like its father, an unspeakable monster that could not be seen by human eyes. The story ends when Henry Armitage and his associates succeed in destroying the monster by singing out incantations, and shortly before the unearthly thing dies, it calls to its father for help in a human voice: "HELP! HELP! ... ff – ff – ff – FATHER! FATHER! YOG-SOTHOTH!" (ibid., 151).

There are two aspects that will interest us in the further analysis – first, the parallels with mythical and religious narratives about the birth and life of heroes, and second the hybridity of the Whateley twins and the threat they represent to the human civilization that originates from their double nature.

The opinions of critics divide as to the extent to which *The Dunwich Horror* is a religious parody or a satire. While Burleson (146-149) and Airaksinen (129-131) tend to see Wilbur Whateley as the central character, the mythological hero, because the story of his birth and short life resemble narratives about the childhood of prophets and heroes, there is evidence suggesting that Lovecraft meant the story to be read differently. Joshi and Shultz quote him saying that he found himself "psychologically identifying with one of the characters (an aged scholar who finally combats the menace) toward the end" (81) – librarian of the Miskatonic University Henry Armitage, who stops the Whateley brothers. Peter Cannon is more careful in his judgement of the story – he quotes James Egan, who is of the opinion that the birth of the Whateley twins "satirically parallels the Immaculate Conception of Christ in the womb of a human mother, Lavinia being the perfect antithesis of the Virgin Mary" (87). In our view, it is crucial that Wilbur Whateley and his brother should be read not as a 'like-Christ', but as the complete opposite, that is, 'anti-Christ', who comes to bring the reign of his father, Yog-Sothoth, on Earth – and destroy humanity. As we read in *Necronomicon*, "*Yog-Sothoth* is the key to the gate, whereby the spheres meet. Man rules where They ruled once; They shall soon rule where man rules now. After summer comes winter, after winter summer. They wait patient and potent, for here shall They reign again" (Lovecraft 118).

The twins in the story, as very often with Lovecraft, have a double nature – they are half-human and half-god (or aliens, as all Lovecraft's gods are entities from the cosmic depths). From this perspective it is possible to read *The Dunwich Horror* as "a story about miscegenation and human/alien hybrids", as Evans does (115).

We can see that Wilbur Whateley and his twin bother have the human and the god-like in different proportions – Wilbur is obviously more human, despite his monstrous lower body; moreover, he develops extremely fast and is fairly intelligent. As Lévy remarks, "monsters that under their clothing hide singular anomalies ... are all the more dangerous because they come and go amid men without usually being bothered" (58). Wilbur's nameless brother, on the contrary, represents the blind and uncontrollable power that destroys everything on its way. But only together they can open the gate and let their father – Yog-Sothoth – come into the world of men. Before his death, old Wilbur Whateley instructs his grandson: "Yew grows – and *that* grows faster. It'll be ready to sarve ye soon, boy. Open up the gates of Yog-Sothoth with the long chant that ye'll find on page 751 *of the complete edition* (emphasis HPL – A.R.)" (Lovecraft 114). Again, like in *The Shadow Over Innsmouth*, the hybrid children are meant to help overcome the boundary between the world of humans and the other world of unearthly, alien creatures. Only here we have two types of hybrids: one that must serve, and the other – more human in his shape and psychology – is to perform the rites and open the gates. By doing this, Lovecraft establishes the supremacy of human nature, because it gives a hybrid the ability to literature and learning that is necessary at least to read out incantations and release the alien forces through the power of word. It appears logical, therefore, that the invisible twin can be defeated by an incantation and not by a crude weapon, because Lovecraft acknowledges the power of a speech act, both through words and the vocalization of intent. Unfortunately for Lovecraft's posthumous reputation, he believed that the ability to learning and changing reality through speech and literature is reserved to the white Anglo-Americans only.

Conclusion

The aim of our analysis was to try and show how hybridity plays the essential role in the creation of the monstrous in Lovecraft's works. The idea that a hybrid itself is monstrous is not new – already Mary Douglas suggested that the abominations of the Old Testament are nothing else but the instances of crossing epistemological boundaries. When she discusses the ide of holy as the whole, Douglas states: "[G]ranted that its root means separateness, the next idea that emerges is of the Holy as wholeness and completeness ... Other precepts extend holiness to species and categories. Hybrids and other confusions are abominated" (Douglas 51-53).

Similar ideas can be found in Lovecraft's works, for whom any type of hybridity is ultimately unholy, abominable and threatening to humanity – less so in the earlier stories like *Arthur Jermyn*, more explicitly in *The Shadow Over Innsmouth* and *The Dunwich Horror*.

Lovecraft's monsters, however, are not only impure – they are torn between two natures, ultimately accepting a more primitive or alien one, while losing their humanity. But the corruption of mankind is not the only reason to avoid miscegenation. For Lovecraft, the main threat of hybrids is that they have the appearance and behaviour of human beings; but at the same time they assist the unknown, threatening forces into the world. These unknown forces plan to destroying humanity, which for Lovecraft is represented by and limited to the Western civilization, but cannot succeed without help of human agents – such as mixed-race children with double nature. For Lovecraft, hybrids represent a much greater danger than the Deep Ones or ancient gods or aliens, and his stories present them as more disgusting, cruel and immoral creatures. Undoubtedly, this is connected with Lovecraft's worries concerning the influx of immigrants to America, who, in his view, were threatening to bring about the fall of the empire. But even more it reflects Lovecraft's weakness to accept his own economical failure and concerns about his "troubled family history" (Lovett-Graff 175).

Bibliography

Airaksinen, Timo. The Philosophy of H. P. Lovecraft: The Route of Horror. New York: Lang, 1999.
Brantlinger, Patrick. Rule of Darkness: British Literature and Imperialism, 1830–1914. Ithaca: Cornell Univ. Press, 1988.
Brittnacher, Hans Richard. "Paranoia als ästhetisches Gesetz. Das literarische Universum des Howard Philips Lovecraft." Vom Zauber des Schreckens. Studien zur Phantastik und zum Horror. Wetzlar: Förderkreis Phantastik in Wetzlar, 1999. 67–95.
Burleson, Donald R. H. P. Lovecraft: a Critical Study. Westport: Greenwood Press, 1983.
Cannon, Peter. H. P. Lovecraft. Boston: Twayne, 1989.
Delpech-Ramey, Joshua. "Deleuze, Guattari, and the 'Politics of Sorcery'." SubStance 39.1 (2010). 8-23. Project MUSE. 9. 2. 2013.
Douglas, Mary. Purity and Danger: An Analysis of Concepts of Pollution and Taboo. New York: Praeger, 1966.
Evans, Timothy H. "A Last Defense against the Dark: Folklore, Horror, and the Uses of Tradition in the Works of H. P. Lovecraft." Journal of Folklore Research: 42.1 (2005 Jan-Apr). 99–135. Project MUSE. 9. 2. 2013.
Joshi, Sunand T. "What Happens in 'Arthur Jermyn'." Primal Sources: Essays on H. P. Lovecraft. New York: Hippocampus Press, 2003.
— and David E. Schultz. An H. P. Lovecraft Encyclopedia. Westport: Greenwood, 2001.
Lévy, Maurice. Lovecraft: A Study in Fantastic. Detroit: Wayne State Univ. Press, 1988.

Lovecraft, Howard Phillips. "Arthur Jermyn." The H. P. Lovecraft Omnibus 2: "Dagon" and Other Macabre Tales. London: HarperCollins, 2000. 65–76.
— "The Shadow Over Innsmouth." The H .P. Lovecraft Omnibus 3: "The Haunter of the Dark" and Other Tales. London: HarperCollins, 2000. 382–463.
— "The Dunwich Horror." The H. P. Lovecraft Omnibus 3: "The Haunter of the Dark" and Other Tales. London: HarperCollins, 2000. 99–153.
— "To James F. Morton" 9 June 1928. Letter 329 in Selected Letters 1925–1929. Ed. August Derleth and Donald Wandrei. Vol. 2. Sauk City: Arkham House, 1968. 240.
— "To Reinhardt Kleiner." 25 November 1915. Letter 9 in Selected Letters 1911–1925. Ed. August Derleth and Donald Wandrei. Vol. 1. Sauk City: Arkham House, 1965. 17-18.
Lovett-Graff, Bennett. "Shadows over Lovecraft: Reactionary Fantasy and Immigrant Eugenics." Extrapolation 38.3 (1997). 175–193 Literature Resource Center. 6. 1. 2013.
Malchow, Howard L. "The Half-Breed as Gothic Unnatural." The Victorians and Race. West, Shearer (ed. and introd.). Aldershot, England: Scolar, 1996. 101–111.
Punter, David. The Literature of Terror. A History of Gothic Fictions from 1765 to the Present Day. London: Longman, 1980.
Rottensteiner, Franz. "Lovecraft as Philosopher." Rev. of H. P. Lovecraft: The Decline of the West by S.T. Joshi. Science Fiction Studies Vol. 19, No. 1 (Mar., 1992). 117–121. Article Stable URL: http://www.jstor.org/stable/4240129.
Simmons, David. "'The Great Race? The African Other and Abject Hybridity in H. P. Lovecraft's Short Horror Fiction." American, British and Canadian Studies Vol. 10 (July 2008). 124–134.
Smuda, Susanne. H. P. Lovecrafts Mythologie: "Bricolage" und Intertextualität – Erzählstrategien und ihre Wirkung. Bielefeld: Aisthesis, 1997.

Grotesque Desire: The Early Horror Films of David Cronenberg and the Limits of Morality

Daniel Illger

From the very beginning, David Cronenberg's films have been criticized for their depiction of violence and depraved sexuality. This paper argues that the shocking imagery of films like *Shivers* and *The Brood* can be seen as part of an overarching aesthetic concept by drawing on theories of the Grotesque. Viewed from this perspective, Cronenberg's films employ a mode of aesthetic experience that aims at putting the spectator into an irresolvable contradiction with him or herself, where his viewing pleasure defies his moral judgment and vice versa.

I.

A scene from David Cronenberg's film *The Brood* from 1979: a woman is raising her gown, in a proud gesture that is somewhat reminiscent of an angel spreading his wings. But what is revealed by this gesture does not evoke heavenly associations at all: the woman's body is disfigured by a sack-like growth that bulges from her belly. The spectator may want to react to this sight like the man who has been talking to the woman and is now recoiling away from her, only to stare in horrified fascination at the morbid spectacle that unfolds before his eyes. What follows is even worse, when the woman bends over to open the growth with her teeth. She then slowly tears the tissue and produces a baby from the bloody inside of the growth. Finally, she takes the creature into her arms and starts to lick it clean, like a cat would do with its offspring.

The woman is Nola Carveth and the man is her husband Frank. Because of her suffering from mental instability, which resulted in separation from Frank, she was given into the care of Dr. Hal Raglan who runs the so-called Somafree Institute of Psychoplasmics. Here, "patients purge themselves of their neuroses by manifesting them as physical changes in their bodies." (Newman 159) In the case of Nola, Dr. Raglan's therapy works all too well. She learns to externalize her rage as a pack of terrible dwarfs, "monstrous simulacra without retinae, teeth, speech, sexuality or navels," (Harkness 24) bent on killing anyone presumably hurting or threatening their mother.

If *The Brood* caused an uproar among contemporary critics, it is not because the film delivers a devastating parody of the more messianic forms of psychotherapy, nor because it can be read as the "eeriest divorce drama in film history," as Georg Seeßlen and Fernand Jung put it. (Seeßlen and Jung 332) No, the most contentious thing about the *The Brood* is the gruesome travesty of the birth process rendered in the film's climactic scene, which I have just described. This scene seems to be the focal point of the many controversies that centered around Cronenberg's early work, notably his horror films from the '70s: *Shivers* from 1975, *Rabid* from 1977, and, of course, *The Brood*.

Particularly leftist and feminist critics were enraged by Cronenberg's depiction of female sexuality, which they took as proof of his misogyny, especially his supposed hatred and loathing of sexually liberated women. Most relevant in this context are the attacks wielded by Barbara Creed and Robin Wood. The former maintains that Cronenberg holds the whole notion of the female, and especially reproductive capacity as monstrous, (cf. Creed 49) while the latter outright condemns the director to the "reactionary wing" of horror cinema, claiming that *The Brood* projects "horror and evil onto women and their sexuality, the ultimate dread being of women usurping the active, aggressive role that patriarchal ideology assigns to the male." (Wood 24)

For my part, I would argue that critics like Wood and Creed failed to see that the drastic imagery of *Shivers*, *Rabid*, and *The Brood* forms part of an overarching aesthetic concept that accounts for the difficulty of coming to terms with Cronenberg's early work on an intellectual as well as on an emotional level. In this regard, *Shivers*, *Rabid*, and *The Brood* can be viewed as typical examples of a certain tendency in the development of Western European and North American cinema during the 1960s and 70s.

II.

In the late 1950s, a new genre cinema began to form. As Hermann Kappelhoff writes, this cinema "owes its appearance to the divided cinema markets. Alongside the big movie house chains, which almost exclusively screened Hollywood productions, drive-ins and smaller movie house chains arose that filled their programs with cheaply made films featuring horror, sex, and violence. Using the label exploitation, this cinema targeted a youthful audience and their pleasure in watching." (Kappelhoff 143)

While largely ignored by contemporary film critics and cineastes, exploitation cinema has increasingly become a subject of scholarly interest since the mid-90s.

By now, the label "exploitation cinema" is almost synonymous with designations such as "cult films," "Eurotrash," "Midnight Movies," or "alternative Cinema," all of which seem to target not only certain economic facts regarding the circumstances of the production and distribution of the films in question, but first and foremost address a cinematic aesthetics that radically transgresses the moral and political boundaries set by the regulations of "good taste."

What Ernest Mathijs and Xavier Mendik claim about alternative European cinema thus may apply to exploitation cinema in general: A recurrent thread

> "appears to be that of resistance, rebellion and liberation. Alternative European cinema sets itself not just against a mainstream culture, but also against a range of ways of thinking, politically and ideologically. Arguably, alternative European cinema … does not always campaign for politically correct perspectives. But at the very least it seems to be championing, almost anarchically, a call for liberty. It is that call that ultimately makes alternative European cinema worthwhile". (Mathijs and Mendik 4)

Of course, one has a hard time understanding what this "call for liberty" is all about, if it obviously cannot be equated to the films – or to their directors and writers – adopting a stance that could be described as politically progressive. The problem is further complicated by the fact that numerous highly disparate subgenres are subsumed under the aforementioned categories.

For example, an exploitation film from the 60s or 70s could be a Gothic Horror flick like Mario Bava's *The Whip and the Body* from 1962, Roger Corman's various Poe adaptations such as *The Mask of the Red Death* from 1964, or the Frankenstein and Dracula cycles produced by the British company Hammer Films. All these films share a proclivity for reveling in lush colors and opulent, if somewhat surreal, period set pieces. At their best moments they thus create a truly morbid beauty, in which the dreamlike landscapes, the ruinous castles, and the lost souls that roam them all bear the mark of an irremediable melancholia, stemming from the downfall of a happier past, itself always already fantasized. But by "alternative cinema" you could also refer to one of the many subgenres of sexploitation. In that case, you should be very precise in what you're talking about. For sexploitation, as it were, is a realm with many regions, some of which are pleasant enough to the eye of the traveler while others may be very harsh and unforgiving. To the former probably belong the films by Russ Meyer – for the most part bizarre and hilarious in equal measure, and, in their own strange way, even emancipatory – or German sex comedies like the famous *Schulmädchen-Report* series with its mockumentary and pseudo-educational style. The latter consist of such notorious subgenres as the W.I.P.-films, nunsploitation and, most outrageous of them all, naziploitation flicks – films which turn jailhouses, monasteries, and even concentration camps into the sites of Sadean debauchery, full of torture, rape, and all kinds of deranged sex practices. Of course, the "cult films" from the 60s and 70s also include American biker movies, erotic (and sometimes pornographic) Vampire films from France or Spain, or Italian cop thrillers whose protagonists make Dirty Harry look like a spokesman for civil rights and a liberal penal system. And the list could be prolonged endlessly.

So, once again, what do all these films have in common, apart from being somehow "different" or boasting "forbidden" imagery? Or, perhaps more to the point, if there really is something "alternative" about exploitation cinema, does it only consist in the gratuitous staging of sex and violence?

In order to answer this question, I'd like to quote Kappelhoff once more. Speaking of the common denominator between American exploitation cinema and the emerging New Hollywood, Kappelhoff argues:

"All of this, however, is not merely a question of breaching moral prohibition. Rather, by breaching the aesthetic order and the perceptive sensations of their audiences, the films try to call into question the very foundations of moral consciousness. The exposed wound, obsessive violence, and deregulated sexuality do not represent any forbidden wishes per se, but refer to aesthetic processes that open up the cinematic visual space as a medium to enjoy the body, which is neither morally reasonable nor sensory, nor is it complacent." (Kappelhoff 145)

Viewed from this perspective, at the core of what we call exploitation cinema we see a certain mode of aesthetic experience, a peculiar idea of the relationship between film and spectator. In order words, exploitation cinema may be defined by an aesthetics of effect that aims at putting the spectator into an irresolvable contradiction with him or herself, where his viewing pleasure defies his moral judgment and vice versa. And if we follow Kappelhoff, this aesthetics of effect does not result from the intensity of the sex and the violence, or a combination of both, portrayed in this scene or that scene. No, its effectiveness depends on "aesthetic processes" which serve to construct a highly precarious spectator position over the course of the whole film.

I would now like to return to David Cronenberg and his early horror films. I think that a closer look, particularly at *Shivers* and *The Brood*, may help us understand how the aesthetics of effect, which I would ascribe to the greater part of European and North American exploitation cinema from the 60s and 70s, actually works, and how the aesthetic processes in question can be linked to precisely determinable techniques of staging.

III.

To begin with, consider the birth scene from *The Brood*: "this short, spectacular scene gets its power from a multifaceted contradiction," as Bettina Papenburg points out. (93) Thus, Nola's angelic posture is contrasting with the almost predatory expression on her face, the loveliness of her body is in contrast with the welts that disfigure it, and the caring attitude with which she licks her offspring contrasts with the horrific circumstances of its birth. As a result, the presentation of Nola conveys an uneasy mixture of conflicting affective qualities to the spectator: there's disgust and wonder, a sense of bizarre beauty, a latent erotic tension, and perhaps some absurd humor as well. The emotional confusion created here results from an aesthetic strategy that can be regarded as typical of Cronenberg's early films. This aesthetic strategy or technique goes by the name of the Grotesque.

As far as I know, Bettina Papenburg is the first to explicitly designate the Grotesque as a cornerstone of Cronenberg's work. In order to do so, she draws on Bakhtin's seminal book *Rabelais and his World* from 1965, and the notion of the grotesque body as it is developed there as part of a comprehensive theory of the Carnivalesque. Papenburg can convincingly show how Cronenberg uses the grotesque body in a way quite comparable to Rabelais, "in order to protest against the sterility and inhumanity of the belief in science and the euphoria over technology in the modern world". (92) Both the French Renaissance poet and the Canadian film director take up a utopian stance and "use the topos of the grotesque body to express a subversive attitude." (ibid.) In this vein, Papenburg writes that Nola's external uterus stresses "her physical and social constructedness as a woman and in particular as fertile. This organ, visibly positioned on the outside, exceeds and distorts female physicality and motherhood, as an aspect of the traditional role of woman, into the grotesque." (94)

However conclusive Papenburg's interpretation may be, I still think that Bakhtin's carnevalesque travesties and parodies are not altogether adequate to comprehend how Cronenberg utilizes the Grotesque – at least not in regard to his horror films from the 70s. I would propose making use of another, decidedly grimmer conception of the Grotesque for the analysis of *Shivers*, *Rabid*, and *The Brood*. Namely, I'm referring to Wolfgang Kayser's book *Das Groteske. Seine Gestaltung in Dichtung und Malerei*, or *The Grotesque in Art and Literature,* from 1957. In this book, Kayser defines the Grotesque as follows: "The Grotesque is 'supernatural' and 'paradoxical', that is, in how it disrupts the order that rules our world. ... Multiple and obviously contradictory sensations are awakened, a smile over the deformations, disgust over the gruesome, monstrous in itself, but as a basic feeling ... amazement, horror, helpless trepidation when the world starts to fall apart and we can no longer get our bearing." (Kayser 31f.) Elsewhere he writes: "The spectator's helplessness is the correlate to that trait singled out as constitutive for all configurations of the Grotesque: that the artist did not provide any meaning, but allowed the absurd to appear as the absurd." (38) Thus, the Grotesque allows for "*the alienated world*," (198) a world that at the same time is and is not the world in which we live, (38) and "the horror assaults us so strongly precisely because it is our world, the reliability of which turns out to be mere semblance. At the same time, we sense that we cannot live in this transformed world. The Grotesque is not about the fear of death, but the fear of living". (199)

In my view, Kayser's conception of the Grotesque provides us with a quite precise description of the aesthetics of effect aimed at by Cronenberg's early films – and much of European and North American exploitation cinema with them. And these aesthetics of effect are in turn centered around images of a violent, desperate, and morbid – in sum grotesque – desire. But this desire does not only afflict the characters of *Shivers*, *Rabid*, and *The Brood*, nor is it limited to the incidents represented on screen. To the contrary, first and foremost it is realized in the minds and bodies of the spectators. By confronting us with a grotesque world, a world without "meaning," Cronenberg forces us to stare in "helpless trepidation" at the fragments of thoughts and emotions that are all that remains of a shattered reality; and in doing so, he also shifts (and this may be the reason Robin Wood and Barbara Creed dislike them so much) the problem from the question of whether capitalism is good or bad, or how we can overcome patriarchal ideology, to the question of who and what we ourselves are, as our craving is always already directed both at creation and destruction, at tenderness and cruelty, at beauty and ugliness.

I think that Steven Shaviro hints at a similar thought – even as he takes a very different perspective – when he writes that the systematic undoing of "traditional binary oppositions between mind and matter, image and object, self and other, inside and outside, male and female, nature and culture, human and inhuman, organic and mechanical" is "the major structural principle of all of Cronenberg's films". (Shaviro 129) And the same is true for Wayne Rothchild's thesis that the "radical character of the political/aesthetic operation in Cronenberg's films is that it is always carried out in a violently double dialectic. Cronenberg, in his cinema, presents a rationalism against reason, a masculinism against itself, and a body that cannot hold in a society that does not work. … His characters cannot deal with either difference nor sameness". (Rothchild 161)

What the positions of Shaviro and Rothchild have in common is that they emphasize the refusal of Cronenberg's cinema to make sense in a conventional way. Moreover, both scholars stress that films like *Shivers*, *Rabid*, and *The Brood* force the spectator to lose his hold on a reality he can trust in and is able to understand, so that the threat arises that he might go astray within the aesthetic experience like in the endless ranges of an uncharted wilderness.

I would like to conclude with some remarks on Cronenberg's breakthrough film *Shivers*, which I hope will clarify the point I'm trying to make.

IV.

Shivers is set in the so-called Starliner Towers, a luxurious and at the same time antiseptic apartment block which is located, quite isolated, on Starliner Island, some miles from Montreal. The Starliner Towers are invaded by parasites, created by one of its inhabitants, Dr. Emil Hobbes, in a misguided experiment. These parasites – which Kim Newman has described, not too subtly but adequately, as "phallic turds" (156) – enter their victims through various bodily orifices to breed among their entrails. In this process, the victims are turned into raving sex fiends who further spread the disease. At the end of *Shivers* there is not a single soul left uninfected in the Starliner Towers, and the whole bunch of lecherous half-zombies is leaving the apartment block in a remarkably disciplined motorcade, heading for Montreal.

Now, if *Shivers* is a textbook case of the Grotesque in the vein of Kayser, it is because Cronenberg's film manages to be alternately, and sometimes simultaneously, disgusting, depressing, hilarious, frightening, and even erotic. So that, considered as a whole, it creates just the feeling of "helpless trepidation" when faced with "a world that is falling apart," which Kayser makes the touchstone for any Grotesque artwork.

For example, the film does everything in its power to undermine the spectator's ability to take up an unambiguous stance towards the parasite's invasion. From the very beginning the Starliner Towers are not described as an idyll that is then destroyed by the forces of evil. They seem more like a hypermodern high-tech cemetery for people who are dead without knowing it. Every single human relationship is depicted as empty, hollowed out from the inside, devoid of affection. That goes for wives and husbands as well as for lovers, friends, or colleagues. Viewed from this perspective, one might be inclined to cheer for the parasites as they begin to take apart the whole hypocritical and claustrophobic routine of mechanical lives, dragged along from day to day.

But then this isn't possible either. For one thing, the parasites themselves are just too repulsive to be a crowd pleaser. More to the point, the consequences of the infection, while they may be liberating in some ways, are at the same time deeply disturbing. The most shocking scenes in *Shivers* "have geriatrics and children making lewd advances" (156), and when they do so, there is a mixture of violence and cheerfulness, cruelty and playful innocence, lust and hate at work which is more profoundly unsettling than buckets of gore spattered against the wall. Perhaps even more so, as the crazed inhabitants of Starline Towers are basically acting out a Freudian infancy nightmare, turning the apartment block into a giant nursery full of polymorphous perverse children who have gone on a rampage. In other words, they are only doing what – at least according to classic psychoanalysis – every one of us once desired and unconsciously still desires: to have intercourse with everyone in any way imaginable regardless of age, sex, degree of relation, or rules of moral conduct.

Finally, it is important to note that Cronenberg refuses to hand the spectator any moral guidelines to *Shivers* by spreading interpretive clues: everyone fails (or succeeds, depending on the point of view), men and women alike, there are neither heroes nor villains, no one commits acts of sacrifice or treachery, and resisting the parasites seems just as pointless as giving in to them. And the parasites themselves are, for all their repulsiveness, not even proper monsters, as Kim Newmann keenly observes: "The *Night of the Living Dead* ghouls only want to eat you; what Cronenberg's parasites intend is unthinkable." (156)

So what are we to make of *Shivers*? Is the film an allegory of the emptiness of modern life? Is it a vigorous attack on conventional ideas of well-regulated desire? Or is it, on the contrary, deriding hippie dreams of emancipation and a communal life? Does it, as Adam Lowenstein claims, present "non-heteronormative sex as the force capable of undermining patriarchal order." (Lowenstein 163) Or is it perhaps suggesting, as Steven Shaviro argues, "that the 1960s bourgeois sexual 'revolution' in fact merely reproduces the aggressive, hysterical logic of a commodified and competitive society"? (Shaviro 133) Does *Shivers* do all of this at once, or none of it? Cronenberg's film denies us any answer to these questions. And this is precisely because in the logic of the Grotesque, as Wolfgang Kayser conceives it, all the bright stars of reason, morality, and political judgment come crashing down into a darkness from which they can hardly be retrieved. It's just this kind of darkness that Cronenberg's early horror films – and many other examples of exploitation cinema – are trying to lead us into.

Bibliography

Works Cited

Seeßlen, Georg and Jung, Fernand. Horror. Geschichte und Mythologie des Horrorfilms. Marburg: Schüren, 2006.
Creed, Barbara. The Monstrous-Feminine. Film, Feminism, Psychoanalysis. London: Routledge, 1993.
Harkness, John. The Word, the Flesh and the Films of David Cronenberg. Cinema Canada, June 1983.

Kappelhoff, Hermann. The Politics of Cinematic Realism. New York, Chichester: Columbia University Press.
Kayser, Wolfgang. Das Groteske. Seine Gestaltung in Malerei und Dichtung. Tübingen: Staufenberg, 2011 [1957].
Lowenstein, Adam. Shocking Representations. Historical Trauma, National Cinema, and the Modern Horror Film. New York, Chichester: Columbia University Press, 2005.
Mathijs, Ernst and Mendik, Xavier. "Introduction. Making Sense of Extreme Confusion: European Exploitation and Underground Cinema." Alternative Europe. Eurotrash and Exploitation Cinema since 1945, Eds. Ernst Mathijs and Xavier Mendik. London, New York: Wallflower Press, 2004. 1–18.
Newman, Kim. Nightmare Movies. Horror on Screen since the 1960s. London et al.: Bloomsbury, 2011 (revised edition).
Papenburg, Bettina. "Der offene Leib. Zu David Cronenbergs Körperbild." David Cronenberg, Ed. Marcus Stiglegger. Berlin: Bertz + Fischer, 2011. 89–110.
Rothchild, Wayne. "The Cronenberg Effect." North of Everything. English-Canadian Cinema since 1980, Ed. William Beard and Jerry White. Alberta: University of Alberta Press, 2002. 160–165.
Shaviro, Steven. The Cinematic Body. Minneapolis: The University of Minnesota Press, 1933.
Wood, Robin. "Introduction." American Nightmare. Essays on the Horror Film, Ed. Andrew Britton et al. Toronto: Festival of Festivals, 1979. 7–28.

Films

Shivers. Dir. David Cronenberg. Cinépix Film Properties (CFD) et al., 1975.
The Brood. Dir. David Cronenberg. New World-Mutual et al., 1979.

Modern-Day Superheroes: Transgressions of Genre and Morality in *Misfits*

Dana Frei and Lars Schmeink

"Thanks to global dissemination and the cross-media phenomenon that drives entertainment media, the hero in his or her superheroic dimension has reached a level of popularity never witnessed before," Angela Ndalianis states, referring to the proliferation of superheroes in film, TV series, games, theme parks and, of course, comic books, and concludes that "the superhero has become part of the wider cultural consciousness" (4). Established in 1938 with the first installment of Siegel's Superman in *Action Comics* #1, the superhero has adapted to the needs and challenges of each society in which he[1] acts. At its most basic level, even without the *super*-prefix: "A hero embodies what we believe is best in ourselves. A hero is a standard to aspire to as well as an individual to be admired" (Fingeroth 14). The hero "has to represent the values of the society that produces him" because he functions as a representative of "the idealized vision we have of ourselves and our society [or even more pointedly,] the idealized vision the entire world has of itself" (ibid. 17, 25).

Heroism, super or otherwise, thus provides a moral compass, charting a society's norms and ethical standards. As the modern day embodiment of mythology, superhero narratives set guidelines for human social behavior, presenting "as natural and inevitable many of the social and political structures of our society" (Reynolds 24) which are truly social constructs, thus allowing us to come to terms with our social environment. Therefore, an examination of the shifts in superhero tropes and observing the ways in which they currently have "become increasingly inverted, questioned, and all out parodied" (Ndalianis 8), uncovers and reflects upon changes in contemporary society. What is it then that is disclosed, one needs to ask, when "the traditional superhero image is scrutinized, deconstructed, reconstructed, and ridiculed" (ibid.) by today's superhero narratives?

In this paper, we would like to examine one such example of modern-day superhero discourse by analyzing the therein suggested shifts within the genre's

---

[1] Whenever the masculine pronoun is used to, the feminine is implied without prejudice.

familiar tropes, the changing attitudes of the underlying morality portrayed in it, as well as to discuss the transitions and transgressions newly taken by the superheroes themselves. The British television series *Misfits* exemplifies the 21st century de- and reconstruction of the superhero narrative to the point.

The show premiered on UK pay-channel E4 in November 2009 and ended in December 2013 after five seasons.[2] The fantasy drama series portrays a group of juvenile delinquents who are thrown together to do mandated community service. From the start, the general tone of the show is marked by strong language, the criminal tendencies of the protagonists and their clear disregard for authorities, as well as drug abuse and strong sexual content. The main characters are united by their status as social outcasts and young offenders, even though they are extremely different from one another in character. The combination of their highly conflicting personalities installs a network of complex relationships. Dialogs are therefore bound to be explosive, provocative and often highly amusing in nature. What eventually binds this diverse group of adolescents is the fact that they get caught in an electrical storm, in which they all accidentally obtain supernatural powers.

The daily routine of community service offers a sense of regularity in the lives of the main characters. Moreover, this orderliness is mirrored by the repetitive narrative structure of the series: each week, the order is disrupted and needs to be restored by the group. As it turns out, the Misfits[3] are not the only people affected by the storm. Other members of the community also develop superpowers, and, even though there are plotlines that take entire seasons to unfold, each individual episode focuses on one specific super-powered evil-doer from the outside, against which the protagonists have to defend themselves. Hence, the series follows a certain "Freak of the Week" (n.pag.) formula, as Owen calls it, which defines the structure of every episode.

The following paper focuses on two predominant forms of transgression as presented in *Misfits*. The first part[4] concentrates on the genre of superhero tales

---

[2] This paper is based on the analysis of the first three seasons only. The fourth season aired during the time of writing, which will briefly be commented on at the end of the article. The fifth season aired while the book was in the editing process.

[3] When referring to the main characters of the show as a group (Nathan, Kelly, Simon, Alisha, Curtis, and in season 3: Rudy), the show's titular grouping "Misfits" is used in this paper, as opposed to the term "ASBO Five", which is a denomination used by the media in episode 6, season 2 of the show. Moreover, the term "Misfits" will be put in italics in reference to the series and used in standard format when referring to the characters.

[4] The first part of this paper is based on the original presentation by Lars Schmeink, whereas the second part is based on the presentation by Dana Frei. For the purpose of this publication, we have aligned our arguments in order to avoid unnecessary repetition and therefore present our analyses together.

and delineates the characteristics traditionally assigned to superheroes, such as their mission or inevitable duality of identities, in contrast to the traits as depicted in the contemporary superhero narrative of the series. In this part, we argue that *Misfits* adapts the superhero narrative of the ordinary individual imbued with extraordinary powers to the social realities of the 21st century. The recognizable transgression of the superhero genre from the perspective of a current social context is thereby illuminated. In the second part of this paper, our argument builds on the insight that the traditional superheroic mission, as well as sense of identity have been radically re-interpreted in the contemporary superhero narrative. The focus here lies on analyzing the morality of the protagonists' actions by reflecting upon their personalities' connection to the superpowers given to them naturally (i.e. via storm) as well as unnaturally (i.e. as a purchased good). In doing so, we aim to uncover underlying values, which initially seem rejected in sum.

Transgressions of Genre

Liquid Modernity and 21st Century Living

Angela Ndalianis describes hero myths on the one hand as universally and continuously present in "cultural memory" and a part of "human socialization" (3) since the beginning of time. On the other hand, she argues that these myths are protean, "dynamic beings who shift and metamorphose to accommodate themselves to specific eras and historic-cultural contexts" (3f.). As the terminology reveals, similarities of superhero narratives with ancient mythology are often argued to reflect the continuous need for myths to "give order and narrative structure to the way humans contemplate the world around them" (10). However, the reality of this world has shifted radically over the course of 75 years since Superman's first appearance, and with these shifts the superheroes' "status as symbolic facilitators and embodiments of civilizing processes" (8) has been called into question.

When examining the superhero genre of the 21st century, we propose to start with a short look at the social and political realities that define this century. According to sociologist Zygmunt Bauman, we live in a world defined by "liquid modernity": A world in which our ordinary systems of stability, such as family, religion and class organization, no longer exist or have been completely liquefied. Nothing, Bauman argues, is fixed or stable anymore:

"Everything or almost everything in this world of ours keeps changing: fashions we follow and the objects of our attention [...], things we dream of and things we fear, things we desire and things we loathe, reasons to be hopeful and reasons to be apprehensive. And the conditions around us, conditions in which we make our living [...]." (*44 Letters* 1)

Bauman even claims that life in a liquid modern world is "the combined experience of *insecurity* (of position, entitlements and livelihood), of *uncertainty* (as to their continuation and future stability) and of *unsafety* (of one's body, one's self and their extensions: possessions, neighborhood, community)" (*Liquid Modernity* 160f., emphasis in original).

In addition, Ulrich Beck says, we are living in a "risk society," in which potential risks become decreasingly natural and increasingly manufactured, and in which the individual is faced with "*industrialized, decision-produced incalculabilities and threats*" (22, emphasis in original) that go far beyond one's capacity of coping, as these threats are mostly global, imperceptible, irreversible. Further, we live in an extreme insecurity of social position, which is reflected in our constant change of wants and needs, and caused by the negation of all existing value systems and institutional factors of stability. Individuality becomes key in our lives, communality is neglected and even frowned upon as a limitation to our individual self-fulfillment. In such a society, the superhero with his "metaphoric malleability" (Coogan 15) to represent a society's hopes and dreams – even the best version of itself – might look quite different from the most prototypical of superheroes, Siegel's Superman, the valiant knight in skin-tight shining armor, "the champion of the oppressed [...] sworn to devote his existence to helping those in need" (Siegel and Shuster 1).

"You lot? Superheroes?" – Misfits and the Question of Genre

Misfits can certainly be seen as such a reflection of the social changes of the 21st century described by Bauman and Beck. Nevertheless, the question remains if *Misfits* is indeed an example of a superhero narrative. In order to answer this question, it might help to consult a definition of the term "superhero" and to examine how this relates to questions of genre distinction. Leaving aside considerations of specific media (i.e. comics)[5] as more or less prototypical of the genre, we propose using Peter Coogan's definition from *Superhero: The Secret Origin of a Genre*:[6]

"A heroic character with a selfless, pro-social *mission*; with *superpowers* – extraordinary abilities, advanced technology, or highly developed physical, mental, or mystical skills; who has a *superhero identity* embodied in a codename and iconic costume, which typically express his biography, character, powers, or origin (transformation from ordinary person to superhero); and who is generically distinct, i.e. can be distinguished from char-

---

[5] Most scholars argue that superhero narrative is prototypically found in the comic, but has been branching out into other media: Fingeroth argues, that the superhero genre suffers from a "continual and historical exploitation [...] across a variety of media" (27), whereas Ndalianis speaks of a "superhero comic book aesthetic" 4) in other media.

[6] Other definitions do not provide as much precision and/or unique criteria (cf. Fingeroth 16f.; Reynolds 12f.), thus Coogan's definition seems preferable.

acters of related genres (fantasy, science fiction, detective, etc.) by a preponderance of generic conventions. Often superheroes have dual identities, the ordinary one of which is usually a closely guarded secret." (30, emphasis mine)

Coogan identifies three elements as prototypical of the superhero narrative – "mission, powers, and identity, or MPI" (39) – which apply to the main character(s) of genre texts. As a qualifier, he adds that due to the non-exclusive nature of genre, these elements might also be found in adjacent text types and that superhero narratives need to be separated from these by looking at "concatenation of other conventions" (43) within the text, found for example in paratext, setting and intertextual reference (cf. 47f.).

In the case of *Misfits*, E4 marketing and PR have clearly positioned the series as belonging to the superhero genre by paratextual markers such as titling their press release "*Misfits* – Who Wants a Superhero with an ASBO?" and sub-heading the accompanying online comic with "ASBOS to Super Heroes" (n.pag.). In addition, the show itself comments directly on the characters as being superheroes and continuously references the genre via intertextual commentary. A definitive positioning within genre discourse, while at the same time ironically subverting it, can be found at the end of the first episode. The series shows the Misfits on the roof of the community center discussing their newly-won powers:

Curtis: Is this it? Are we meant to be like this forever?

Simon: What if we are meant to be … like … superheroes?

Nathan: You lot? Superheroes? … No offence, but in what kind of fucked-up world would that be allowed to happen?

Alisha: I did not sign up for that?

Nathan: Superheroes? I love this guy … you prick!

Kelly: What if there is loads of people like us, all over town?

Nathan: No, that kind of thing only happens in America. This will fade away. I am telling you, by this time next week, it will be back to the same old boring shit.[7]

During this scene the camera is tracking the conversation in a series of medium shots, followed by a long shot from behind that reveals the Misfits as a group and establishes an ensemble – similar to the group images of comic superheroes such as the X-Men, the Justice League or the Avengers.[8] The irony of the scene lies

---

[7] *Misfits*, Season 1, Episode 1. In the following, all references to the show will be shortened to the format S01E01.

[8] For an example of the ensemble imagery see the website for Joss Whedon's *The Avengers* (2012). Also, the musical cues of the scene with its dramatic string arrangements bear strong generic resemblance to the scores of superhero films such as *The Avengers*.

in the juxtaposition of Nathan's commentary, that superheroes like the Misfits do not conform to genre conventions. At the same time, the show makes explicit its meta-fictionality by referencing viewer expectations through Nathan. The specific cultural reference of superhero narratives as a form of an American utopia or fantastic imagination is mocked by the following fly-over tracking shot, which directs the viewer's attention from the roof-top towards the world in which such characters actually could become superheroes: the working class ghetto of Thamesmead in South East London in a classic 1970s social development estate.

Both the show's metafictionality and intertextual reference to the genre are repeatedly highlighted over the course of the series, mostly to add irony to the characters' superhero status. To give just a few examples: When Curtis attempts to break up with his girlfriend Sam, he tries dozens of different approaches but never succeeds until he quotes a line from *Spider-Man*, which Sam finds tacky and immature enough to leave (S01E05). The melodramatic movie line becomes the only thing that works because Curtis' life itself has become theatrical. At the end of S03E01, the Misfits again find themselves on the rooftop of the community center, discussing their superhero status and its relevance to their lives. At one point, the new member of the ensemble, Rudy, asks: "Are we doing catch-phrases?" and argues that they will need them "for when the shit goes down" because it seems unlikely that they would be spending the next weeks "ambling about picking up litter," thus revealing a metafictional understanding of the shows' mechanics and the nature of superhero narrative in general.

"We are lazy and incompetent – leave it to the police!" – A Superhero's Mission

Having established *Misfits* as part of the superhero genre, the stature and pride of these heroes' of being anti-social delinquents and self-absorbed adolescents may seem shocking. They are not quite prototypical of superheroes who, according to Coogan's definition, need a mission, something that guides their behavior and justifies their actions:

"The superhero's mission is pro-social and selfless, which means that his fight against evil must fit in with the existing, professed mores of society and must not be intended to benefit or further himself. The mission convention is essential to the superhero genre because someone who does not act selflessly to aid others in times of need is not heroic." (31)

These parameters of the mission, even though they do not always apply neatly, as Coogan concedes, help differentiate between superheroes and supervillains, the latter of which pursue their own interests "at the legal, economic, or moral expense of others" (ibid.). Fingeroth, in a similar argument, points out that the most obvious defining aspects of a superhero are "some sort of strength of character (though it may be buried), some system of [...] positive values, and a determination to, no matter what, *protect* those values" (17, emphasis in original). What differentiates him from the supervillain, who shares those same characteristics, is that the superhero "represents the values of the society that produces him," doing the right thing – and "more importantly, *he knows what the right thing is*" (ibid., emphasis in original). The superhero stands for ethics a society will recognize as superior to the practical considerations of any applied justice system.

It is exactly in this context that *Misfits*, in a general sense, manages to show that establishing a value system might be problematic in our liquid modern world. For one, the Misfits have all been placed under an "Anti-Social Behaviour Order (ASBO)", a civil order that allows institutions of governmental authority to sanction anti-social acts, that is, behavior "in a manner that caused or was likely to cause harassment, alarm or distress to one or more persons" ("Anti-Social Behaviour Orders" n.pag.). ASBOs are under heavy critique in the UK, their numbers having escalated and their intentional uses having been thwarted (cf. "Memorandum" n.pag.). Especially because breaching the conditions of an ASBO is a criminal offense (punishable with up to 5 years in prison), the National Association of Probation Officers (Napo) has estimated that "around 50% of those who are subject of an ASBO eventually end up in jail," even though "the original offence was not itself imprisonable" (ibid.). As Christian Lenz points out, ASBOs are generally aimed at youths? deviating from normed social interaction: drinking, sexual conduct, vandalism, and harassment. The order is supposed to mark the deviance and re-establish institutional control over the anti-social subject (cf. Lenz, n.pag.).

For the Misfits, the ASBO is ironically marked as both justified and linked to a more specific institutional blindness: both Kelly and Simon have acted out violently (assault and arson respectively), justifying the order, but would have clearly benefitted from more socially integrative measures such as psychological treatment instead of driving them deeper into anti-social patterns. Professional runner Curtis is made an example of for minor possession of illegal drugs, his sentence only reflecting the institutional need to name and shame the sports star as perpetrator. All of the Misfits display an anti-social behavior typical of youth deviancy, but over the course of the series, this is explained as psychological insecurity due to neglect, as mistakes of impulsive action, or simply as defense mechanisms. Their anti-social behavior is merely a reflection of the anti-social, anti-communal life that surrounds them. That the group is not inherently criminal is even pointed out by Nathan when Kelly is held hostage and the others need to buy her freedom. The Misfits use their powers to steal money from a security transport and Nathan realizes that they could have done so many times before: "A bunch of young offenders develop superpowers and not one of us thinks of using them to commit crime. Shame on us." (S02E04). Incidentally, they never return to this kind of thinking, and when Simon needs money later on in the series, he borrows it from Seth instead of repeating the robbery.

In terms of the superhero's mission of service and protection towards his community, the ASBO thus ironically underscores the general values and expectations of society, which has never lived up to its own standards. In the series' pilot, the probation worker states the purpose of the ASBO in a speech that is oddly reminiscent of a superhero's mission:

"This is it. This is your chance to do something positive, to give something back. You can help people. You can really make a difference to people's lives. That is what community service is all about. There are people out there who think you are scum. You have an opportunity to show them they're wrong." (S01E01)

Nathan's dead-pan answer perfectly expresses the insecurity of values present in society and general attitude towards social norms that the series showcases: "But what if they are right?" Clearly this lost generation does not value community but rather thinks of themselves and their own situation. When confronted with a delusional gangster killing another young offender, the group discusses what "doing the right thing" means. Nathan, in complete agreement with the social stigma that the ASBO has placed on him, defers the heroic action to the authorities: "We are lazy and incompetent. Leave it to the police." (S02E04) The group itself, their own physical integrity and social stability, becomes the communal order to be preserved. Interestingly then, the Misfits actually "do the right thing" in most episodes, and restore that communal order (even beyond their group). Even though Simon tries to establish a motivation for the Misfits, the group's mission does not go beyond securing their own existence. As such, one could compare them with a character like the Hulk, who, Coogan argues, "fights primarily for self-preservation but inadvertently does good" (41).

The inadvertent good that comes from fighting supervillains, another "one of the significant markers of the superhero genre" (ibid. 61) is similarly complicated in *Misfits* though. Typically, a given episode's simple "villain" threatens an individual or the group as a whole and forces them to react: a girl from Simon's past wants his affection and starts taking over the identities of the other Misfits in order to cause mayhem (S02E01); an overprotective father kills everyone that gets too close to his daughter (S02E05). Interestingly, most of these conflicts are of a personal nature revolving around the impact of dysfunctional social institutions such as community, family, love relations, employment and living environment on the individual: the Misfits are superheroes who fight the insecurity, uncertainty and unsafety of living in a liquid modern world.

In the season finales, however, larger-scale "supervillains" emerge to threaten the community beyond the Misfits group. In the last episode of season one, a girl named Rachel uses her power of persuasion to start a chastity organization similar to the American "True Love Waits" and to radically alter the values and norms of today's society. The organization, "Virtue," speedily turns into a reactionary group, forcing formerly unpopular behavior standards onto a helpless youth. The proclaimed chastity, piety and conformity of "Virtue" are representative of a time in which institutions such as religion, family and community stood against the precariousness of our reality. By oppressing the former loose and raucous youth of the estate, by enforcing a conservative, white middle-class dress as a uniform and violent brainwashing any opposition, Rachel and her organization force lost values (as they were common in the 1950s) onto our liquid modern age. Juxtaposing these outdated morals with today's urge towards instant gratification, ever-changing offerings of sexual partners and entertainments, the series equates these values with fascist ideology. In a sermon-like speech, Nathan takes the role of the savior of the sinful and spokesman of liquid modern non-morality and non-existence of fixed social values:

"She's got you thinking, this is how you are supposed to be. But it is not. We're young! We're supposed to drink too much, we're supposed to have bad attitudes and shag each other's brains out. We are designed to party! [...] If you could just see yourselves. It breaks my heart. You're wearing cardigans. We had it all, we fucked up bigger and better than any generation that came before us. We were so beautiful. We're screw-ups. I am a screw-up. And I plan to be a screw-up until my late twenties, maybe even early thirties." (S01E06)

Nathan then struggles with Rachel and they both fall to their deaths, ending season one with him discovering his superpower of immortality – in the grave, after having been buried. His resurrection from the dead then turns him into a superhero, his mission statement: embracing liquid modernity to the fullest. His mission of saving everyone's hedonistic individuality is a bitter commentary on society's status quo, placing value solely in pleasure and individual gratification. Ironically, though, he does act like a superhero in not abandoning his friends and community (as hedonistic and self-centered as they might be) to the fascist regime, and in sacrificing his life for others.

"We don't need to be caught up in all this bullshit!" – Unwanted Superpowers

In the finale season two, a frustrated priest – again a symbol of the lost values and broken moorings of community and religion – turns into a supervillain by buying superpowers and using them to appear as the second coming of Christ, calling himself Jesus. He starts by walking on water and stripping a robber of a gun via telekinesis, but soon he abuses his powers by extorting money and having the same criminal rob and kill for his own purposes. He continues to buy more powers, becoming power-hungry both literally and figuratively. Similar to Rachel, Jesus represents religion with its moral values of a bygone era being corrupted in our contemporary world. The institutional stability provided by religion is shown as broken, corrupt, and concerned with self-interest and instant gratification.

An additionally interesting point about this episode is that it explicitly comments on another prototypical element of the superhero narrative: superpowers. Coogan argues that superpowers determine the superhero, in that his power "amplifies the abilities" (32) of other heroes – where a hero might be strong, Superman is superstrong, an exaggeration of human abilities beyond proportion. The superhero possesses "skills and abilities normal humans do not" (Fingeroth 17), and the "extraordinary nature of the superhero will be contrasted with the ordinariness of his surroundings" (Reynolds 16), so as to showcase these skills. Ordinary beings are needed so that the sense of wonder the superhero evokes is not blunted by there only being extraordinary characters.

In the mentioned episode (S02E07), two aspects are important for the analysis: First, the Misfits at one point lose their powers and return to being ordinary people, thus contrasting strongly with the remaining supervillain and, more to the point, with the superhero characters they were before. And second, a character is introduced into the series (becoming a recurring character in season three) who can absorb superpowers and store them, thus generating an economy of powers and the option to add or subtract elements from the superhero status.

In a self-reflexive moment, triggered by Alisha's discontent with her inability to be intimate with her boyfriend due to her power of sexual frenzy, the Misfits discuss the advantages and disadvantages of having a power. The offer made by the power dealer Seth to buy their powers and restore their lives to normal is a strong temptation for the young group.

Nikki: What has any one of us really achieved with our powers?

Nathan: You mean apart from saving all our lives?

Alisha: We would not need saving if it wasn't for the powers. We don't need to be caught up in all this bullshit. (S02E07)

The discussion turns on the question of choice, of being charged with a "selfless mission" and of the fate that comes along with it. Within the course of the season, most of the characters express practical day-to-day problems with their powers. Kelly becomes afraid of any social interaction because of her telepathy and the constant tirade of lies that surround her. She falls in love with a gorilla-turned-man because his thoughts are honest and reflect his actions (S02E05), but he gets shot and dies. Curtis is frustrated because his power does not allow him to turn back time at will, and his girlfriend Nikki, similarly complains about her power of teleportation: it shifts her at the most inappropriate moments, i.e. when she is experiencing an orgasm (S02E07). The Misfits, wishing for normal life without "this bullshit," consequently turn to the power dealer Seth and sell their powers, becoming ordinary again. Simon, who still believes that their powers are connected to a mission, confronts them and explains the danger of giving up their power in an intertextual reference that draws upon the self-doubt convention of superhero comics and films:

Alisha: What are you doing here?

Simon: I wanted to know what he was doing with the powers. Why are you here?

Kelly: Twenty-fucking-grand!

Simon: You sold your powers?

Kelly: Yeah, mate!

Simon: You shouldn't be doing this. We were given them for a reason.

Nikki: And what reason is that?

Curtis: I give you twenty-thousand reasons for getting rid of them.

Simon: It is like in *Superman 2*, when Superman gives up his powers so that he can be with Lois Lane.

Kelly: And?

Simon: General Zod took over the world!

Curtis: That is totally relevant, except there ain't no General Zod and that's twenty-thousand pounds. Later... (S02E07)

In liquid modernity, the ordinary is without security, without safety. Values are corrupted and life itself is a precarious adventure that could go wrong with any decision. No institution exists that is willing or able to step in and save you. Hence, when Fake-Jesus sends out his robber to bring more money, that criminal decides to rob the bar where Curtis works and the Misfits hang out. In the ensuing struggle, a stray bullet hits Nikki. Her unnecessary death drives home the point of a precarious reality and the purpose of the superpowers for the group. Nathan could have acted as a human shield, Nikki could have teleported out of the way and Curtis could have just rewound time to undo the robbery. But ordinary as they are, the Misfits are unable to intervene. They feel the pressure of normality, being confronted with ordinary life and its consequence of a meaningless death. In a heroic decision to accept their mission – as unclear and unstated as it still is – they decide to act against the supervillain and get back their powers at all costs. They confront him, steal his money and in a nice plot twist make him kill himself with his own powers.

At the end, they are then confronted with an even more problematic choice. Since their old powers have died with Fake-Jesus, they now get to choose new powers. With the introduction of Seth, the power dealer, the series again calls upon a superhero genre convention while subverting the original element into a liquid modern revision.[9] The ensemble, defined by their characteristic superpowers, now undergoes a radical change in that the dynamic of the group shifts. Instead of adhering to the convention of a "linkage between biography or personality and powers" (Coogan 256, note 16) as in the first two seasons, the third season of *Misfits* uses superpowers as yet another commodity that can be traded, sold, bought, stolen or extorted. The moral implications of this break with convention will be discussed in the second part of this paper in more detail; it is worth mentioning at this point, however, that the ideology representative of such a shift is obviously closely related to liquid modernity.

"Why do I have to be the Invisible Cunt?" – Secret Identity, Silly Names and Costumes

Third and last on Coogan's list of prototypical elements is the superhero identity. In his argument, this "identity element comprises the codename and the costume, with the secret identity being a customary counterpart to the codename," both of which usually "firmly externalize either their alter ego's inner character or biography" (32). In Coogan's view, the costume and name of a superhero function as iconic markers of their identity, in their stripped-down simplicity amplifying the meaning that the superhero itself transports. Furthermore, "the mask", as Fingeroth argues, "is recognized as bestower of power as well as disguiser of identity" (51).

In *Misfits* this conception is subverted and deconstructed on several levels. Most obviously in the sense that the protagonists have no codenames, a point which they comment on, again foregrounding a metafictional knowledge of the genre and its conventions:

Nathan: Think about it, we could have really cool superhero names: Captain Invincible. Mister Backwards.

Curtis: I sound retarded.

Nathan: The Invisible Cunt.

Simon: Why do I have to be the Invisible Cunt?

---

[9] There are superhero comics that explore the question of "different powers" for known superheroes, most famously the "What if the Fantastic Four Had Different Super-Powers?" issue of *What If* (cf. Coogan, 255f., note 16).

Nathan: Because you just are, man, get over it. What is the point of us all having superpowers if we can't use them. Make obscene amounts of money and shag lots of drunk, impressionable girls. It is clearly what God intended for us, and I for one will not let him down. (S02E06)

In this scene, Nathan picks up on the idea that codenames refer to inner character or biography, and that they represent a superhero's personality. In his own charming way he thus bestows names on the male Misfits. Simon, the shy guy who never gets noticed and who suddenly manifests the power to turn invisible, thus obtains the codename "The Invisible Cunt." Taking Curtis' reaction as an indication, the show here mocks the "foppish alter egos" (Coogan 32) that superheroes tend to project with their codenames.

Whenever the show does allow codenames, they seem either ironic or somewhat ridiculous and non-befitting a superhero. When in S02E06 the group is found out because of a superpower media frenzy, one character is named "Monsieur Grand Fromage" because of his ability to manipulate dairy products – "the shittiest power ever", as Kelly so aptly puts it – whereas the Misfits are referred to as the "ASBO Five". As discussed above, ASBO and superheroism are already ironically juxtaposed in regards to the selfless, communal mission. In addition, the group here does not get individual names, as would be befitting superheroes and mark them as extraordinary individuals. The group name rather functions, as does the ASBO itself, to lower the visibility of the deviant behavior and to eliminate all individuality.

Moreover, just as the group name functions to undermine the superhero identity, their costume is equally un-heroic. The community service overall on the one hand fulfills Reynold's claim that a "costume functions as a uniform, binding together all super-beings and costumed characters in contrast to the non-costumed ordinary world" (26) but only by deliberately denying the individual identity and reducing the heroes to non-persons. It is precisely their anonymity and status as pariahs that mark their identity. As Lenz notices, there is, of course, a slight adjustment to the costume that does set apart each individual from the others, as each character wears the overall differently, by accessorizing it or by simply negating the uniformity of fabric and cut (i.e. Curtis wears only the bottom half, knotting the top; Alisha uses a belt to enhance her figure). Nonetheless, the costume does not yield power to the Misfits. Masks and superhero costumes are used for different reasons: for protection, intimidation of enemies, as a source of power, a symbol for immortality, or to avert danger from loved ones by hiding behind a second identity (cf. Fingeroth 47-61) – the first and original identity thus becoming secret. For most of the show, the group ironically adheres to this concept of a secret identity in the sense that their anti-social manner, reflected in their ASBO and thus their overall non-costumes, actually keeps them under everyone's radar as individuals – even in their "real" identities.

In S02E06, this status quo is upset, however. The Misfits are found out and superpowers go public. When faced with their identity being revealed and their invisible making costumes being stripped from them, the group turns to Simon to find out what will happen next and he paints the grim picture of genre convention:

Simon: They'll treat us like freaks. They'll lock us up in a secret military facility and conduct experiments on us.

Nathan: Hey, no one's experimenting on me. I'm not a monkey.

Kelly: What we gonna do?

Simon: We have to go into hiding. We assume new identities. We break off all connection with our family and friends. We wear disguises and only go out after dark.

Curtis: I am not loving the sound of that?

Nathan: Yeah, do you expect me never to see my mom again? Who's gonna do my washing, huh? Ah, you have not thought this through.

Simon's solution to the problem is adopting a conventional superhero secret and dual identity, which is then ridiculed in a gesture of adolescent ignorance by Nathan. For the group, with the sole exception of Simon, the solution lies in becoming media stars, profiteering on the attention and letting a manager take over their lives. All their misdeeds – which have increased considerably over the course of the series, by mistake or accident – are glossed over by their newly found popularity. The manager aptly spins the group's deviance into an asset: "I would say that these people you may or may not have killed were evil, you were protecting society. You are not murderers, you are heroes. Superheroes. Rich, famous superheroes." (S02E06)

But again, as with the loss of superpowers, the loss of secrecy turns out to be a disaster that kills the whole group, which can only be reversed by Curtis travelling back in time. The disaster does not strike against the superheroes' sense of family and security, however, as the enemy does not attack their loved ones. Rather, it is the media hype, the attention span of society, always looking for that bigger spectacle, that better deal, that causes another superpowered being to retaliate, as he realizes that he cannot compete as a hero and needs to turn to being villainous. His "Big Cheese" ability to manipulate dairy-products only makes headlines as long as no one else with a better, more interesting power is around. With the ASBO Five along, his power is not worth the attention. Media frenzy starts to move towards people with powers from the "A-list", as Nathan calls it – people like the young woman Daisy. "She can heal people. Any illness, any disease. She plans to heal the world. She is like a pretty modern day Mother Theresa with a superpower. She is going to make a fortune" (S02E06), the manager reckons, and thus perfectly showcases liquid modernity's economy of attention. The shows ironic commentary on this self-less superheroic mission of world-healing is that Daisy suffocates on a latte macchiato, while at the same time impaling herself on her Mother Theresa humanitarian award. When asked why he killed the others, "Grand Fromage" says: "Because the only time people like me ever get noticed, is when we kill a shitload of people. They will talk about this for years. They will talk about me. Monsieur Grand Fromage." (S02E06) The series satirically comments upon contemporary media saturation in this instance, as well as on the fact that not even superheroes are exempt from the constant sway of audience attention and public opinion changes. Ordinary people become extraordinary superheroes who in term become ordinary media entertainment, which is then replaced by something more extraordinary like a supervillain and so on. Stability of values and categories is completely dissolved.

Last but not least, the show's only "real" superhero, a man in a mask, with a codename, a sense of self-less mission and superpowers needs to be addressed. In terms of Coogan's definition and within the concept of the show, this character functions as the prototype, the classical superhero character, who is contrasted to the rest of the Misfits. At the end of the first season, a guy in a hoodie rescues Nathan from the Virtue-mob with perfect timing for the escape (S01E06). Later on in the series, the savior returns, disguised by a black paintball mask, and helps the group over and over again, displaying clairvoyance as well as great acrobatic skills. He is mockingly named "The Guy in the Mask" in the series,[10] and his mannerisms (the mask, saving people etc.) are made fun off several times by the characters. It is specifically the use of superhero conventions that is repeatedly commented upon. When "The Guy in the Mask" rescues Peter, a comic book fan, he easily identifies him as a superhero by genre conventions: "You are a superhero. I know you can't tell me who you are. That's why you have a secret identity, right?" (S03E03)

When the show finally reveals his identity as Simon's future self who travelled back in time to rescue Alisha from death, the secret identity convention becomes more poignant as (present) Simon now really has another secret (future) identity. Future Simon needs to remain secret as knowledge about his presence would alter

---

[10] Interestingly, fans of the series as well as the official E4 website do not pick up on the in-text nomination but rather refer to the character as "Superhoodie" ("Superhoodie" n.pag.), thus drawing the connection not with the black paintball mask but with the hooded sweatshirt he is wearing. This, of course, ironically undercuts public perception of youth in hoodies as hooligans or threats and bestows a positive image on youth in such a garment. In both cases though, the name-personality connection is non-existent and the name is simply a statement of "masked-ness."

the time line, radically changing his present self's development and thus risking the chance that he will later not become "The Guy in the Mask". This is metafictionally commented upon by the series in S03E03. Peter, the comic book fan, has the power to draw comics, which then become reality. When he meets "The Guy in the Mask" and later recognizes Simon, he makes him become his friend. During that episode, Peter forces Simon to choose between the superhero's mission and his individual fulfillment, at which point Simon (and thus "The Guy in the Mask") realizes the limitations of his own belief in superhero conventions. He confronts Peter and for the first time negates his own statement from the shows very first episode: "I am not a superhero. They are a fantasy. Your fantasy, not mine." In the end, though, by drawing a sacrificial death for himself and a change of heart for Simon, Peter ensures that Simon will become "The Guy in the Mask": "You did it. You saved her. A superhero has to be prepared to die for what he believes in." (S03E03). The series here openly calls into question the conventions of superheroism, especially its mission of selflessness. Even the most convinced superhero of the series is not selfless by choice but rather because the convention (as enacted through the comic book fan) needs him to be.

To sum up, the superhero narrative functions as a representation of and adaptation to the societies out of which it is born. *Misfits* shows us that rigid value systems do not exist anymore; that a moral code is fluid and adaptable; that powers can shift, reverse or even be bought and sold in order to adapt to new situations; that superhero identities become complicated by media attention; and that the low-profile non-costume of uniformity turns out to be much more efficient than any high exposition costume of alter ego reflection.

Dealing with Misfitting Powers

As mentioned before, the third season of *Misfits* introduces a number of storylines that deal with the effects of an altered set of preconditions which is caused by the introduction of a new character: the power dealer and initially cold-blooded businessman Seth. As a result of the new possibilities he offers to the characters, this season differs from the first two in that it is marked by a variety of transgressions and boundary crossings, which are implicitly portrayed as going too far – arguably, as a result of the abuse of an 'unnaturally' obtained power. The aim of this section is to analyze the dissolving of moral and social boundaries in the aftermath of the introduction of this power dealer as depicted in selected storylines of *Misfits'* third season, and to discuss in particular the values and ideologies latently reflected and debated within them.

Personality Extensions and the Process of Maturation

Initially, the powers distributed to the various characters in the electrical storm at the very beginning of the series display a clear connection to the respective personalities of their bearers. The show thus clearly adheres to the conventional linkage of either biography or personality and the adopted powers, as described above (cf Coogan 256, note 16). They seem, in fact, to reflect, amplify or adapt to certain traits of the person they append to. In short, they function as a hyperbolic reflection of who their bearers are. For instance, there is Alisha who is portrayed as highly sexual and no stranger to the idea of taking advantage of her natural powers of seduction. After the storm and due to her newly acquired superpower, she can no longer touch a man without causing arousal, and even raging lust. Then, there is Kelly, who has been stereotyped as a simple-minded, lower class 'chav' by people all her life, due to her accent and style. In the past, she had repeatedly reacted insecurely and aggressively to people's untenable judgments. Kelly now has the ability to hear exactly what people think of her: she has obtained the power to read minds. Moreover, there is shy and introverted Simon, who has always felt isolated and invisible to most of society, and especially the opposite sex. He suddenly obtains the ability to literally turn invisible. Even newly introduced characters who join the Misfits at a later point in the story display a clear connection between their powers and personalities or biographical backgrounds: Rudy, for example, who is clearly torn between a number of contradictory personality facets, obtains the ability to literally split his multiple personality into two separate and independently acting characters.

Based on these and other similar connections between an acquired superpower and a respective character with a given personal history, we view the powers gained in the storm as a form of personality extension and their allocation as purposely aimed. This circumstance adds a sense of 'naturalness' to the possession of a given power – the power belongs to a character and appends to him or her, as if drawn by a natural attraction. We would suggest, even, that they hold up a mirror to the characters' personalities, and especially their weaknesses, and thereby have a function of teaching them a lesson about themselves. When the characters thus have to learn to deal with their powers, as well as to control them, they are simultaneously forced to come to terms with who they really are.

Reckless and cocky as he is as a person, Nathan, for example, is given the power of immortality, a power that emphasizes his natural hubris. Whilst now rendered incapable of being too reckless to lose his own life, he has to learn regard for other people's wellbeing and save lives by turning his recklessness into bravery and his egomania into at least a certain amount of empathy. The same applies to Curtis, the athlete, who has ruined his career with one idiotic mistake, been struggling with the consequences of his actions, and become so driven by remorse and regret, that he receives the ability to turn back time. Despite his power, however, he still has to come to terms with the consequences of his own actions and accept the past. Curtis is doing community service and has been banned from athletics because he was caught buying drugs. His girlfriend Sam who was also involved in this event was sent to prison as a punishment for her actions. As Sam had been sent to prison mainly because she took the blame for Curtis, he is in debt to her. When she is finally released after six months in jail, Curtis is confronted with what he had done to her. As she nevertheless wishes to be reunited with her lover in S01E04, he is faced with the harsh reality of not having waited for her and being in a new relationship with Alisha instead. Ridden with guilt, he decides to prevent the drug bust from happening in the first place. A number of failed attempts to undo these harmful events and actions, however, painfully teach him the lesson that he cannot simply avoid taking responsibility by using his power, but can only make things right for those he has hurt by accepting the blame and reacting to the consequences of his choices accordingly.

The stories told in *Misfits* are enriched by the addition of supernatural powers to a very human plot. They are, however, much more about the difficulties of being a teenager than about the fantastic elements of the storylines: The protagonists are 'misfits' not mainly because they have powers – even though they initially believe to be the only ones that do. Also, they are not 'misfits' mainly because they are delinquents – although that, of course, amplifies their 'misfit-ness' as well. Mostly, however, they are 'misfits' in the sense that adolescents could generally be seen to be. The teen-age of the protagonists symbolizes the transition from childhood into adulthood, and the development of maturing into fit members of a society. They have not finished their maturation yet, and the lessons they are supposed to learn from their powers are merely a hyperbolic version of the challenges posed to any juvenile, trying to develop a full personality and come to terms with the traits given to them by nature.

In this sense, *Misfits* matches the general tendency of teen drama to feature coming-of-age storylines. Moreover, as Ross and Stein argue, television formats which focus on teen characters and/or are aimed at a teen audience offer "a crucial space for the negotiation of political, social and cultural issues […] television featuring the lives and experiences of teens not only touch on coming of age issues, but also on questions of self, identity, gender, race, and community" (1). Hence, the series can also be seen as a platform, based on which norms, values and possible forms of identity as reached within a maturation process, can be negotiated – a trait that is also associated with the superhero genre.

Thus reading the series as a form of coming-of-age drama, the protagonists are not so much super-heroes, but mostly super-teens. *Misfits* tells the story of how a group of juveniles forcedly convene every day, dressed in their orange jumpsuits (in subversion of the usual fancy superhero attire as discussed above), and *re*actively (instead of *pro*actively) fight against all threats directly coming at them in their secluded world of community service (instead of saving the world with a sense of duty that stereotypically defines the superhero[11]). Nevertheless, the flawed and immature natures of the Misfits can also be aligned with the tragic heroes of classic tales. As Neuhaus and Wallenborn argue, the dramatic hero in such narratives is traditionally equipped with a fatal flaw, the so-called 'hamartia', which he has to overcome within the process of his heroic journey and for which he is commonly severely punished (233). The maturation process of the young protagonists in *Misfits* can thus also be read as a hyperbolic version of the necessary learning process of a classic hero who is equipped with both remarkable and superhuman powers as well as tragically human flaws.

Freaks of the Week and the Failure to Grow

As argued, the powers given to the characters in the series can be seen as personality extensions in all cases, i.e. also in the cases of the so-called Freaks-of-the-Week against which the protagonists have to defend themselves. These antagonists are individuals who have also been given a power amplifying a character trait, a weakness, an experience or fear. What differentiates them from the protagonists, however, is that they do not manage to overcome or learn from these extremely emphasized negative traits and are thus bound to fail. Lucy, for instance, a highly insecure girl who has always wished to be someone else, is turned into a shapeshifter by the storm (S02E01). As she is jealous of Simon's new circle of friends and feels rejected by him, she begins to turn them against one another by adopting their form and seemingly forcing them to do unacceptable things to each other. She ends up getting killed. Brian, the afore-mentioned master of lactokinesis who abuses his power to take revenge on those who have deprived him of his long-craved and finally received (media) attention does not manage to survive either, as he proves incapable of finding any sense of self-worth that is independent of the view of others (S02E06). Another character, who has been entrapped in a computer game reality since the storm, refuses to listen to reason and insists on remaining in his escapist version of the world. He never gives in to the pleads of his begging victims, maintaining the world-view that all characters he meets

---

[11] According to Barbara Kain, there is a widespread tendency to depict a new form of anti-heroes who are not in the least interested in saving the world in (pseudo-) superhero comics, films and parodies of the genre. *Misfits* certainly fits neatly into that trend as well: "Die Tendenz neigt zu realistisch dargestellten, im Alltagstrott gefangenen und an ihrer Existenz zweifelnden, ambivalenten Problemcharakteren, sogenannten Antihelden – zumindest was das männliche Heldengeschlecht betrifft – sowie zu amüsanten und verspielten Superhelden-Parodien" (8).

are automatically enemies who must be destroyed for points in the game. Hence, he does not return to humanity, refuses to learn empathy and therefore cannot survive (S02E04). Moreover, the tattoo artist who can manipulate the emotional attachments of people is eventually punished for forcing Kelly to love him, as a punishment for his refusal to recognize that true affection has got to come freely and love has got to be earned (S02E03).

Based on a number of examples like these, we would like to argue that the Freaks-of-the-Week that attack the protagonists in every episode are always characters who have failed to turn their powers, as well as their natural personality traits, into tools of strength and a base for personal growth. Hence, they have failed to mature and their fatal flaw eventually destroys them. Nevertheless, the consequences of this kind of failure do not only exist for the weekly attackers in the show, but also for the protagonists. They too are punished when they try to take advantage of their power. When Alisha starts using her power to sexually seduce any man she desires, for example, she nearly initiates her own rape (S01E03) and when Curtis attempts to undo the past, he ends up killing half of his friends (S01E04). Hence, the supernatural gifts given to the individuals in *Misfits* can help them overcome their fears and insecurities by making them go through a typical hero's journey and learning process, thus initiating and accelerating the maturation process of a teenager, as well as teaching them as super-powered beings about the responsibility of a superhero as mentioned in the Spider-Man edict: with great power comes great responsibility.[12] Alternatively, the characters can choose to abuse their newly given powers in order to take revenge on others, satisfy their personal desires or simply provide them with an easy way out, i.e. to ignore the weaknesses they have. In case of the latter, the character gives in to sin and is therefore punished for his or her failure.

Disruption of Order and the Abuse of Power

The first two seasons of *Misfits* are marked by the refusal of characters to grow as a person, i.e. to mature and to learn something from their 'naturally' given character flaws that are expanded into superpowers. Their refusal usually leads to horrific consequences. In the third season, this general code is mostly continued, but it is taken one step further. A supernatural dealer is introduced to the show, who exhibits the ability to take and give powers by touching someone. All of the sudden – in a scene that has been discussed in detail above – the characters are thus given the opportunity to change their fates and dispose of the sometimes paralyzing personality extension that is their power. As this new character opens

---

[12] According to Simone Ofenloch, this credo can be seen as motto of all classical superhero conceptions (17).

up a trading business, they are suddenly given the option to purchase, dispose of, abuse or steal powers not originally meant for them. Hence, the afore-mentioned punishable abuse already begins with the possession of the power.

The third season of *Misfits* thus alters the turn of events and features a number of storylines that deal specifically with the effects of this precondition. Interestingly, the person responsible for this change is called Seth. He is thus given the name of the Egyptian god of Chaos, and chaos is indeed what he spurs. Seth himself initiates a series of catastrophic events when his greed for money and power lead him to selling a number of very dangerous abilities to a disillusioned vicar pretending to be Jesus (S02E07). He does not care that Elliott uses Alisha's former power to rape women. He does not even ask what good the power of sexual seduction could do to a religious leader when he sells Alisha's power to Elliott. He simply does not care, thus refusing to take responsibility for his actions and violating Spider-Man's credo once again.

As a general tendency, the largest scale horrific events in the series seem to occur when some kind of moral, physical or social boundary is crossed. When powers are taken and used that do not truly belong to a personality, i.e. when they are bought for one's own benefit, things go wrong. That is especially the case when these powers are chosen for selfish reasons. Because of Seth, the distribution of powers is no longer controlled by nature or an outside force, such as any form of godly creature. It has become an object of capitalism and human culture instead. Naturally given powers are sold like commodities, these former personality extensions thus become marketable and their bearers thereby corruptible.

Curtis, for example, buys the power to switch his gender back and forth (S03E02). Even though he never had any real interest in this power in the first place – it had simply been the only one left to buy – he soon recognizes its potential, as his newly acquired female alter ego provides him with a second chance to return to athletics. Moreover, he increasingly takes advantage of his female body for pleasure. When he thus begins to abuse his power for the purpose of an intensified form of masturbation, to alternate between male and female orgasms, he accidentally self-inseminates and eventually has to dispose of his power again, in order to avoid either pregnancy or abortion. The power can thus be seen as refusing to be abused for self-gratification or any other selfish motifs without consequence. Instead of dealing with that, however, Curtis chooses to avoid the problem by simply giving up his female side, and trading his gender-switching power for the horrific new power of bringing back the dead. This power is then abused as well by someone it does not belong to, in order to resurrect a former girlfriend. Seth asks Curtis to bring back to life a woman whom he himself was responsible for killing. He does not do so for her sake, however. He neither wants to get together with her again, nor does he simply wish to give her a new life. Instead, he merely wishes to relinquish his own personal sense of guilt. Once again, this truly selfish motivation is punished, as resurrecting the dead eventually turns them into cannibalistic zombies (S03E07). This episode is a clear reminder of the idea of hubris: It is not a human's place to play God by deciding over life and death.

Even in the Nazi-episode (S03E04) where a 75-year old Jew purchases the power to travel back in time in order to kill Hitler, everything goes wrong. Of course, trying to avoid the Holocaust seems like a very noble and altruistic plan at first glance. After all, it would not simply benefit one person, but potentially all of society. It would eradicate one of the most horrific genocides in the history of the world. Nevertheless, we would like to argue that his real motivation is not purely altruistic either, but really quite personal in nature. As he himself states in his motivational letter, he has to do this in order to dispose of his feeling of guilt for never having done anything against the Nazis when he was younger. He does not want to die knowing that he did nothing. If he had had purely altruistic motives, he could have bought the power and given it to someone strong and young who could have potentially killed Hitler. Instead, this physically fragile old man confronts Hitler on his own, and risks not only failure, but also the loss of this precious power and humanity's single chance to ever alter the past. When he thus attacks Hitler, he is not only overpowered with ease, but Hitler even comes into possession of the old man's mobile phone. With this future technology now in the wrong hands, the world transforms, and we are presented with an alternate reality, in which the Nazis are still in power.

The third season of *Misfits* is marked by a vast number of transgressions and boundary crossings, which are implicitly portrayed as going too far. As opposed to the first two seasons, where things tended to go wrong as the result of a selfish abuse of power, the third season takes 'going wrong' even further when the abilities that are abused are 'unnaturally' obtained powers to begin with. Suitably, Seth eventually pays for his carelessness in selling any power to anyone as well, when he is forced to rob people of their power and give them to the Nazis in the episode just described. In the course of this episode (S03E04), Seth is eventually taught a lesson about the necessity of a sense of morality and responsibility for the powers he holds. Unfortunately, this lesson is rendered temporarily ineffective by the end of the episode, as Kelly remains the only one who remembers the alternate Nazi reality. Nevertheless, the relationship between Kelly and Seth begins to form within this storyline and eventually leads to their relationship, which then leads to Seth finally learning his lesson in the zombie episode S03E07 described above.

Morality and its Christian Legacy

At first sight, the overall tone of the series *Misfits* seems rather 'immoral' in many ways. It perfectly fits into what Perry recognizes as a trend in superhero comic books and film to focus on "deliberately amoral and decadent characters" (171). The protagonists in this case are delinquents with countless character flaws. According to Oropeza, however, the flawed nature of contemporary heroes simplifies identification even in narratives in which superheroes are still presented as nobler, better versions of the self: "we also see the flaws in heroes, which make them humans rather than gods, creatures instead of Creator" (269). Hence, the non-Christ-like hero figure of modern superhero narratives such as *Misfits*, i.e. characters who may not automatically be selflessly willing to sacrifice themselves to save humanity, but arrive at doing so nonetheless, are much more suitable to a predominantly secularized audience. In addition to the flawed heroes, *Misfits* features a vast amount of drug abuse, coarse language, vulgarity, unprotected promiscuity and, last but not least, numerous cases of homicide, which – despite the fact that fiction has a tendency to differentiate clearly in its evaluation between "evil violence" and "violence against evil" (cf Gutmann 113) – is still in clear violation of legal as well as religious guidelines.

Nevertheless, certain core values are implicitly promoted by the show, as we would like to argue, and there is a deep-seated sense of morality transported through the effects caused by the supernatural abilities. The powers given to individuals are the dice dealt to them by nature, fate or possibly even a higher power. Despite the fact that the existence of God is literally ruled out in S03E08 by the highly disappointed, formerly Christian ghost of Rachel – the leader of the Virtue movement who was killed in S01E06 – the presence of implicit religious themes is easily uncovered. In fact, there is a general sense of morality in *Misfits*, which seems to be formed by Christianity's cultural legacy. This is only true to a highly selective extent, though, as the commandment not to kill is clearly ignored, for example. Also, the characters repeatedly commit blasphemy and ridicule Christian values in the show, as seen in the analysis of the first and second seasons' finales above. Nevertheless, the notion of the 'doctrine of original sin' seems to lie at the core of the value system as presented in the depicted world. As Perry defines it, original sin "names the bias toward evil conduct that infects all human beings [...,] accounts for the widespread structures and acts of moral evil [... and] does not absolve anyone of responsibility" (182). Consequently, sins such as envy, wrath, greed, pride and even lust are punished severely in *Misfits* whenever they are taken too far. The consequences then can only be reversed or avoided by regard and compassion for others, maturity of personality and selfless courage. This circumstance additionally mirrors the earlier argument that the show is really about youth and the difficulties posed by coming of age.

Outlook on Season Four

During the writing process of this article, E4 aired the fourth season of *Misfits*, shifting several aspects of the show's dynamics and almost completely exchanging the main cast. While there has been too little time to fully analyze this new season and to engage it with as much depth as the other three seasons, we feel that it still warrants mentioning within the scope of a short outlook. During season four, three new characters, Finn, Jess and Abbey, are introduced in order to replace the vacancies left by Simon, Alisha and Kelly (who remains in Africa to clear landmines, aided by her superpower of "rocket science", we are told). By mid-season, Curtis, the last remaining original Misfit, is killed, leaving Rudy the only character to promote a certain form of narrative continuity. Especially in regards to realizing an overarching plot for the whole show (or even just the fourth season), this break proves to be impossible to overcome.

More interesting, from the point of view of this article at least, is that with Simon gone and thus no one acting as superhero expert and moral compass of the group, the show's thematic and ideological emphasis shifts completely. Whereas the superhero narrative was emphasized continuously via metafictional commentary and intertextual reference in the first three seasons, in season four it almost completely fades from the show. Without Simon making certain problems of super-heroism explicit and connecting the events to a greater meta-narrative, the show comes close to ignoring the superpowers given to the characters. Even though Jess, Finn and Abbey have superpowers, the plot no longer features these powers as prominently as before. Instead, the series focuses on the teenage drama aspect, on coming-of-age plots and stereotypical problems of adolescence such as working out one's relationship with parents (in all patch-worked forms) and potential partners. The natural order of superpowers (Seth leaves for Africa after using his power one last time in S04E02) is present throughout the season. Nevertheless, the powers now simply function as exotic motivational devices instead of the origin of the dilemmas that are faced by the group. What this means for both the question of *Misfits* representing changes in our society via its subversion of traditional superhero narratives as well as the question of superpowers reflecting moral challenges posed to teenagers as a means to imagine the transition of adolescents becoming adult members of society, remains to be analyzed in full at a later point.

Conclusion

Misfits begins with a group of young offenders paying back their debt to society and by accident becoming superheroes of sorts. From the start, the show presents its heroes as problematic, unconventional and "misfitting" in today's society, and their community service as a meaningless and futile attempt to engender conformity. By subverting the traditional superhero conventions of mission, power and identity, the show plays on the changes in society itself. Ironically, however, the plot of the show actually is focused on the rehabilitation of these delinquents. *Misfits* is all about the turn of self-centered individuals into morally acceptable members of society, as well as the difficulties of transitioning from youth into adulthood. Slowly but surely, the protagonists learn to deal with the traits that make them misfits. And it is only their potential for personal growth that eventually turns their superpowers into an actual source of strength.

Bibliography

"Anti-Social Behaviour Orders on Convictions (ASBOs)". http://www.cps.gov.uk/legal/a_to_c/anti_social_behaviour_guidance/, 28.02.13.

Bauman, Zygmunt. *44 Letters from the Liquid Modern World*. Cambridge: Polity 2010.

Bauman, Zygmunt. *Liquid Modernity*. Cambridge: Polity 2000.

Beck, Ulrich. *Risk Society: Towards a New Modernity*. Trans. Mark Ritter. London: Sage 1992.

Coogan, Peter. *Superhero: The Secret Origin of a Genre*. Austin: Monkeybrain 2006.

Fingeroth, Danny. *Superman on the Couch: What Superheroes Really Tell Us about Our_selves and Our Society*. New York: Continuum 2004.

Gutmann, Hans-Martin. "Gewalt". In: Fechtner, Kristian, Gotthard Fremor, Uta Pohl-Patalong and Harald Schroeder-Wittke (Eds.): *Handbuch Religion und Populäre Kultur*. Stuttgart: Kohlhammer 2005.

Kainz, Barbara. "Einleitende Worte". In: Barbara Kainz (Ed.): *Comic. Film. Helden. Heldenkonzepte und medienwissenschaftliche Analysen*. Wien: Löcker 2009, 7–15.

Lenz, Christian. "'You can be so much better': Deviant Ideology in the TV Series Misfits". Conference Paper. "Übergänge und Entgrenzungen in der Fantastik." 3rd International Conference of the Gesellschaft für Fantastikforschung. 13.09.12. University of Zurich.

"Memorandum submitted by Napo". http://www.publications.parliament.uk/pa/cm200405/cmselect/cmhaff/80/80we20.htm, 03.03.13.

Misfits. TV-Series. Created: Howard Overman. E4. Five Seasons. November 2009 – December 2013.

"*Misfits* – Who Wants A Superhero With An ASBO?" E4 Official Press Release. Aug 9, 2009.

"*Misfits* – A Graphic Adventure". http://www.e4.com/misfits/comic.html, 25.02.13.

Ndalianis, Angela. "Comic Book Superheroes: An Introduction." *The Contemporary Comic Book Superhero*. Ed. Angela Ndalianis. New York: Routledge, 2009. 3–15.

Neuhaus, Volker and Markus Wallenborn. "Held". Hans-Otto Hügel (Ed.): *Handbuch für Populäre Kultur. Begriffe, Theorien und Diskussionen*. Stuttgart: Metzler 2003. 233–240.

Ofenloch, Simone. "Antihelden als Superhelden, Superhelden als Antihelden. Die Pseudo-Comicfilme der *Darkman*-Reihe und *Hancock*." In: Barbara Kainz (Ed.):

Comic. Film. Helden. Heldenkonzepte und medienwissenschaftliche Analysen. Wien: Löcker 2009, 17–33.

Oropeza, B. J. "Conclusion: Superheroes in God's Image". In: Oropeza, B. J. (Ed.): *The Gospel According to Superheroes. Religion and Popular Culture*. New York: Peter Lang 2005. 269–271.

Oropeza, B. J. "Introduction: Superhero Myth and the Restoration of Paradise". In: Oropeza, B. J. (Ed.): *The Gospel According to Superheroes. Religion and Popular Culture*. New York: Peter Lang 2005. 1–24.

Oropeza, B. J. "The God-Man Revisited: Christology Through the Blank Eyes of the Silver Surfer". In: Oropeza, B. J. (Ed.): *The Gospel According to Superheroes. Religion and Popular Culture*. New York: Peter Lang 2005. 155–169.

Owen, Dan. "TV Review: Misfits, 2.1". *Dan's Media Digest Blog*. http://whatculture.com/tv/tv-review-misfits-2-1.php, 20.01.13.

Perry, Tim. "Mutants That Are All Too Human: The X-Men, Magneto, and Original Sin". In: Oropeza, B. J. (Ed.): *The Gospel According to Superheroes. Religion and Popular Culture*. New York: Peter Lang 2005. 171–187.

Reynolds, Richard. *Super Heroes: A Modern Mythology*. Jackson: U of Mississippi Press, 1992.

Ross, Sharon Marie and Louisa Stein (Eds). *Teen Television: Essays on Programming and Fandom*. Jefferson: McFarland 2008.

Siegel, Jerry and Joe Shuster. *Action Comics #1*. DC Comics. June 1938.

"Superhoodie". http://e4-misfits.wikia.com/wiki/Superhoodie, 02.03.13.

"The Avengers Movie". http://marvel.com/avengers_movie/, 28.02.13.

"Love is a Psychopath": The Postmodern *Doppelgänger* in Steven Moffat's *Jekyll*

Inken Frost

The 2007 BBC series *Jekyll*, written by Steven Moffat, is certainly not the latest in a long line of adaptations, parodies and sequels referring to R. L. Stevenson's *Strange Case of Dr Jekyll and Mr Hyde*, but one that is worthy of note as it deals with its relationship to its source in a fantastically self-conscious way in the manner of postmodern fiction and imbues one of modernity's haunting spectres, the *doppelgänger*, with some thoroughly (un)canny new twists. Indeed, the construction of the 21st century Hyde to a contemporary Jekyll relies, as we shall see, very much on the play between adaptation and original – the *doppelgänger* here not only transgresses the boundaries of identity, but also those of history, in a fantastical play between reality and fiction.

The Original and its Adaptations: The Conundrum of the Double

The original pair of doubles is, of course, well known; has even become proverbial. The story has been a raging success from the day it has been published in 1886, and everyone knows the plot: The mild-mannered, morally upstanding Dr Jekyll devises a potion that turns him into his evil other, the vile and repulsive Mr Hyde.

The really strange thing about this case of a divided identity, however, is that nobody seems to have read the book; as Elaine Showalter puts it in the preface to *Recent Reinterpretations*, "many who think they know the story of Jekyll and Hyde are responding to its various cultural adaptations, rather than Stevenson's original text." (i) Indeed, the well-known summary given above, while not *entirely* wrong, misses much of the point of Stevenson's story as it fails to capture the complex relationship of Jekyll and Hyde as it tries to define in oppositions a duality that can never be completely reconciled.

With Jekyll's hypocrisy and the far-reaching *identity* between the characters, the story also often looses many of the spectres that, in proper Gothic fashion, haunt it. Jekyll/Hyde embody "these deep fears and longings in western readers that the Gothic both symbolizes and disguises in 'romantic' and exaggerated form" and that "so *contradict* each other, and in such intermingled ways, that only extreme fictions [...] can seem to resolve them or even confront them." (Hogle 4)

The objects of fear and desire have changed in 250 years of Gothic fiction, but they are always "the fundamental inconsistencies that prevent us from declaring a coherent and independent identity to ourselves and others", what Kristeva calls the "abject". (Hogle 7)

The Gothic displaces the threat to cultural, familial and individual identity into the monster, the past or future, and distant places. Thus it is never quite 'here' and 'now' and certainly not 'us' (though it *might* be), enabling us to confront it as something external in ghostly disguises of blatantly counterfeit fictionality to confront the roots of our beings in sliding multiplicities (from life becoming death to genders mixing to fear becoming pleasure and more) and to define ourselves against the uncanny abjections, while also feeling attracted to them, all of this in a kind of cultural activity that as time passes can keep inventively changing psychological and cultural longings and fears. (Hogle 16-17)

The ghosts of the abject returning in fantastical guises are not just a theme in Gothic fiction, but also work at a structural level of the texts: "the Gothic is the material repository for that which language fails to touch but which haunts it like an 'unsayable', unreachable core." (Berthin 3) In typical Gothic fashion, *Jekyll and Hyde* abounds with things that will not be named and cannot be said, with curious and blatantly obvious absences of voices, most notably, as has often been remarked, those of women, but also that of Mr Hyde. And while language cannot fully grasp the other, the other, by insinuating itself into the text, attacks the very foundations of language: "The symbolic can only function as long as a series of barriers has been elaborated between the subject and object, inside and outside, and the entry into the symbolic can only be completed if the subject accepts these various forms of separation." (Berthin 82f.)

The Gothic ghost of the abject, the monster, the other of the text threatens the well-set definitions of the subject and can, where it confuses the boundary between self and other, even undermine the boundaries that define language itself, as evidenced by Jekyll's final confession. In his introduction to the Oxford edition of *Jekyll and Hyde*, Roger Luckhurst puts it in a nutshell:

"Yet for all this carefully constructed architecture of stories [that situates the fantastic confession in the world of the possible], *Jekyll and Hyde* does not end with a resounding resolution of the mystery. Indeed, the book finishes with an utterly puzzling sentence: 'Here then as I lay down the pen and proceed to seal up my confession, I bring the life of that unhappy Henry Jekyll to an end.' This is, as Mark Currie has pointed out, not only an impossible attempt 'to narrate the end of narration', it also splits between first and third person, leaving one radically uncertain about who in the end is writing these words, for who is the 'I' in this utterance?" (loc. 178)

This conundrum, of course, here rests on the construct of the double: Hyde is given no voice, and the inability of everyone to describe him renders him curiously absent as he "moves fluidly in the gaps of a complex narrative structure" (Miller 10), alluding to the abject of Victorian society as its undefinable, unbound other. He stems from Jekyll's psyche, it is his "fortress of identity" (Stevenson, loc. 1497), specifically, that he violates, destroying his ability to, literally, express himself: "To be haunted by another, by a spectre, is uncanny enough, but to be haunted by yourself strikes at the foundations of identity." (Dryden 41)

What many adaptations gloss over is the fact that Jekyll, before ever taking the potion, is *already* Hyde, the "real stab of the story", as Chesterton puts it, that "is not in the discovery that one man is two men" – a thoroughly moral Jekyll and an evil Hyde – but in "the discovery that the two men are one man." (loc. 448) The stab is usually taken out of the story by introducing the potion right at the beginning of the narrative, and/or – interestingly enough – by introducing women, often as Jekyll's fiancée, a disreputable counterpart to Hyde or, sometimes, by turning Hyde female; seldom do these woman more than gloss over that particular empty space in the narrative.

The tradition began with Sullivan's play (1887), where a love interest was needed, and that, as the very first adaptation, started "the endless retelling in theatre, film and television, the constant stream of rewritings and updatings", that, as Luckhurst puts it, "all take us further away from the original until it lies forgotten under the rubble of its imitators. *Jekyll and Hyde* immediately evokes chemistry sets and bubbling potions, werewolves and damsels in distress" (loc. 64).

Of course, the idea of an 'original' invoked here is also one of those haunted modern concepts, and particularly charged in the case of *Jekyll and Hyde*. The story has its own double in the first manuscript that Stevenson burned at his wife's behest and which remains largely unknown to us, but still plays, as an implied subtext, a significant part in many a scholarly discussion of the rewritten version that has been published.[1]

All in all, the claims of authenticity and reliability usually attached to "originals" is a bit fickle in this strange case, and so the BBC series not only tells its story as a kind of sequel, detailing the struggles of Jekyll's (or rather Hyde's) descendants, merrily incorporating the highlights of the texts – fictional as well as scholarly – generated by Stevenson's tale, but also making the original text(s) a central plot device.

---

[1] There is also, of course, the matter of the dream in which Stevenson's "Brownies" fashioned for him the germ of the story, as detailed in Stevenson's essay *A Chapter on Dreams* (1888).

Identity at Risk: Playing With Layers of Unreliability

How reliable is Stevenson's narrative, with its silences and absences? For series' protagonist Tom Jackman, filling in the blanks means, in many ways, saving his identity from the forces that try to shatter him.

Initially, Tom – as a foundling – is a man without a past, but a wife that is his soulmate and his twin sons Harry[2] and Eddy give him a family, while his mentor and benefactor Peter Syme has provided him with an education and well-paid position at Klein & Utterson. Even without a history to his name, Tom could be secure in what he has and who he is, were he not threatened by another who has recently started at intervals to take over his body to commit violent and miscreant deeds. Tom desperately tries to control the fiend and, above all, does anything to keep him from his family.

The division between Tom and the other is, of course, based on a timesharing basis; at the outset of the series, Tom hires a secretary to keep their schedules straight. The two personalities live in a precarious balance of control and retribution: Jackman uses modern technology to cheat the boundaries of time, cameras, a GPS to track the other's movement, a Dictaphone to communicate, a combination lock to chain the other up. The other, for his part, marks Tom's body: cigarette burns, nicotine addiction, hangovers, sleep deprivation and lipstick traces.

The uneasy *modus vivendi* cannot last, however. Tom's wife, Claire, gets suspicious and hires two private detectives, which find out that he lives a double life (though they do not tell her about the other). The other is approached by an American who calls him by the name of Hyde and hails him as superman; Hyde takes the name for himself, but throws the American out of a skylight instead of consenting to work for him. Jackman and Hyde share no memories (and little communication), but Tom learns from the P.I.s that someone wants to own Hyde, and they disclose to him the first layer of the secret of his miscreant other and the people that try to capture him.

Stevenson's narrative – of which Tom knows approximately what everybody 'knows' – is not a fiction, they tell him; Stevenson wrote it after a factual account that his friend Jekyll gave him. Once we have accepted the premises, however, we get told that the factual account is actually a carefully crafted lie. Plato, for once, is justified in saying that authors are liars; there is a valid reason for the misdirection, though: In a flashback to Victorian times, we see Jekyll express his fears someone might recreate Hyde, take possession of his power. Stevenson guesses at the fundamental secret at the core of Hyde that Jekyll kept silent about, but we

---

[2] Obviously this name is a nod to the original Jekyll and Hyde – though Jekyll's first name in the book is given as Henry, the narrator Utterson calls him Harry half the time.

cannot, from our point of view, see what he writes on the paper he shows Jekyll and subsequently burns.

The parallels to the scholarly pursuit of Hyde's nature is obvious: While the burned manuscript is fancied to hold the secret to the text's omissions and thus to the repressed that Hyde is supposed to represent, the incinerated note contains the key to Jackman's Hyde. And this, he desperately needs: Hyde discovers Tom's family, and while he does not harm them, Jackman threatens war. While they fight each other worse than the original doubles toward the end, Jackman learns that his life has been a carefully constructed lie: Klein & Utterson have controlled his life from the day he has been found as a baby, his supposed benefactor Syme steering him into the arms of the firm that has been founded in Victorian times with the sole purpose to recreate Hyde, to contain him and control his power.

Not only does Hyde, in accordance with the novel, gain ever more control in their fight over supremacy, the series thoroughly shatters Jackman's identity as the "original and better self" (Stevenson, loc. 1591). His "fortress of identity" is a mirage constructed by Klein & Utterson, to whom he is inconsequential as anything other than the 'father' of Hyde. His only solution is to find the secret of *Hyde's* origin, to destroy his enemy from within as well as thwart his pursuers from without. If "to be haunted by yourself strikes at the foundations of identity" with the intuition that you yourself might be the other, how much worse to discover you had no proper existence in the first place.

Who is what? Navigating Through Self and Other(s)

Theories about Hyde abound in the series. At first Tom thinks of a nervous breakdown, developing a split personality, denying Hyde an existence of his own. Later, Hyde readily accepts that he is Tom's dark side, but what does that mean? He is called Tom's repressed urges, his Id, his ego gotten too big and walking away. Werewolves are mentioned. While in the original story being called an ape or caveman, Klein & Utterson hail him as a superman, the next step in human evolution. Hyde old and new are called child, and hate, rage, greed, lust. And as he is, in all these explanations, tied to Tom as his other, how did he come about? Tom never took a potion.

In the novel, the marked physical difference between Jekyll and Hyde is a central plot device since it enables Hyde to hide in Jekyll and leaves the crucial discovery that "the two men are one man" to the very end. Also, Hyde's small stature and his indescribable but very acute ugliness mark him not only as an 'underdeveloped' part of Jekyll's personality, but also as deficient, as lacking in spiritual faculties, as thoroughly less than Jekyll's whole personality.

In the very first adaptation of the novel, Sullivan's play, both Jekyll and Hyde are played by the same actor, Richard Mansfield, who used no makeup or other devices apart from his acting skills to present the different personalities. The BBC series resurrects this fascinating approach; both Tom Jackman and Billy Hyde (as well as the original Hyde[3]) are played by James Nesbitt, while there are hardly any artificial means used to distinguish them physically. While the play, in keeping with the novel, lets its characters simply react to Hyde's presence instead of having them try to describe him – leaving him undefined in spite of his appearance on stage – the series has, starting in the very first scene, a number of people enumerate the differences between Jackman and Hyde: The general consensus is that he is altogether sexier than Tom. While there is no way to confuse Jackman and Hyde – Nesbitt's acting thoroughly transports the differences in character – the fact everyone notes the similar-different halfway convinces the viewer of even the physical differences.

The great exception is Claire Jackman. Right at their first meeting, as soon as she realizes that Hyde is not her husband – and says so – she adds: "You look just like him." While she still believes Hyde to be Tom's cousin Billy, she alone notes the different similar.

At the point in the story where she learns of the double identity of Tom/Hyde, she is very angry at having been deceived – by Symes as well as by Tom and Hyde – but she instantly accepts that she married both of them. In fact, she tells Hyde he had better listen to her, since she is his wife.

Shortly after, she, her husband and her children are kidnapped by Klein & Utterson. Since the firm is only interested in Hyde, they effectively erase Tom, leaving Hyde 'free'.

While Tom's identity had crumbled, Hyde had started to become ever more aware when it was Tom's turn to run the body, even been able to communicate with him. Now that Tom is gone, he gets all of his memories – and those of the original Jekyll and Hyde.

One of the memories he accesses is the exact double of the flashback to Victorian times in which we witnessed Stevenson talking to Jekyll. But whereas we were confined to the camera's view, Hyde is able to freely move through the scene, so he can see what we could not: Stevenson writing, "There is no potion. It is the girl."

The girl, Alice, is revealed in one of the original Hyde's memories, in which Edward and Billy are actually able to interact with each other. Edward is about to kill Alice, who is an exact double of Claire Jackman (or rather, vice versa) and he tries to talk Billy into murdering Claire, because, as he says, the girls are what

---

[3] Jekyll only appears in a photograph for which Nesbitt stood model.

brought them into being, but also what keeps their Jekyll around, making them weak. Emerging from the memory, Billy Hyde very pointedly does nothing of the sort.

Klein & Utterson tried to recreate the potion, then tried to clone Jekyll – resulting in faulty copies caught somewhere between Jekyll and Hyde. Tom, finally, was an exact genetic copy out of nowhere – and so they cloned Alice, creating Claire and shaping her life just like Tom's to create the love of his life that would bring out Hyde.

But both Claire and Billy refuse to resign themselves to the role of Tom's other, and for one moment Hyde looses the manic behaviour, making him indistinguishable from Tom. He tells Claire, "I'm so strong, I walk through this funny little world of yours and I don't notice it. It bores me. But you – you, Mrs. Jackman, you make me weak. I notice you." Other than Alice, and despite being her clone, Claire is very much her own woman. She sets Billy boundaries, enabling him to define himself. In the very moment where he finally accepts an identity of his own, he is, paradoxically, closest to Tom. As a being defined, however, he also realizes that they can only tackle the threat of Klein & Utterson as an actual unity, because now he has something to lose. Being a superman does not safe him now, because he does not know how to deal, so he resurrects Tom.

Tom, finally, strikes an actual truce with his alter ego, for Claire. And we learn what Hyde really is – their mother, who has been flitting in an out of the story like a ghost, tells Claire: "What was the first day you knew you could kill anyone?" – "The day I first held my children?" – "It's our oldest, deadliest impulse. The need to protect our own at the expense of any other living thing. And we give that impulse such a nice name, don't we? Hyde is love. And love is a psychopath."

In the end, Billy Hyde sacrifices himself for Claire, the twins and even Tom, sparing Tom the bullet wounds on his body. All is well, it seems, as the sacrifice turns him into a hero, the act seemingly making him comprehensible, making us wonder, for a moment, whether love might not be such a psychopath after all.

This is not, however, how the series ends. After everything is ostensibly solved, Tom seeks out his mother to have a last question answered. Even though Jekyll had died a virgin, by now Tom at least suspects that actually Hyde could be his ancestor. His father, however, was not a Jekyll, and that baffles him. Exactly why, as a man of the 21st century, he thinks Jekyll has to be male remains unanswered as the nice, quiet, ethereal old lady turns into Hyde – the sharp, crisp, controlled businesswoman Ms Utterson, of Klein & Utterson.

Hiding and Haunting: Doubles Everywhere

Clearly, doubles abound in this story. There is, for one, the plethora of *doppelgängers* we are confronted with: The Victorian Jekyll/Hyde and the contemporary Jackman/Hyde, and of course Jackman is the genetic twin of Jekyll while Billy is Edward's look-alike. Claire is Alice's clone, and while the Jackman's twins are not identical, we learn that they can "switch" personalities and appearances between them. And finally, as we have just seen, there is the mother who turns into Ms Utterson.

There is also a constant doubling of meaning. While Stevenson's text uses silences and absences to hint at a hidden layer that haunts the text, the series revels in ambiguity. When Jackman meets Syme at the beginning of the series, he answers his questions in a way designed to appear innocuous while turning every sentence into a double entendre referring to his situation with Hyde. While Jackman probably thinks himself miserable, but clever, Syme of course catches the double meaning, and while Tom is deceived into believing he answers innocuously back, he does in fact say that he knows much more about the situation than Tom does.

In similar fashion, when Hyde first meets Tom's family, the conversation on Claire's part is an obscure welcome, while Hyde's comments, to the viewer, contain a hidden menace. Finally, she tells him to bring a knife for the cake and the scene ends with Hyde regarding a knife in the manner of a thousand Hollywood serial killers, stating: "What a perfect start to the evening", the exact same sentence he used in the scene he was introduced to us in where the "perfect evening" consisted of brutal violence. Cut to Jackman waking up, realizing Hyde discovered his family, entering the house, ascending the stairs and standing in the bedroom of his sons. Part of this is overlaid with the voice of Ms. Utterson from Klein & Utterson, saying: "He can't control Hyde. Not forever. Eventually Hyde will do something. Something that Jackman cannot forgive. Eventually he will know that he cannot contain him. And then WE begin." The way the scene is cut, the image of the disorderly house, Jackman standing in the door to the boys' room where two motionless bundles lie under the blankets on the bed add a plethora of horror-movie clichés to the overabundance of signifiers that tell us that Hyde has murdered Jackman's family.

In fact, everybody is fine. Kelly Hurley, who depicts Gothic writing at Stevenson's time, recounts the aspects of the Gothic after a long tradition so that the list contains among "sensationalist and suspenseful plotting" and the active search to "arouse a strong affective response" inevitably also "narrative innovation despite the frequent use of certain repetitive plot elements". (194) The series does, in fact, create suspense to arouse a strong response not in spite, but because of the ability to fall back on repetitive elements. The scene is overdetermined with a jumble of signals quoting a standard horror movie plot that vividly unfolds in the viewer's mind without ever actually happening. While Stevenson's text hints at some horrific secret, the series hints – with a surplus of signifiers – at a horror become cliché, of which Stevenson's text (the version that everybody knows and has seen in countless movies) has long since become a part: the signifier is devoid of meaning, so nothing really happens.

In Stevenson's time, the "Gothic negotiated a cultural moment within which traditional constructs of human identity were breaking down on all fronts." (Hurley 203) Linda Dryden details the Victorian fears at length, and while the individual narratives quoted in the monograph are usually consistent in their construction of a desired self versus an immoral other, the texts read together do not add up to a coherent, encompassing structure.

Such it is no wonder that "abhumanness *spreads* in the modern Gothic. It is not just socially problematic or marginalized individuals – feminists, "natives", homosexuals – who are liable to degeneration, devolution, and other bizarre transfigurations. All human subjects, it would seem, are potentially liminal, potentially abhuman." (Hurley 203) No wonder Hyde is such a mismatched creature, in body as in mind, and his Victorian contemporaries simply have no words to describe him. The postmodern subject, on the other hand, is all to conscious of the underlying structures, and exposing them in all their contradictory, jumbled awkwardness has become something of a reflex.

What distinguishes Gothic from Horror, Misha Kavka maintains, is that the horror movie "demands that we see – not that we always answer the demand. In fact, we are not necessarily meant to, for a dialectic between seeing and not seeing is played out in horror cinema between the film and its viewers." The visualization of the Gothic, on the other hand, incorporates this dialectic in its structure, "the feared object of Gothic cinema is both held out and withheld through its codes of visual representations. [...] It is thus not just that we *do* not see, but precisely that we *cannot* see", echoing the structure of the Gothic and the uncanny in general, but also grappling the "impossibility of representation actually grasping the thing 'beyond'". (227)

In the series, the point is rather that we *cannot be sure what we see, or what we know*. From the supposed physical differences bestowed on Hyde to the scene described above, the postmodern text replaces the silences of the original with an overabundance of signifiers in the spoken as well as in the visual language.

The characters are obsessed with minutely describing Hyde's appearance, the theories about his nature pile up after decades of discourse about the other, the visual codes point to a tradition that forever loses its once-innovative vocabulary to convention in the hunt for the next sensation, and language tries to double and treble what it can express.

Doppelgängers multiply, each pair as little a clear-cut dichotomy as the Victorians' attempts at dualities that divide the world into an unambiguous 'us' and 'them'. And like the Victorian's diverse attempts at constructing a system of dualities failed in making them translatable into each other, the *doppelgängers* of the series are to varied, to complicated in their internal dynamics as well as in their relationship to the others to be superimposable onto each other.

While this is, of course, thoroughly uncanny, the series does not simply replace the fraught silences with an endless play of signifiers devoid of meaning. For one, a shadow of the signified always remains; in the scene detailed above, the once evoked structure is not cancelled out; the murder did not happen, but it could have, and thus the scene does not only foreshadow the sinister machinations of Ms Utterson and her underlings, but also echo the actual murder Edward Hyde commits when he kills the woman Jekyll loves.

Also, the secret at the heart of the narrative is presented much in keeping with tradition. In the vein of Gothic cinema, it is at once presented to us quite early – the fictional Stevenson, in the flashback, writes it down in plain sight – and also withheld from us, as the camera fails to bring the writing into focus.

The novel, as we have seen, delivers its stab by withholding it to the last to administer it with all the more force. The secret of the potion can only be revealed at last, or the complexity of horror is reduced to ineffectuality. Faithfully, the series reveals the heart of its retelling – that there is, in fact, no potion – towards the end, and explains the meaning of this even later.

Anything else would turn the relationship between Jekyll and Hyde into that of mere opposites, and would draw a clearly defined boundary that would render the device of the *doppelgänger* into a mere platitude. The relationship between *doppelgängers* is, by definition, a complex one, and so is that of a text to any and all kinds of transtexts it enters into a relationship with.

The most prominent transtext of Stevenson's novel is one that is distressingly absent: the burned manuscript. As a double to the novel, its relationship to the published version is very much like that of Jekyll and Hyde, shadowing it on the meta-level of scholarly discussion. Rumored to fill in the gaps in the narrative, it promises to detail Jekyll's unnamed vices and deliver the key to Hyde's nature; but it continues to elude us, and so Hyde remains undetermined, continuing to move through the gaps. As Jekyll, the burned text has claims to originality and authenticity, but is forever superseded by its inexplicit double.

By turning the actual author Stevenson into a fictional character, his formerly fictional utterances are made into a factual account. At first glance, this creates a dual structure mirroring that of the original novel: In detailing his origin, the book contains Jackman's past and with it, the key to Hyde. But as a factual account, the novel turns from a fictional narration into a lie, and the supposedly faithful shadow-text is transported with it into the world of fiction as the truth written on a subsequently burned paper.

We do have, in fact, a ternary structure made up of Jackman's present, the misleading account of the past and the hidden truth, reflected by the ternary structure of burned manuscript/published novel/television series. As the burned manuscript supposedly fills in the gaps of the narrative, the truth in the burned note integrates a woman into the text where females had hitherto been absent. In Alice's case, this is a mere addition, like in many adaptations. As the object of Victorian Jekyll's love, she is not able to engage Hyde and thus merely acts as a personification of the impurity in the powder, that fickle device of the potion.

Claire, however, despite being a clone made for Jekyll, refuses to let her identity be a lie and actively chooses her love for Tom, while she has the power to impress Hyde. This enables a ternary structure in the relation of the characters, too, creating a trinity of Tom/Billy/Claire.

There has been much talk of 'third spaces' to offset the inevitably imbalanced dualities western culture constructs;[4] and indeed, it seems that the addition of a third element into the relationship of the *doppelgängers* actually makes the relationship between self and other work. We have to remember, however, that even as Billy sacrifices himself, that this is not a device to glaze over the cracks in the old structure, and certainly not one to finally, after a long history of failed attempts, to capture the other.

Conclusion: The Frightening Power of Love

The seemingly neat solution in the trinity of the three main characters is offset by another ternary relationship that does a lot to foreground the message that love is, indeed, a psychopath.

Jekyll couches his relationship with Hyde in terms of father and son, as does Billy Hyde in referring to Tom. The series, then, inserts the missing person into this relationship: the mother. This seems, from a critical perspective, like a thoroughly laudable move; however, the other is not so easily appeased when it is finally revealed that she is the double of Ms Utterson.

In the novel, Utterson is the nexus that holds together the complicated structure of the narrative; in him, all the different strands of information run together, which puts him at the very heart of the narrative's unreliability, while he remains curiously undefined. In this context, the novel's final ceding of Jekyll's will to Ut-

---

[4] The most prominent example would be Homi K. Bhabha's *The Location of Culture* (2004).

terson makes sudden chilling sense: "[I]n place of the name of Edward Hyde, the lawyer, with indescribable amazement, read the name of Gabriel John Utterson." (loc. 1331)

Like Utterson in the novel, Ms Utterson remains remote throughout the series; in a clear parallel, she pulls all the strings, the other at the very core of the plot. Also, it is the mother that reveals the final truth; taking Gabriel Utterson's role into account, this renders this and every other ready-made solution in the series doubtful. If Ms Utterson, as Hyde, is love, than she clearly is not the nurturing motherly kind. We kill for the sake of love, as the series states, but we also know that we kill those we love, and that love can easily turn into selfish obsession.

The love of a mother, the devotion of a good wife, the death for the love of king and country: love makes for powerful constructs; but dare we dismantle them, to expose the workings of oppressive or destructive structures, just like all the common topoi of deconstruction listed in the course of this paper we so readily (and maybe arrogantly) dismiss as follies of the past? Love is intertwined with many a moral and social structure, can be their fiercest enemy or freedom from the need to think in categories. The kind of love exhibited by Tom, Billy and Claire in the end does seem valuable and true, and we cannot simply expose one without loosing them all, turning Hyde's sacrifice truly empty and rendering the tale wholly amoral.

The series does allow for the possibility of taking an individual stance, of actively choosing our position according to ourselves, not against the abject we see in the other. Still, this is frightening, as it lacks the assurances of the great narratives, an ultimate point of reference, as even love may be a treacherous value.

No small wonder that Tom, in the end, returns to his mother to demand answers, to solve the last mysteries to be able to turn his story into a consistent whole. And of course, he – and we – are left, in the end[5], with the image of an other, a creature born of love at the heart of the tale, that, after 250 years of monsters, still succeeds in being frightening.

Bibliography

Primary Sources

Jekyll. Dir. Matt Lipsey and Douglas Mackinnon. Wr. Steven Moffat. Perf. James Nesbitt. BBC 2007, DVD [BBC, 2007.]

Stevenson, Robert Louis. The Strange Case of Dr Jekyll and Mr Hyde and Other Tales. Ed. Roger Luckhurst. New York: Oxford 2006. Kindle Edition.

---

[5] According to IMDb, Steven Moffat did have a second season finished, but so far the BBC has not agreed to continue the series. As it stands, this image is very strong and evocative precisely because it stands for the failure to wrap up the inconsistencies.

Sullivan, Thomas Russell. Jekyll and Hyde Dramatized. Ed. Martin A. Danahay and Alex Chisholm. Jefferson, NC: McFarland, 2011. Kindle Edition.

Secondary Sources

Berthin, Christine. Gothic Hauntings. Melancholy Crypts and Textual Ghosts. Basingstoke, New York: Palgrave Macmillan, 2010.

Chesterton, G. K. and Nicoll, Robertson W. (The Original) Robert Louis Stevenson. New York: Dodd, Mead & Company, 1928. Kindle Edition.

Dryden, Linda. The Modern Gothic and Literary Doubles. Stevenson, Wilde and Wells. Basingstoke, New York: Palgrave Macmillan 2003.

Hogle, Jerrold E. "Introduction: The Gothic in Western Culture." The Cambridge Companion to Gothic Fiction, Ed. Jerrold E. Hogle. Cambridge et al.: Cambridge University Press, 2002. 1–20.

Hurley, Kelly. "British Gothic Fiction, 1885–1930. The Cambridge Companion to Gothic Fiction, Ed. Jerrold E. Hogle. Cambridge et al.: Cambridge University Press 2002. 189–207.

IMDb (International Movie Database): Jekyll (2007-). 30. 3. 2013

Kavka, Misha. "The Gothic on Screen." The Cambridge Companion to Gothic Fiction, Ed. Jerrold E. Hogle. Cambridge et al.: Cambridge University Press, 2002. 209–228.

Miller, Renata Kobetts. Recent Reinterpretations of Stevenson's Dr. Jekyll and Mr. Hyde. Why and How This Novel Continues to Affect Us. Lewiston, Queenston, Lampeter: Edwin Mellen 2005.

TRANSFORMING NARRATIVE

Good Fences Make Good Neighbours? On the Dialectics of Genre Formation and Hybridization in Contemporary Fantasy Fiction

Dieter Petzold

Building, Mending, and Rejecting Walls in Literary Studies

There is no way of pinpointing what Robert Frost was having in mind when he wrote his famous poem *Mending Wall* (1914), but since (as George MacDonald once observed) "a genuine work of art must mean many things" (17) we may be excused for applying the speaker's neighbour's insistence on the usefulness of walls in the poem metaphorically to literature – or, more precisely, to the necessity of creating boundaries, and of transcending boundaries, when discussing literary genres like fantasy fiction.

 Of course we are dealing here with a phenomenon that is by no means unique to fantasy fiction, nor to fantastic literature in general, indeed not even to literature and other products of the human mind. After all, forming categories creates order out of chaos: it is the essence of human thought and human language.

 Yet when this basic human activity is applied to cultural products like literature, it is also a highly frustrating one. For while natural objects – stones, trees, flowers, animals – are fairly solid things, cultural products – customs, literature, the arts – are extremely volatile: they keep changing, and any attempt at *definitio* (which is the Latin word for drawing borders) is doomed to at least partial failure because it is certain to elicit disagreement among some observers. And it is likely to provoke protest from those engaged in production because they feel that borders inhibit the free play of creative imagination. "Something there is that doesn't love a wall" is the first line of Frost's poem, but what that "something" is remains a mystery. (Later in the poem, ll. 36–37, the speaker rejects the idea that it is elves that quietly tear down walls; that was before the word 'entropy' had become common use.)

One person who apparently doesn't love walls is Michael Moorcock, the famous and prolific author of countless fantasy and science fiction stories. In his "study of epic fantasy", *Wizardry and Wild Romance* (1987), he states:

"It has always been my belief that category definitions in the arts are destructive both of the thing they try to describe and of the aspiration of the artist. They produce an unnecessary self-consciousness. They are convenient only to substandard academic discussion and cynical commercial exploitation.

'Schools' and 'movements' exist, usually for very short periods, because conservative and authoritarian elements force individuals to club together against them. A school prolonged past its immediate necessity for existence becomes, like sf, itself conservative and rigid, producing rivals." (141)

While Moorcock's fears of "category definitions" as impediments to the freedom of creation is certainly understandable it is also true that in literature and the arts the grouping of texts – creating a consciousness of genres, "'schools' and 'movements'" – is in fact an important, if not *the,* motor of progress. *Creatio ex nihilo,* the creation out of nothing, is the prerogative of Gods: humans, in general, create by imitating, rejecting, changing, improving patterns already in existence.

The Uses of Pigeonholes

The emergence of 'fantasy literature' is a case in point. Today most critics regard it as a genre situated within the large field of fantastic fiction (also known as fantasmatic, speculative, non-mimetic, heterocosmic and extra-empirical fiction or simply – and confusingly – as 'fantasy'). According to the *Oxford English Dictionary*, the meaning "a genre of literary composition" was attributed to the word 'fantasy' for the first time in 1949;[1] but its acceptance among a large public is closely tied to the phenomenal success of Tolkien's *The Lord of the Rings* (1954–55) in the 1960s and 1970s. When it appeared, that book seemed to be something entirely new, a work *sui generis*, but of course we know that it was inspired by a great number of other texts that are somehow similar yet different: fairy tales, ancient Greek, Germanic, Celtic and Finnish myths and epics, the artificially medievalized tales of William Morris, etc. Nevertheless, Tolkien *had* created something new out of all these ingredients, and since it was also highly successful there was a need for a new label: among the critics, who needed to name what they were faced with, among his fans, who needed a word to express their desire for more of the same, and among authors, publishers and booksellers, who needed it to signal that they were ready to satisfy the new demand.

---

[1] In the title of the American *Magazine of Fantasy and Science Fiction* (cf. *OED*, s.v. "Fantasy").

This is not the place to discuss the endless attempts to define the (seemingly) new genre. One thing that critics soon began to point out is that although the label 'fantasy' (alias 'fantasy fiction' or 'fantasy literature') is fairly new, the object it describes is much older, dating back to the Age of Enlightenment or even to the very beginnings of literature. Another is that it is next to impossible to draw a clear dividing line between texts that are somehow like Tolkien's *Lord of the Rings* and texts that defy the principles of mimetic fiction in other ways and thus bear different labels, like "fairy tale", "Gothic fiction", or "science fiction". In the light of these circumstances, the idea that genres should not be regarded as clearly defined entities but rather as "fuzzy sets" that have a centre but no fixed borders and whose members may have no more than a vague 'family likeness' (propagated, e.g., by Brian Attebery in his seminal *Strategies of Fantasy*) seems to be the best way to deal with this recalcitrant matter. At its widest meaning, 'fantasy' denotes nothing more precise than a 'mode' of writing characterized by its wilful violation of the principles of mimesis, at its narrowest, it is applied to texts that are similar to Tolkien's *Lord of the Rings*, featuring a rambling action full of heroic adventures but with a 'happy ending', set in a slightly medieval-looking otherworld (cf. Attebery ch. 1).

Why, one might ask, can we not leave it at that? Why this impulse, or need, to differentiate, to find new labels, draw new boundaries? According to Moorcock, who represents one author's point of view, it is "conservative and authoritarian elements [who] force individuals to club together against them". Moorcock does not name those "elements", but it is safe to assume that as a successful author he will have been familiar with the culture industry of the 1980s when he wrote these sentences. He may have had certain professional critics and publishers in mind, but since he does not name them, it seems equally possible that he was just venting some vague general paranoia. In any case he felt it is the restrictions inherent in rigid genre definitions and thus in the expectations of the market that drives innovative authors to "club together" and declare what they are doing to be a new thing by giving it a new label. Seen from this angle, the formation, and indeed the existence, of genres have a lot to do with power relations (cf. Frow 2). To this one might add that there is also a simple economic incentive: If you have invented something new, you need a good label to make the public aware of the new product.

While authors, and publishers in particular, have a vested interest in the existence of labels that help them sell their products, the public, too, have a stake in this labelling business. For one thing, there is the very basic observation (stressed in most recent discussions of genre theory) that our socially acquired knowledge of genres determines the way we read any specific text. Secondly, and perhaps even more obviously, we find genres useful because they help us choose, and name, what we like and what we dislike, and to share our preferences with like-minded people. The latter is particularly important for lovers of genres outside the mainstream: belonging to an in-group of connoisseurs united by the tastes, predilections and cultural habitus they have in common provides security and a sense of cosiness; it is, indeed, a form of self-identification. In this process, a common language – a jargon that provides an arsenal of labels – is essential. Still in this context, yet another group that has a vested interest in the existence of such labels are the journalists who take an active part in the coining and establishing of new labels in their endeavour to find a common language to connect with their clientele, the fans.

Diversification as a Fine Art

And then, of course, there are the academics, in particular lexicographers and literary historians, whose very business it is to create order out of chaos by establishing and describing categories and thus subjecting seemingly random phenomena to more or less rigid systematization. Their work, again, involves recognition of, and a readiness to re-negotiate, boundaries, for each one will inevitably build on the concepts and terminologies of predecessors. Since works of reference carry an implicit claim of authority, the principles and theoretical foundations that underlie their entries (whether spelled out in introductions or afterwords or left to be deducted from the entries themselves) are worth examining.

Due to lack of space, a somewhat closer look at one single example will have to suffice. Apart from the now almost canonical *Encyclopedia of Fantasy* by John Clute and John Grant (1997) – still authoritative, if perhaps a little dated after 15 years – Brian Stableford's more recent, and more handy *The A to Z of Fantasy Literature* (2009)[2] is particularly interesting with respect to generic labels.[3] Apart from articles on individual authors, those on the various kinds of fantasy constitute the bulk of entries. All in all, Stableford (himself an author of fantasy and science fiction first and foremost, in addition to being an academic critic) lists no less than 82 modifications of the word 'fantasy', thus defining (and creating?) a great number of sub-genres, from "afterlife fantasy" to "wish-fulfilment fantasy".

To a certain degree the great number of these entries is the result of Stableford's broad definition of the term "fantasy literature", which comprises many texts that also bear other generic labels (like "Gothic fiction" or "science fiction"),

---

[2] First published in 2005 under the title *Historical Dictionary of Fantasy Literature*.
[3] Other rich sources for this kind of investigation would be, e.g., *A Short History of Fantasy* by Mendlesohn and James or *The Cambridge Companion to Fantasy Literature* (ed. James and Mendlesohn).

having no more than a vague 'family likeness' based on their common use of the fantastic mode.

Furthermore, Stableford's "Fantasy Literature" covers a huge historical expanse, since he refuses not only to regard fantasy fiction as a product of the 20th century but also argues against the frequently voiced notion ("the Clute/Attebery strategy" (xl), in Stableford's nice shortcut term, although Clute and Attebery were by no means the first to formulate this concept) that our sense of the fantastic (and hence of fantasy fiction) is the product of the empiricist turn of the early modern period:

"The improvisation of a historical divide between modern fantasy literature and earlier manifestations of the materials that it recycles and transfigures is a brutal artifice. […] it is true that the Enlightenment refined ideas about the definition and determination of 'reality,' but it is certainly not true that previous storytellers were unaware of any contrast or tension between the naturalistic and supernatural elements of their stories." (xlii)

Instead, Stableford stresses the historical continuity of fantasy by identifying the processes of "recycling" and "transfiguration" as the central means of innovation in the field of fantasy literature:

"Fantasy writers routinely recast old stories in order to extract presently relevant morals, import presently relevant metaphors, update or culturally revise the settings, demonstrate artistic virtuosity, or simply because they have licence to do it and it saves creative labor." (Stableford 409, s.v. "transfiguration")

There is, then, a constant diversification process within the field that makes it difficult to speak of fantasy literature as a single 'genre'. Another way to deal with this diversity, suggested by Farah Mendlesohn and Edward James in their *Short History of Fantasy* (2009), is to think of the many fantastic genres (and sub-genres) as forming a "literary braid" (117) – a useful metaphor since it neatly encapsulates the dialectics involved in the description of the genres of fantasy literature: the need to distinguish *and* to unify at the same time.

Another reason for the large size of Stableford's list is that the labels offered are based on many different criteria, so that any concrete text can belong to several of these groups at the same time. Some refer to geographic provenance (e.g., Australian fantasy, Canadian fantasy, French fantasy, German fantasy, etc.), some to the sources used for recycling or transfiguration (e.g., Arthurian fantasy, Biblical Fantasy, Odyssean fantasy, Shakespearean fantasy), some to the topography or time of the secondary world (e.g., Arcadian fantasy, Edenic fantasy, urban fantasy, prehistoric fantasy, contemporary fantasy), some to dominant agents (angelic fantasy, animal fantasy). A large (and rather fuzzy) group is based on criteria like 'ideology' or 'belief systems': Christian fantasy, Jewish fantasy, messianic fantasy, theosophical fantasy, etc., another on the dominant mood or effect they aim at: dark fantasy, erotic fantasy, Gothic fantasy, humorous fantasy. A small but important group is formed with regard to narrative form and patterns: Commodified fantasy, epic fantasy, picaresque fantasy, high fantasy, low fantasy, science fantasy. Within this group, especially the terms portal (quest) fantasy, immersive fantasy, intrusive fantasy, and liminal fantasy, introduced comparatively recently by Farah Mendlesohn, have become useful tools for a classification of fantasy text according to the way they introduce the reader to their worlds, and to the way these worlds are structured and presented.

Long as this list of different 'fantasies' may seem, it is not even complete, for there are quite a few terms (duly listed in Stableford's dictionary) that denote still more kinds of 'fantasy' without using the actual word "fantasy". Some of these have been around for a long time, like (literary) fairy tales, legends, ghost stories, sword and sorcery, science fiction, utopian and dystopian fiction; others are present-day buzzwords: magical realism, slipstream, steampunk, paranormal romance, the New Weird. In fact, no list of this kind can ever hope to be complete, for new terms will continue to be coined as the critics', and the public's, views change; and, of course, the field itself keeps changing and developing as authors stretch, distort and transcend generic boundaries.

Delightful Monsters: Hybrid and Chimerical Texts

Although this is difficult to measure, there are some indications that this continuous process of recycling and transfiguration has accelerated in recent times. Any attempt to demonstrate this extensively would definitely transcend the boundaries set by the editors of this volume for one single essay. A somewhat closer look at just one recent development within the field of fantasy literature (excluding, due to lack of space, other media like films, illustrations, comic strips, graphic novels, video games etc.) will have to suffice: hybridization, or the mixing of genres.

According to Stableford's *The A to Z of Fantasy Literature*, hybrid texts are "texts in which elements drawn from different sources are combined in such a way as to harmonize their content" (209). Stableford mentions specifically the welding of science fiction and fantasy fiction to 'science fantasy' where "rational explanations" are offered "for motifs that would be seen as magical or supernatural in other contexts" (209). He insists on distinguishing this phenomenon from "chimerical texts" which "juxtapose motifs from very different sources […] in order to derive narrative energy from a combination of apparently incompatible materials" (74). I suspect that in practice, this distinction will be difficult to maintain since harmony, like beauty, rests at least as much in the eye of the beholder as in the object itself. All the same, it is true that some mixtures are more conspicuous than others, depending on their relative compatibility.[4] In order to produce a sense of *frisson,* the generic terms involved need to be defined on the same systematic level (cf. Baßler 52) and to imply sufficiently distinct *structural* features. Thus, terms like "quest story", "adventure story" or "coming-of-age story" (themselves rarely used to denote proper genres) are naturally compatible with the basic formulae of fantasy fiction while genres like "school story", "detective fiction" or "romance" have distinctive structural features that do not mix quite as easily with the typical structure of fantasy fiction because they imply different relationships between the fictional and the empirical world. In addition we might distinguish between meta-fictional allusions to other genres and their systematic use on the plot level. Thus, for instance, the characters in Terry Pratchett's *Witches Abroad* (1991) or Jasper Fforde's *The Fourth Bear* (2006) move (partly) in a fairy tale world, mixing with fairy tale characters, but the plots of the stories are basically those of the quest fantasy and the detective story respectively. In actual practice though, it might be more useful to envision a gliding scale of the prominence of "contaminating" genres, from structural dominance to mere allusion: "hybridisation is a matter of degrees" (Seibel 137).

It is true that although hybridization, even in a broad sense, is more specific than the general recycling/transfiguration process in the production of fantasy texts, it has also been quite common in the history of the genre; in particular, the boundaries between fantasy fiction and science fiction and between fantasy fiction and 'horror' have never been watertight.[5] What is new in the recent development is a greater tendency to mix genres that are structurally quite distinct, and a heightened awareness, both among authors and the public, of (sub-) genres and, consequently, of hybridity when it occurs. The latter aspect is particularly significant: to a certain extent, hybridity, too, rests in the eye of the beholder, for the consciousness of a violation of borders presupposes an awareness of the existence of borders.

Due to lack of space, only a few examples can be mentioned here.[6] The one that comes most readily to mind, perhaps, is Joanne K. Rowling's *Harry Potter* heptalogy (1997–2007). Not only does the author subject the whole range of traditional fantastic motifs, from 'afterlife' to 'wizardry', to a process of recycling

---

[4] Cf. Seibel, who distinguishes between "weak contamination" ("the elements of the fictional world of the contaminating genre are taken from a generic repertoire that is subject to the same accessibility relations as the contaminated genre" (142) and "strong contamination" which is the case when "the elements of the fictional world of the contaminating genre are taken from a generic repertoire that is subject to different accessibility relations from the contaminated genre" (142).

[5] Witness terms like "science fantasy" and "weird fiction" or "dark fantasy". For an account of the former cf., e.g., Attebery, ch. 7; for the latter, Kincaid 44–46 and Kaveney.

[6] For many more examples of "genre coalescence," cf. Wolfe.

and transfiguration; on a structural level, she combines the typical fantasy plot (a hero's struggle with forces of evil that threaten the whole world) with features of the school story, the love story, the crime novel, and horror fiction. Similarly, Jasper Fforde's *Thursday Next* and *Nursery Crime* series (2001–) make use of the basic plot structure of the detective story, combined with elements reminiscent of the 'alternate history' genre (itself widely regarded as a sub-genre of science fiction), of Gothic fiction, of romance and of fairy tales (cf. Mohr 307–322). The same ingredients, in various combinations, can be found in Terry Pratchett's *Discworld* novels (1983–), some of which are, in addition, based on the plotlines of specific texts like Shakespeare's *Midsummer Night's Dream* or *Macbeth*. Yet another example are Eoin Colfer's *Artemis Fowl* novels (2001–) that combine basic plot elements of the crime novel with elements of fantasy and science fiction, and Jonathan Stroud's *Bartimaeus* books (2003–10), once again 'urban fantasies', which employ conventions of the 'alternate history' and the spy thriller in combination with the transfiguration of the traditional motif of 'spirits serving humans' familiar in Western tradition since *Dr Faustus* and the publication of the *Arabian Nights*.

Another combination of genres that seems to be quite popular currently is the mixture of fantasy and historical fiction. The result may be "historical fantasy", in which 'real' historical events are enhanced by fantastic elements (e.g., Susanna Clarke's *Jonathan Strange and Mr Norrell,* 2004), but the opposite strategy is equally possible: texts whose secondary worlds are basically fantastic (containing dragons or magic etc.) while their main interest is not on fantastic elements but on political aspects such as heredity, intrigue, and war: e.g., George A.A. Martin's *A Song of Ice and Fire* series (1996–).[7] As with most urban fantasies that apply conventions of the 'alternate history' genre, the hybridity of these texts creates stronger connections with extra-literary reality than is normally found in 'straight' fantasy fiction.

Yet another 'genre mix' that is popular at the moment is 'paranormal romance' or 'romantasy', in particular the combination of the 'Gothic' vampire story with 'highschool romance' (love stories with a specifically middle-class American background, cf. Mohr 285–98), as in Stephenie Meyer's *Twilight* (2005–08) series, which contains also elements of the fairy tale of redemption and of apocalyptic fiction (Kegler). Because of the erotic element which has been inherent in vampire stories from the very beginning of the genre, this seems to be a particularly smooth blending, but we can also see here how hybridization entails modifications of the original elements: In this case, vampirism is 'sanitized' in order to

---

[7] For Clarke's novel and more examples, cf. Schanoes; for a discussion of the *Game of Thrones* series, cf. Schultchen.

allow a vampire to become the dream hero of teenage readers. Even such highly specific female preadolescent wishful dream products as 'horse and pony stories' have been combined with fantasy fiction – simply by replacing the horses with dragons![8]

Although many more examples could be mentioned, this short list of very successful recent fantasy novels will suffice to make the point that hybridity is indeed a prominent feature of present-day fantasy fiction. What remains to be discussed is an assessment: What are the reasons for this development, and what is its significance?

Jumping Walls: the Games of Hybridization, Metalepsis and Medialization

As authors following Rowling's example must have discovered quickly, there is a commercial aspect to this vogue of hybridization. Nor is this a completely new thing. "Wer vieles bringt, wird manchem etwas bringen" ("He who offers many things will offer something to many"), says the commercially-minded theatre manager in Goethe's *Faust* (13); and long before that Shakespeare makes fun of this salesman's trick by having Polonius advertise the players at the Court of Denmark as being "the best actors in the world, either for tragedy, comedy, history, pastoral, pastoral-comical, historical-pastoral, tragical-historical, tragical-comical-historical-pastoral, scene individable or poem unlimited" (*Hamlet* II, 2, 379–382). Given a fundamental attraction based on characters, suspense and readability, stories appeal to many readers if they work on several levels of experience and desire: providing not just the "sense of wonder" Manlove (1) and Attebery (15–17) see at the centre of the 'fantasy experience', but also the satisfaction of a mystery resolved and justice victorious offered by detective stories, the love interest of romance, the specific experience of social adaptation schoolchildren have to deal with, the thrill of horror contemplated in security, etc.

It would be rash, however, to attribute the new vogue of hybridization solely to authors' and publishers' commercial strategies. In the best of these texts, I should like to suggest, the main attraction lies not in the recipe 'diverse things for diverse readers' but in their fundamental playfulness. This is not to say that hybrid fantasy texts are invariably 'funny'; but many (if not all) display a more or less conspicuous ironic stance that foregrounds the artificiality of the literary text

---

[8] Cf. Mohr 259–268, who discusses the "Drachenwelt" novels by 'Salamanda Drake' as prime examples. – According to Wikipedia, 'Salamanda Drake' is a pseudonym for the authors known as "The Two Steves", Steven Lowe (aka Steve Barlow) and Steve Skidmore; the original titles of the "Drachenwelt" books are *Dragonsdale* (2007) and *Riding the Storm* (2008). – Cf. "Dragonsdale".

without foregoing the charm of the story – its suspense, its emotions, its 'sense of wonder'. Frequently this ironic detachment finds expression in parody and satire, most prominently perhaps in Terry Pratchett's novels, but also clearly in evidence in Jasper Fforde, Eoin Colfer and Jonathan Stroud.

In passing I should like to point out books that display this ironic stance frequently also feature other kinds of transgression, in particular metareference and metalepsis, which make the reader aware of the artificiality of fiction in even more striking ways. Probably the best-known example of metareference using metalepsis are, again, Jasper Fforde's *Thursday Next* novels which are set in a world where the fictitious worlds of books have the same ontological status as the world the characters of the story move in: in other words, they are both 'real', so that in *The Eyre Affair* (2001), for instance, it is possible for the protagonist, Detective Sergeant Thursday Next, to enter the world of Charlotte Brontë's *Jane Eyre* (1847), and for Brontë's character Rochester to be abducted from his world into that of Thursday Next.[9]

Another way of describing this peculiar kind of serious playfulness found in many recent fantasy texts is to observe that contemporary fantasy has become part of the broad movement of postmodernism – which, like fantasy, has always been informed by its scepticism about the ability of literature (or, for that matter, human thought) to describe 'reality'. There are two ways (by no means mutually exclusive) to assess this observation: it seems (a) to argue that postmodernism has lost its elitist air (if it ever possessed it) and has definitely reached popular culture; and (b) to corroborate the impression that "fantasy [is] moving from the margins into the cultural mainstream" (Mendlesohn and James, 216–217).

The fact that both views appear plausible can be seen as evidence that the conventional distinction between 'high' and 'low' culture (with genres like fantasy fiction belonging clearly to the latter) is increasingly being eroded in our times. If this (admittedly rather commonplace) observation is correct, one final question remains: Is this post-modern dissolution of boundaries – including, in particular, this trend towards generic hybridization – to be welcomed or to be deplored? The answer, as is to be expected, depends on one's basic attitudes, one's own value system. Purists may disapprove of texts in which (to borrow Dr Johnson's famous phrase describing metaphysical poetry) "the most heterogeneous ideas are yoked by violence together" while adepts will find them exciting and exhilarating rather than irritating and confusing.

The ironic stance that comes with the mixing of disparate genres (as well as with metareference) demands sophisticated readers who are not only able to recognize the various generic patterns employed but also flexible enough to appreci-

---

[9] For more examples, cf. Klimek; for a general assessment, cf. Wolf.

ate the *frisson* produced by their apparent incompatibility. The huge popularity of authors like Terry Pratchett, Jasper Fforde or Eoin Colfer seems to indicate that there is indeed a large readership today with these faculties and tastes. As to the reasons for this development, we can only speculate. Perhaps this readerly competence and flexibility is, at least in part, the result of what has been described as the 'medialization' of contemporary society. It seems plausible that the digital generation's easy moving between media – from narrative fiction to films to graphic novels to computer games – enhances the awareness, and the acceptance, of the artificiality of all products of the 'culture industry', creating a 'participatory culture' or, in Henry Jenkins' terms, a "convergence culture". The existence of a whole huge cosmos of 'fan fiction' in the internet seems to support this supposition, for it indicates that a large section of consumers is independent and sophisticated enough to treat the products they 'consume' as public property free to play with and to transform (recycle/transfigure) into new fiction – fiction that, incidentally, frequently employs generic hybridization and at the same time is subjected to rigorous generic classification by webmasters and the fan fiction community.[10]

One might argue that this new sophistication in popular culture is to be welcomed as a sign that popular culture is 'coming of age' by creating – and responding to – a less stratified, more self-reliant public. One might also argue that this excessive self-awareness is to be deplored as a sign of decadence, and that autonomy and sophistication come with a price: the loss of naiveté, of unconditional immersion, of being carried away by the powerful feelings produced by strong stories.[11] Seen from that angle, it appears possible that there will eventually be a swing of the pendulum towards more 'earthy', clear-cut fantasy – to a "mending of walls". On the other hand, we all know that readers can temporally 'switch off' their awareness of disillusioning elements in order to enjoy a 'ripping good story'. Indeed, I propose that the success of some of the books I have mentioned will be durable because they combine the liberating experience of boundary-crossing with the security of a 'good read' that has little to do with 'escapism' and much with the complex way they deal with basic human experiences. After all, in Wolfe's words, "a healthy genre, a healthy literature, is one at risk, one whose boundaries grow uncertain and whose foundations get wobbly" (51).

---

[10] Witness the jargon the fan fiction community has developed in order to compartmentalize its products, featuring words like "het" and "slash" (subdivided into m/m and f/f), h/c (hurt/comfort), angst, AU (alternate universe), dark, etc. Cf. Kroner 109–111 and Silver 207–210.

[11] Cf. Wolf, who considers both options (38-40). Similarly, Wolfe talks about the danger of "an accelerating inward spiral, resulting in a kind of genre implosion or collapse" (52) but is nevertheless optimistic because "the fantastic genres [...] seem evolutionary by their very nature" (53).

Bibliography

Attebery, Brian. Strategies of Fantasy. Bloomington: Indiana University Press, 1992.
Baßler, Moritz. "Gattungsmischung, Gattungsübergänge, Unbestimmbarkeit." Handbuch Gattungstheorie. Ed. Rüdiger Zymner. Stuttgart: Metzler, 2010. 52–54.
Casey, Jim. "Modernism and Postmodernism".The Cambridge Companion to Fantasy Literature. Ed. Edward James and Farah Mendlesohn. Cambridge: Cambridge University Press, 2012. 113–124.
"Dragonsdale". Wikipedia. 13 Feb. 2013.
Frost, Robert. "Mending Wall". The Norton Anthology of Poetry. Third ed., shorter. New York: Norton, 1970. 539.
Frow, John. Genre. London: Routledge, 2006.
Goethe, Johann Wolfgang. Faust: Eine Tragödie. Werke in zehn Bänden. Ed. Ernst Beutler. Vol. 4. Stuttgart: Deutscher Bücherbund, n.d. 8–394.
James, Edward, and Farah Mendlesohn, eds. The Cambridge Companion to Fantasy Literature. Cambridge: Cambridge University Press, 2012.
Jenkins, Henry. Convergence Culture: Where Old and New Media Collide. New York: New York University Press, 2006.
Kaveney, Roz. Dark Fantasy and Paranormal Romance. The Cambridge Companion to Fantasy Literature. Ed. Edward James and Farah Mendlesohn. Cambridge: Cambridge University Press, 2012. 214–223.
Kegler, Adelheid. "Wir werden verwandelt, und die Toten ersteh'n unverweslich": Das Märchen vom steinernen Edward und der Stolper-Bella." Inklings – Jahrbuch für Literatur und Ästhetik 27 (2009): 111–130.
Kincaid, Paul. American fantasy 1820–1950. Cambridge Companion to Fantasy Literature. Ed. Edward James and Farah Mendlesohn. Cambridge: Cambridge University Press, 2012. 36–49.
Klimek, Sonja. Paradoxes Erzählen: Die Metalepse in der phantastischen Literatur. Paderborn: mentis Verlag, 2010.
Kroner, Susanne. "Still Not King" – The Very Secret Diaries: Tolkien fan fiction between book-verse and movie-verse." Inklings – Jahrbuch für Literatur und Ästhetik 28 (2010): 107–117.
MacDonald, George. "The Fantastic Imagination". Fantasists on Fantasy. Ed. Robert H. Boyer and Kenneth J. Zahorski. New York: Avon, 1984. 11–21.
Manlove, C.N. Modern Fantasy: Five Studies. Cambridge: Cambridge University Press, 1975.
Mendlesohn, Farah, and Edward James. A Short History of Fantasy. London: Middlesex University Press, 2009.
Mohr, Judith. Zwischen Mittelerde und Tintenwelt: Zur Struktur Fantastischer Welten in der Fantasy. Frankfurt/M: Lang, 2012.
Moorcock, Michael. Wizardry and Wild Romance: A study of epic fantasy. London: Gollancz, 1987.
Schanoes, Veronica. "Historical Fantasy". The Cambridge Companion to Fantasy Literature. Ed. Edward James and Farah Mendlesohn. Cambridge: Cambridge University Press, 2012. 236-47.

Schultchen, Ricarda. "A Game of Thrones, Indeed: A Lot of Politics and Just a Bit of Magic in George R. R. Martin's A Song of Ice and Fire". Inklings – Jahrbuch für Literatur und Ästhetik 30 (2012): 122–34.

Seibel, Klaudia. "Mixing Genres: Levels of Contamination and the Formation of Generic Hybrids". Gattungstheorie und Gattungsgeschichte. Ed. Marion Gymnich, Birgit Neumann und Ansgar Nünning. Trier: wvt, 2007. 137–150.

Shakespeare, William. The Tragedy of Hamlet, Prince of Denmark. The Norton Shakespeare. Ed. Stephen Greenblatt. New York: Norton, 1997. 1668–1756.

Silver, Brenda R. "Popular Fiction in the Digital Age". The Cambridge Companion to Popular Fiction. Ed. David Glover and Scott McCracken. Cambridge: Cambridge University Press, 2012. 196–213.

Stableford, Brian. The A to Z of Fantasy Literature. Lanham: Scarecrow Press, 2009.

Wolf, Werner. "Is There a Metareferential Turn, and If So, How Can It Be Explained?" The Metareferential Turn in Contemporary Arts and Media: Forms, Functions, Attempts at Explanation. Ed. Werner Wolf. Amsterdam: Rodopi, 2011. 1–47.

Wolfe, Gary K. "Evaporating Genres". Evaporating Genres: Essays on Fantastic Literature. Middletown, CT: Wesleyan University Press, 2011. 18–53.

Parody Upon Parody Upon Parody: Narrative Myth and Mythic Narration in the American Metafiction of the 1960s

Michael Heitkemper-Yates

> Revolutionary periods are times in which the linguistic code of a generation or dominant social group of a culture comes under attack and gets revised.
> *Hayden White, "The Problem of Change in Literary History"*

1. Crisis, Change, and the Context of American Metafiction

Not only were the 1960s a decade of extreme social change, political upheaval, and cultural/sub-cultural/counter-cultural revolution in America, this period witnessed a complete re-evaluation of the human experience and the ways and means of communicating that experience. Through the use of mind-altering drugs and spiritualities, through the manipulation of various types of media and technology, through psychological explorations of self, identity, and persona, and especially through a comprehensive overhaul of literature, language and narrative systems, young American writers of the sixties co-opted, subverted and attempted to re-draft the very concept of reality.

As Patricia Waugh writes in *Metafiction: The Theory and Practice of Self-Conscious Fiction*, the sudden emergence in the sixties of a highly influential youth counter-culture, "with an attendant growth in political and psychological awareness about issues such as race, war, gender and technology," led to a disavowal of orthodox literary practices and precepts (especially those incapable of articulating this new awareness) and initiating a turn towards absurdism, black humor, and innovative literary means of parodic subversion (115). The consequence of this literate, self-critical, and highly psycho-politicized awareness, Waugh states, "has been a strong tendency in US writers to respond to the anonymous, frenetic and mechanized society they see around them with fiction that is similarly depersonalized, hyperactive and over- or under-systematized" (115-16). And the literary form that emerged from this frenetic matrix is what is commonly referred to as "metafiction."

According to Waugh, the metafictional impulse that began in the sixties "represents a response to a crisis," a crisis not simply in culture, but in the act of narrative communication itself (65). The metafictional response to this crisis that developed in the sixties represents an attempt to, in Waugh's words, "'defamiliarize' fictional conventions that have become both automated and inauthentic, and to release new and more authentic forms" (65). The young American vanguard that ushered in this age of metafiction applied parodic means to attack these "automated and inauthentic" literary structures because, as Waugh explains, "Parody as a literary strategy, deliberately sets itself up to break norms that have become conventionalized" (65). In the sixties, metafictional practice became an invaluable mechanism of change by virtue of its capacity to expose and make *explicit* these literary norms – through parody and other ironic formal inversions – and, thereby, critically interrogating the "*implicit* cultural and literary codes" that were revealed to be imbedded in these literary conventions (66, Waugh's emphasis). Through this fundamentally *meta*-fictional process of critical deconstruction and ironic reconstruction, Waugh writes, "parody thus discovers which forms can express which contents, and its *creative* function releases them for the expression of contemporary concerns" (69). For American writers in the sixties, metafictional parody suddenly became at once a powerfully subversive literary tool and an innovative means of describing authentic experience.

Paradoxically, this new and supposedly more authentic means of articulation is also, by virtue of its *meta*-fictional nature, more fictional, more artificial, and even makes this artificiality the very selling point in its claims of enhanced authenticity. However, the ironic feedback of this paradox is that fictionalized experience *is* no less vital and authentic for its inherent artificiality, in fact, fictionalized experience *is* reality to the extent that reality is capable of being or becoming manifest through articulation (artificial or otherwise) – recalling Paul Ricoeur's omnipresent reminder in *Time and Narrative* that, "human action can be narrated … because it is always already symbolically mediated" (57). And if reality is, indeed, an inherently manufactured, narrative construct, the closer one gets to that event, to that precise act of articulation or narration, the closer one gets to the vital moment of experience itself. As Jacob Horner states in John Barth's *The End of the Road* (1958):

"To turn experience into speech – that is, to classify, to categorize, to conceptualize, to summarize, to sanctify it – is always a betrayal of experience, a falsification of it; but only so betrayed can it be dealt with at all, and only in so dealing with it did I ever feel a man, alive and kicking." (366-67)

The upshot of this realization of a fundamentally narrative/narrated reality, as Mas'ud Zavarzadeh points out in *The Mythopoeic Reality*, is an awkward, postmodern awareness of the impossibility of any "central, all-encompassing view" or "comprehensive scheme of reality" (9). As a result, such totalizing, grand Modernist narratives as monadic subjectivity, autonomy, and institutional authority suddenly lose their ethical and political sustainability and are replaced by the proliferating idiolects, rhizomatic multiplicities, and globalized paranoias of postmodern discourse. "Consequently," Zavarzadeh writes, "the forms of recent narrative literature have changed so radically that the present seems to be more a mutation than a continuation of the past" (9). But, given that literary and cultural change is constant, has this radical postmodern "mutation" of consciousness and literary practice actually distanced the present from the past, experience from articulation, or has it brought them closer together?

According to Hayden White, this type of revolutionary mutation is a necessary element of literary innovation and signals a "historically significant" reassessment of the linguistic nature of culture and human experience. As White claims in *The Problem of Change in Literary History*:

"Literary innovation must be presumed to be going on all the time, in the same way that speech innovation must be conceived to be continuous. But *historically significant literary innovation* is possible only at those times in which the potential audiences for a given form of literary work have been so constituted as to render unintelligible or banal both the messages and the modes of contact that prevailed in some preceding era." (108)

This revolution of the literary field through deconstruction, White argues, "represents a transformation in the relationship between 'literature' and 'language in general,'" such that the "whole linguistic code" becomes an object of revisionary attack and, once transformed, gives rise to an entirely new sense of reality (110-11). As this process takes place, antiquated systems of communication are jettisoned and new linguistic connections are established. And central to this transformation is the expansion of the act of narration, which places an increased emphasis on the participative experience of the reader's involvement with the text and institutes an entirely new relationship between author and audience.

This literary revolution, White contends in *Metahistory*, occurs at the level of mode, specifically the mode of irony (10–11). Essentially following the cyclical system of modal progression proposed in Northrop Frye's *Anatomy of Criticism*, White alleges that the rhetorically and tropologically subversive nature of modal irony, concordant with its "awareness of its *own* inadequacy as an image of reality" (10), anticipates an imminent return to the mode of myth. However, does a return to the mode of myth actually explain the postmodern metafictional project of deconstructing and parodically re-articulating the narrative structure of reality?

As the following section of this paper will attempt to illustrate, critical analysis of this theory of modal progression, examination of the Aristotelian basis of this theory, and the application of modal theory to metafictional practice indicates an urgent need to revise this concept of modal progression.

Rather than following the prescribed cyclical pattern that Hayden White, Northrop Frye, and other theorists have proposed,[1] the course of modal progression appears to be fixed to a threshold of experience: an experientially normative axis which describes the narrative protagonist's power of action relative to an assumed neutral audience. Analysis of this revised course of modal progression reveals that as the self-contained, textual object of modern fiction changes to the self-reflexive, intertextual vehicle of postmodern metafiction, a definitive shift occurs in the presence and agency of the narrative voice such that the narration itself begins to inhabit and expand the role of protagonist. Not only does this shift correspond to the postmodern movement away from more directly representational means of literary practice (especially in the metafictional elevation of signifier over signified), it also suggests the appearance of a new dominant ironic mode.[2]

As will be argued, the increase in the narrator's power of action typical of postmodern metafictional literature does not necessarily indicate an abrupt return to the mythic mode (though it does suggest a trend in that direction). Instead, what emerges is a decidedly advanced species of "high irony" that, while maintaining its distinctly ironic quality, displays an enhanced tendency to deconstruct and reconstruct myth, folklore, and other archetypal elements of cultural narrative (including popular media iconography and other culturally resonant miscellanea such as jokes or nursery rhymes) into a discursive, highly self-reflexive type of parody. This high ironic parody is especially noticeable from the mid-sixties onward and is frequently encountered in the metafictional works of Kathy Acker, Laurie Anderson, John Barth, Donald Barthelme, Richard Brautigan, Robert Coover, Don DeLillo, Steve Katz, Clarence Major, Joyce Carol Oates, Thomas Pynchon, Ishmael Reed, and Kurt Vonnegut (to name but a few).

As the parodic, metafictional structure of the high ironic mode may or may not lead to a return to the mode of myth – attendant with the significant political,

---

[1] While the theory of a cyclical modal structure is most famously expounded in Northrop Frye's *Anatomy of Criticism* (1957) and *Fables of Identity* (1963),this theory of a modal cycle also plays a prominent role in the narratological studies of Hayden White's *Metahistory* (1973), Robert Scholes's *Structuralism in Literature* (1974),and Robert Foulke and Paul Smith's *An Anatomy of Literature* (1972).

[2] Linda Hutcheon writes: "If language, as these [metafictional] texts suggest, constitutes reality (rather than merely reflecting it), readers become the actualizing link between history and fiction. But this does not occur on the model of traditional historical fiction, where history is meant to authenticate fiction on a product, or representation, level, but in a new (or at least newly articulated) mode," see Hutcheon, *Narcissistic Narrative*, xiv.

ethical, and social ramifications of such a return – such an hypothesis remains merely a presumption until a substantial connection is proved to exist. It is this modal connection that this paper proposes to scrutinize through a brief analysis of the high ironic mode and its relation to myth in metafictional practice.

2. Modal Theory and its Basis in Aristotelian Poetics

In the first essay of his *Anatomy of Criticism* Northrop Frye enumerates what he terms the five modal elevations of the fictional hero's "power of action" (33). Beginning, ostensibly, with the mode of myth, the fictional hero descends from an initially powerful state of divine eminence and supremacy into a cyclical pattern of ever-diminishing agency. According to Frye, this cycle essentially follows a progression of "displacements" whereby the narrative patterns of each mode are subsequently re-cast in ever more realistic terms (51).[3] With each modal descent the hero's power of action gradually dwindles, culminating in the mode of irony where the hero is rendered all but powerless.

These five modes and their respective protagonists (taken in fragments from Frye's analysis) may be paraphrased along the following lines:
– Mythic hero: "superior in *kind* both to other men and to the environment of other men, the hero is a divine being."
– Romantic hero: "superior in *degree* to other men and to his environment, the hero is the typical hero of romance."
– High mimetic hero: "superior in *degree* to other men but not to his natural environment, the hero is a leader."
– Low mimetic hero: "superior neither to other men nor to his environment, the hero is one of us."
– Ironic hero: "inferior in power or intelligence to ourselves, so that we have the sense of looking down on a scene of bondage, frustration, or absurdity." (33-34, Frye's emphasis)

Frye goes on to employ this table as the basis for his formulation of a revolving model of modal shift (35). He claims that the re-emerging "dim outlines of sacrificial rituals and dying gods" indicates the "reappearance of myth in the ironic," and concludes that, "our five modes evidently go around in a circle" (42). From such an analysis one might assume that the increasing incidence of mythical figures, fragments, and traces within the ironic mode presupposes a modal return to myth.

---

[3] Robert D. Denham writes: "'Displacement' is the term Frye uses to describe the tendency of fictions progressively to move, throughout the sequence of modes, from myth to verisimilitude," see Denham 17.

One immediate problem with this revolving, circular conception of modal shift is the fact that, if indeed the literary center of gravity has followed this rotating tendency to strip the fictional hero of his power of action and has progressed directly from mythopoesis to verisimilitude, how then does the ironic hero spuriously affect to scramble back onto the vacant mythic throne and re-proclaim his ascendancy? And further, does the ironic appraisal of the mythic mode – attendant with its characteristic inter-twisting of satirical critique, philological pastiche, and other parodic deconstructions of archetypal structures – necessarily imply its direct proximity to the mythic mode? Consideration of these problems reveals a number of significant weaknesses in this proposed cycle of modal progression.

Firstly, in considering the progressive fall in the hero's power of action from the mode of myth to that of irony, would not a direct modal shift from the ironic back into the mythic mode suggest an interminable erosion of the hero's power of action? And, ignoring the possibility for some completely random leap in power of action, what kind of mythology could support such an impotent, anti-heroic protagonist? Furthermore, where does the problematic duplicity of postmodern metafiction figure into Frye's structural mechanism? For example, what are we to make of such parodic, metafictional "possessions" of literary myth and archetype as John Barth's *Chimera*, Donald Barthelme's *Snow White*, Robert Coover's *Briar Rose*, Steve Katz's *Creamy & Delicious*, and Ishmael Reed's *Mumbo Jumbo*? And finally, assuming that the progressive shift in the dominant mode has not yet completed its full return to myth, then, where are we now, and why is everything still so ironic?

The answer to these riddles is found – in part – in the very basis of the theory of modal shift that Frye derives from Aristotle's *Poetics*. Summarizing the second paragraph of the *Poetics* (1448a1-5),[4] Frye writes that, "In some fictions, [Aristotle] says, the characters are better than we are [*spoudaios*], in others worse [*phaulos*], in still others on the same level [*toioútos*]" (33). While scholars of the *Poetics* tend to vary in the definition of these terms, a general translation of *spoudaios* (σπουδαῖος) is likely to include: serious; of high character; heroic; figuratively weighty – and a definition of *phaulos* (φαῦλος) might include: frivolous; of low character; ordinary; figuratively light.[5] Although the precise English definition of these terms appears elusive, what this paragraph does clearly indicate is that in Aristotle's dialectical assessment of the protagonist's power of action a definite threshold of experience is implied as an axis.

This threshold, which marks the line between Aristotle's opposed classes of *spoudaios* and *phaulos*, not only designates the point at which these terms di-

---

[4] See *Aristotle's Ars Poetica*, ed. R. Kassel (Oxford: Clarendon, 1966): 1448a 1-5.
[5] See Butcher 11, Else 68; 77-78, Frye *Anatomy* 33, and House 82.

verge/converge, but might also perform the role indicated by Aristotle's mysterious intimation of an ordinary average or "third class" (Else 79). Although highly contested, this third class is inferred through Aristotle's use of the term *toioútos* (τοιοῦτος) in the phrase: "ἢχαίτοιοῦτος" (1448a5), which has been rendered as: "or also men like (it?)" (Else 68); "or exactly as they are" (Twining 7); "or exactly such as we ourselves are" (Warrington 5). Seeing this to indicate an independent category, this passage has been interpreted by Johannes Sykutris as a suggestion of a tripartite synthetic rather than a bipartite analytic (Else 79, n. 54) and by Augusto Rostagni as a discrete "Mean" or intermediate character type in Aristotle's system (Rostagni 9). However, regardless of whether this phrase indicates an intermediary type, a synthesis, or simply represents an awkward addendum to the original (Else 79-82), Aristotle's dichotomy makes a threshold not only logically necessary as a means of delineation between *spoudaios* and *phaulos*, but also necessary as a means of relating the specific conditions of this delineation to an audience that might provide the normative function of projecting itself as an intermediary device, and thereby, in a very real sense, becoming the threshold itself.

Such a threshold of experience would suggest that the shift in the level of the fictional hero's power of action is relative to this projected, normative audience (i.e., a reader presumed to be more or less neutral in power of action). As a normative axis or "degree zero" to the protagonist's power of action, this threshold also marks the border between two separate realms of literature, referred to here as the realm of identification and the realm of abstraction. As far as the fictional hero's power of action is concerned, the realm of identification contains and is defined by those narrative modes wherein the hero or narrator's power of action and level of experience is either inferior to or equivalent with that of an assumed neutral audience, such as in the low mimetic and ironic modes. Likewise, the realm of abstraction contains and is defined by those narrative modes wherein the hero or narrator exhibits a power of action discernibly superior to that of an assumed neutral audience, as in the high mimetic, romantic and mythic modes.

However, in order for the power of action dialectic that this threshold delineates to have any stable critical application at all, a revised model of modal shift must permit the literary mode to shift toward the mythic not as the next stage in a rotating cycle, but only when describing a helical pattern of perpetual, repetitive difference. In this revised model, the dominant fictional mode gradually passes downward into the realm of identification – charting the decrease in the hero's power of action as observed in the shift from the high mimetic toward the ironic – before entering a pre-mythic stage of modal ascent – marking the discernable increase in the narrator's power of action as the mode shifts from the ironic to a higher modal position. As the dominant mode follows this spiral movement through the realms of this dialectic, narrative patterns, archetypes, and other aesthetic forms of the past are projected diachronically forward through the matrix of the constantly evolving dominant mode, providing the linguistic fundament upon which each successive literary or linguistic act is superimposed, like beams of light being cast from the lower levels of a spiraling glass staircase, reflecting, refracting, and sending up shadows from the depths.

This spiral structure explains the profound presence of the mythic in the high ironic mode, for from a certain perspective (i.e., looking back through the modal matrix), these two modes appear to occupy a similar modal and semiotic position, however, the temporal distance between these modes explains their obvious differences in epistemology and linguistic structure. Though this model indicates that an actual return to the mode of myth might be deferred indefinitely, such a model would suitably account for both the temporal component of epochal gravitation (i.e., the perpetual progression of the dominant mode through the two realms of the dialectic) and the modal variance in power of action without resulting in the inexplicable "leap" that would obtain in the resolution of Frye's modal cycle.

As indicated above, such a dialectical spiraling precludes an abrupt return to the mythic mode (though it would seem to suggest a certain semiotic trend in that direction, as will be explored shortly). Instead what is seen to develop as the dominant mode ascends into the realm of abstraction is an advanced mode of irony, or "high irony," wherein the protagonist continues to be shackled by the bondage of narrative irony while the narrative voice begins to exhibit a power of action that tends to be equivalent to or greater than that of the reader. Within this emergent mode of irony, the narrative environment surrounding the protagonist is also typically subject to compositional modulations that alter both the protagonist's and the narrator's power of action, identity, and narrative environment. As a result, the line separating the protagonist and the narrative environment often appears arbitrary, absent, or reversed, such that the narrative world seems to morph and twist capriciously, without apparent purpose to the progress of the narrative, or simply at the whim of the narrator.

Analysis of the process behind this parodic metafictional practice reveals that the extreme heightening of the degree of the artificiality – through structural innovation, the use of bizarre vernacular or nonsense language, random or protracted digression, disorienting shifts in narrative direction or point of view, emphasis on the arbitrary nature of the narration – has the effect of enhancing the degree of the narrator's power of action by severely undermining any presupposed limitations to the exercise of that power. And attendant with this sense that anything could happen at any moment, the expansion of the narrator's power of action suggests a modal trajectory away from the realm of identification and ever further into the realm of abstraction.

These shifts in the protagonist's and narrator's power of action thereby appear to maneuver the mode to an intermediary position between the mode of "low irony" (i.e., Frye's "ironic mode") and myth. However, unlike the low ironic mode, which typically derives its narrative structures through "the application of romantic mythical forms to a more realistic content" (Frye 223), the high ironic mode is more: the application of low ironic forms to a more surrealistic, absurd, or fantastical context. And as a form of paradoxical reversal it is more open to the free mixing and re-configuration of parody and parodic forms – political satire upon picaresque lampoon, such as in Kathy Acker's *Don Quixote* or Donald Barthelme's *The Dead Father,* parody upon parody, as in William H. Gass's *Willie Masters' Lonesome Wife*, or even the *risus purus* of parody upon parody upon parody, as in Robert Coover's "On Mrs. Willie Masters" – thereby providing a means of simultaneously interrogating and revitalizing the art of parody. As Linda Hutcheon writes in *A Poetics of Postmodernism*, "The collective weight of [postmodern] parodic *practice* suggests a redefinition of parody as repetition with critical distance that allows ironic signaling of difference at the very heart of similarity" (26). And few modes of literature are riper for metafictional parody than myth and romance. However, rather than simply re-telling myth in a contemporary and, therefore, automatically ironic setting (as is common of low ironic parody), high ironic parody is typically an accentuation of the already fabulous narrative source material and is most often set in a mutated world, altogether unlike any world previously experienced by the reader in any kind of extra-textual, terrestrial context.

3. Myth as a Formal Template

The semiotic transparency of myth also makes it an ideal framework for metafictional parodic re-appropriation. In fact, according to Claude Lévi-Strauss, this perpetually plastic capacity is perhaps the defining characteristic of myth:

"[The] substance [of myth] does not lie in its style, its original music, or its syntax, but in the *story* which tells it. Myth is language functioning on an especially high level where meaning succeeds practically at 'taking off' from the linguistic ground on which it keeps rolling." (430–31)

Because myth is made to be passed from generation to generation, voice to voice, in an always already parodic style of narrative transmission, its ephemeral, easily manipulable semiotic structure makes myth a ready template for metafictional parody. Within this mode myth becomes, in a sense, a formal "stencil" to be traced and refashioned to suit whatever target the parodist deems worthy of attack. Case in point is Donald Barthelme's parodic *Snow White* (1967).

Although Donald Barthelme's *Snow White* could never, by any stretch of the imagination, be categorized as a more realistic reinterpretation of Jakob and Wilhelm Grimm's *Little Snow-White* (1812), nor even akin to Walt Disney's *Snow White and the Seven Dwarfs* (1937), Barthelme certainly owes the reader's familiarity with the tale's characters and plot structure to precedent versions of the tale. As Barthelme remarks in an interview with Larry McCaffery, "Again, the usefulness of the Snow White story is that everybody knows it and it can be played against. ... Every small change in the story is momentous when everybody knows the story backward. ..." (LeClair and McCaffery 42-43). And as is typical of narrative irony, this familiarity (e.g., the reader's expectation that the princess be lovely, the witch evil, the dwarves loyal) is methodically drawn upon and subverted during the course of the novel. But what makes Barthelme's high ironic version of the tale more of a parody *on* parody – rather than a formal low ironic parody or a simple retelling of the myth – are the following:

1. Barthelme's *Snow White* employs a host of shifting narrators (each character randomly throwing in a new voice and perspective), thereby constantly undermining the development of any sense of narrative coherence or identity and expanding the power of the narrator beyond a single position.
2. Barthelme's *Snow White* maintains a self-conscious, deceptively transparent attitude towards its borrowed theme, the narrative forever on the verge of establishing thematic parallels to the traditional form of the narrative only to see them systematically destroyed.
3. Barthelme's version uses the hollowed-out shell of the myth to conduct carefully structured intertextual attacks on the very cultural discourses that directly and indirectly act to maintain the "Snow White" narrative pattern and system of logic as cultural institutions (e.g., phallocentrism, psychoanalysis, rationality, courtly love).
4. Barthelme's *Snow White* relies more upon the rhetorical mixing and juxtaposing of various patterns and forms than upon the dislocation of a single narrative pattern (e.g., Barthelme's paraphrase of Freud's "On the Universal Tendency to Debasement in the Sphere of Love" which introduces Snow White's exhaustive list of potential princes [82-83]).

Another important feature of the multi-layer parody used in Barthelme's *Snow White* is the fact that, although the historical time period within the narrative has been warped beyond recognition, the modern terms and phrases scattered throughout the novel (e.g., references to trench warfare [63], Snow White as a "goddamn degenerate" [98], *National Geographic* [124], etc.) never seem to resonate any "real world" environment, but instead establish the sense of a hybrid, fairytale-meets-quotidian "textscape" that seems ever on the verge of collapsing under the weight of its own bloated linguistic structure.

Barthelme's use of parody as a platform for the forensic dissection of parody and, indeed, the narrative act itself, provides a perfect example of the attitude many postmodern authors have towards myth and mimesis as the mode tends ever more towards what Mas'ud Zavarzadeh describes as "…a zone of experience where the factual is not secure or unequivocal but seems preternaturally strange and eerie, and where the fictional seems not at all that fictitious, remote and alien, but bears an uncanny resemblance to daily experience" (56). Although this topsy-turvy zone between factual fiction and fictional fantasy can be, at times, a disorienting experience for the reader to navigate, it is a necessary reminder that there is not, nor could there ever be "an accurate representation of the way the world is in itself" (Rorty 4). There are only the narrative accounts of encounters with this, that, or another world – all of which can be read ironically.

While the extraordinary absurdity that develops in this zone beyond experience, in this realm of abstraction, inversion, and paradox, derives in large degree from the dialectical opposition inherent in experience itself. However, when ironic parody begins to stretch and re-imagine the boundaries between mimetic representation and mythopoesis, and the heroes and villains of yesterday merge into the Janus-like antiheroes of today, there is often no telling where the fiction ends and the reality begins because they have been ironically superimposed. Whether or not this modal ascent into abstraction will lead to a subsequent pre-mythic mode or a further evolution in ironic extremity, is yet to be seen. But one thing is certain: the emergence of this new dominant mode has had an impact on the world of letters that is impossible to ignore.

Bibliography

Aristotle. Aristotele Poetica. 2nd ed. Trans. Augusto Rostagni. Torino: Chiantore, 1945.
— Aristotle's Ars Poetica. Ed. R. Kassel. Oxford: Clarendon, 1966.
— Aristotle's Poetics and Rhetoric, Demetrius on Style, Longinus on the Sublime. Trans. Thomas Twining. (1812) London: J. M. Dent, 1953.
— Aristotle's Poetics, Demetrius on Style, Longinus on the Sublime. Trans. John Warrington. London: J. M. Dent, 1963.
— Poetics. 3rd ed. Trans. S. H. Butcher. London: Macmillan, 1902.
Barth, John. The Floating Opera and The End of the Road. New York: Anchor, 1988.
Barthelme, Donald. Snow White. New York: Scribner, 1967.
Barthes, Roland. Roland Barthes. Trans. Richard Howard. New York: Wang & Hill, 1977
de Man, Paul. Romanticism and Contemporary Criticism: The Gauss Seminar and Other Papers. Ed. E. S. Burt, Kevin Newmark and Andrzej Warminski. Baltimore: Johns Hopkins University Press, 1993.

Denham, Robert D. Northrop Frye and Critical Method. University Park: Pennsylvania State University Press, 1978.
Else, Gerald F. Aristotle's Poetics: The Argument. Cambridge, MA.: Harvard University Press, 1957.
Frye, Northrop. Anatomy of Criticism: Four Essays. Princeton: Princeton University Press, 1957.
Hassan, Ihab. Paracriticisms: Seven Speculations of the Times. Urbana: University of Illinois Press, 1975.
House, Humphry. Aristotle's Poetics. London: Rupert Hart-Davis, 1961.
Hutcheon, Linda. A Poetics of Postmodernism: History, Theory, Fiction. New York: Routledge, 1988.
— Narcissistic Narrative: The Metafictional Paradox. New York: Methuen, 1984.
LeClair, Tom and Larry McCaffery. Anything Can Happen, Interviews with Contemporary American Novelists. Urbana: University of Illinois Press, 1983.
Lévi-Strauss, Claude. The Structural Study of Myth. The Journal of American Folklore. 68.270 (1955): 428-44.
Ricoeur, Paul. Time and Narrative. Trans. Kathleen McLaughlin and David Pellauer. Chicago: University of Chicago Press, 1984.
Rorty, Richard. Contingency, Irony, and Solidarity. Cambridge: Cambridge University Press, 1989.
Waugh, Patricia. Metafiction: The Theory and Practice of Self-Conscious Fiction. London: Routledge, 1984.
White, Hayden. Metahistory: The Historical Imagination in Nineteenth-Century Europe. Baltimore: Johns Hopkins University Press, 1973.
— The Problem of Change in Literary History. New Literary History. 7.1 (1975): 97-111.
Zavarzadeh, Mas'ud. The Mythopoeic Reality: The Postwar American Nonfiction Novel. Urbana: University of Illinois Press, 1976.

Deconstructing Dracula: The Vampire as Semiotic Body in Stephenie Meyer's *Twilight*

Nils Jablonski

Reading the Vampire

The popularity of Stephenie Meyer's *Twilight*[1] depends, in particular, on her depiction of Edward, the novel's vampire protagonist. Unlike the most well-known vampire of the 20th century, Count Dracula, his 'grand-child' Edward is no longer a scary, blood-sucking revenant, but rather a sympathetic 'teenager' with a strange 'eating disorder' who tries to withstand the seduction of first love. This characterization of Edward highlights how he is the ideal protagonist for one of the most successful trivial love stories in contemporary popular literature.

Although the concept of the vampire can be traced back to ancient tales of blood-drinking creatures (Pütz 15), the modern prototype of the vampire is much younger: The literary figure of Count Dracula, the antagonist in Bram Stoker's novel from 1897, became the most important model for the many other revenants in western literature, fine arts, and cinema (Pütz 12). In *Dracula* the 'special powers' of the vampire are described by Abraham Van Helsing as follows: The vampire is "cunning" and as strong as twenty men, but afraid of "garlic and a crucifix" (216); he can "appear at will when, and where, and in any of the forms that are to him; he can […] direct the elements […]; he can command all the meaner things […]; he can grow and become small; and he can at times vanish and come unknown" (252). Supernatural abilities are as essential for vampires as special attributes are for monsters[2]. Since "nothing is emphasized more consistently in the

---

[1] All quotations from *Twilight* will be cited with the abbreviation 'TL' followed by the page number(s).

[2] In his essay "Monster Roundup", David J. Russell develops a taxonomy in order to classify the horror genre by its monster types. He bases his approach on Robin Wood's formula for the horror genre as normality threatened by the monster (Russell 238). The threat to normality is evoked by the monster's special powers, abilities or features which challenge the rules and characteristics of the diegetic space of the literary work or film. Russell's taxonomy is quite useful, though he does not reflect on his mimetic concept of literature underlying his theory:

Twilight saga than Edward's physical appeal" (McMahon 198), this close reading of the text will explore the depiction of Edward by focusing on the narratological question: Who describes Edward and, more importantly, how is he described? Since he is presented to the reader via Bella's perception of him, Edward can be analyzed as a construct, both as an artificial as well as a semiotic body. Reading the vampire in a semiotic way, namely as a 'body' (or 'sign') which "signifies something other than itself" (Cohen 4), is not a new idea: Jeffrey Jerome Cohen points out that the monster is "an embodiment of a certain cultural moment" (14) and therefore to be considered as a "cultural body" (4). Applied to the most prominent monster in "print literature since the 18th century" (Ames 37), Cohen's first thesis reveals the vampire as the signifier of the human fear of death and as the embodiment of "the anxiety we have about our bodies" (McMahon 197). Thus, monsters are both "a construction and a projection" meant "to be read" (Cohen 4) – but perhaps not just through the lens of cultural studies; the structuralist approach offers a means to analyze their semiotic formation and literary use.[3]

The taxonomy sets the monster in relation to the diegetic space in which it appears. However, it would be more efficient to describe the monster and its 'threat to normality' with the help of the Russian Formalists' concept of alienation. This would be a reasonable amendment to Russell's approach, since he does not take into account that 'normality' is a relative category: Within the diegetic space, 'normality' does not necessarily have to be 'realistic' according to the reader's/viewer's reality, but according to its depiction, which has to be mimetic in the sense of Aristotle's concept of a possible or probable depiction. In general, 'normality' presented in a (mimetic) literary work corresponds to the reader's/viewer's own (or extraliterary) reality. However, it is not necessary that the diegetic 'reality' corresponds to the natural laws of physics present in the reader's/viewer's own reality. Thus, any figure or event which challenges or deviates from the rules constituting the diegetic (or 'inner-literary') normality, could be described as a monster or monstrous.

[3] Except for Dennis Knepp's essay from 2009, there is, to my knowledge, no other semiotic approach among the increasing number of scholary texts about *Twilight*, most of which focus on (pop-)cultural aspects from a feminist perspective. In his essay "Bella's Vampire Semiotics", Knepp seems to offer a semiotic reading of the vampire in *Twilight* by focusing on Bella's 'epistemic progress' while revealing Edward's vampire identity. Promising at first sight, Knepp's approach disqualifies itself by comparing Bella's biography to Charles Sanders Peirce's biography (211). Thus, Knepp analyzes the triadic structure of Bella's argumentation (which follows the classical rhetoric pattern of a syllogism) rather than her reading of "the signs that point to *vampire*" (209, italics in the original text). In his essay Knepp confuses Peirce's triadic typology by saying that the coldness of Edward's skin is interpreted by Bella as an iconic sign, becoming one of the first clues to reveal Edward's vampire existence (211). An icon is defined as an analogical relation between signifier and signified (Knepp does not use Ferdinand de Saussure's terminology, though it might have helped him to apply Peirce's terminology in a correct way). Undoubtedly, 'coldness' cannot be an icon, it is an index of Edward's vampire existence.

(Re-)Constructing the Vampire

"The vampires in *Twilight*," Jennifer L. McMahon points out, "do deviate from the archetypal vampire in important ways. They are undeterred by garlic and invulnerable to stakes through the heart. They don't sleep in coffins – indeed, they don't sleep at all. Daylight isn't deadly, either. Instead, vampires glisten in it. Most important, they aren't exactly monstrous" (McMahon 202). In fact, Edward seems to be the opposite of a typically threatening monster, since he is depicted as a kind of "celebrity" in *Twilight* (Stevens Aubery et al. 227). Edward may be a vampire, but he is not an evil one and, like a 'real' celebrity, "[h]e is not ordinary" (227). On the contrary, his vampire existence makes him as extraordinary as possible: "He is supernatural; he is magical" (ibid.). Thus, Edward completely 'fails' in following in the tradition of his 'grand-father' Dracula. Due to the "countless films, literary renditions, graphic novels, television commercials, cartoons, and children's programming throughout the years", Dracula has become the "most influential" (Ames 42) vampire figure in mass media-dominated western society. Dracula is the prototype of an evil, scary, blood-sucking revenant, while Edward is the opposite. The two could not be more dissimilar, and yet there is one aspect both have in common: They are artificial constructs.

The vampire as a literary figure first appeared in the 18th century (Claes 20), promoted by the increasing popularity of the emerging genre of the Gothic novel in England (Pütz 24), and Stoker's *Dracula* marked the real breakthrough of the literary vampire at the end of the 19th century (29). Although the figure of Dracula dominated the image of the prototypical vampire, two major developments concerning the depiction of the vampire stand out in the 20th century: first, an increasing 'descent' of the motif through trivial and/or pop-cultural adaptations and transformations (Claes 21), and, second, a shift in narrative perspective which increasingly covers more the point of view of the vampire than of his victims (Pütz 163).

In a diachronic perspective *Twilight* marks an anachronistic development in the genealogy of the vampire novel: Since the narrating voice in *Twilight* takes up Bella's position and perspective in the form of a first-person narrator, the novel deviates from the modern development of covering the vampire's perspective. Furthermore, *Twilight* is printed proof that the vampire in 20th and 21st century literature does not necessarily have to be a metaphor for the failure of human relationships and the impossibility of love (Claes 26) because Edward and Bella fall in love – and the obstacles their love has to overcome are the main catalysts for the story's progression throughout the four books of the *Twilight* saga.

As mentioned previously, Edward and the other vampires are presented to the reader via Bella's perspective, whereby two discourses are constituted: On the one hand, Bella refers to Edward's celestial origin, and, on the other, to his relation to art. During her first encounter with the Cullens at school, Bella not only takes notice of Edward and his brothers and sisters, but 'stares' at them (TL 16). She then directly points out their uniqueness by saying: "They don't look anything alike" (TL 16). The appearance of the Cullens is extraordinary, since all of them are "chalky pale" but with "very dark eyes," and "purplish, bruiselike shadows" under them (TL 16). Bella describes the features of their faces as "straight, perfect, angular" (TL 16) – a triad of attributes rather more convenient for geometric constructs in art or architecture than for faces. Thus, the three adjectives refer to the vampires' 'supernatural' appearance, and they are one of the text's first hints of the artificiality of the vampire as construct.

The impression of artificiality is also evoked by Bella's metaphors concerning Edward's vampire sisters, who are "statuesque" and "pixilike" (TL 16). These two meta-artistic or meta-literary terms refer to the fine arts on the one hand, and to the literary genre of the fairy tale on the other. Finally, Bella summarizes her impressions of the Cullen children by stating that they are "devastatingly, inhumanly beautiful" (TL 17). Furthermore, they are perfect enough to cover "the airbrushed pages of a fashion magazine" because they seem "to be painted by an old master" (TL 17). Contemporary fashion magazines and the works of old masters are a strange and (certainly unintentionally) weird juxtaposition; this is supplemented by Bella's thought that Edward and his brothers and sister look "like a scene from a movie" (TL 35).

During the course of the story, Bella's observations shift from the vampires as a group to Edward. In the beginning, she notices two characteristics of Edward: his "quiet, musical voice," and his "clear, elegant script" (TL 37). Apart from their similar linguistic structure in the form of a noun phrase attributed with two adjectives, both 'voice' and 'script' are two means of potential artistic expression. This occurs again later in the text when Bella describes Edward's voice as "melting honey" (TL 88), and then again when she mentions his "quiet, musical laugh" (TL 262). The motif of Edward's artistic vocal expression is repeated yet again, whereby the artificial aspect of his voice is stressed even more because he has "the voice of an archangel" (TL 272). Finally, Bella says to herself during Edward's performance on the piano that "[t]he music grew unbearably sweet" (TL 285). This comment seems like metapoetical irony because it is not only a reference to Edward's musical voice, but also an indirect reflection on this over-romanticized scene.

When describing Edward's appearance Bella notices not only his "gray-colored eyes" (TL 49), but also "a set of perfect, ultra white teeth" (TL 43). She realizes that Edward moves "swiftly and [...] gracefully," and, generally, she thinks of him as a "bizarre, beautiful boy" (TL 43). In these examples, the pattern of two adjectives in a noun phrase is used again to describe Edward's attributes. They underline his unusualness and, at the same time, his artificiality, which is stressed even more when Bella refers to Edward with the metapoetical term "figure" (TL 44) while listing his extraordinary features. After this closer introduction to Edward, Bella thinks about him and reflects on her perception of him. She wonders whether Edward could "merely [be] an invention of my imagination" (TL 61) because she finds it hard "to believe that someone so beautiful could be real" (TL 75). She comes to the conclusion that Edward does not "belong in the same world" (TL 88).

Bella's reflections play an important part in the construction of the text: On the one hand, they suggest to the reader that she or he should share Bella's hesitation and doubt concerning Edward and his extraordinary attributes. Thus, the text evokes *par excellence* the 'phantastic effect'. This effect is constituted by a figure's hesitation or doubt which is shared with the reader (Todorov). On the other hand, the reader is made aware of the depiction of Edward, who is more than obviously presented as an artificial construct.

As Bella checks out different vampire myths on the internet, she compiles a "catalogue" (TL 117) of the most common characteristics of the vampire. The catalogue is interesting because of three aspects. First, it is one of the oldest literary forms. Second, Bella's catalogue has the same function as van Helsing's descriptions of the vampire's abilities in *Dracula*. Furthermore, both Bella's catalogue and van Helsing's descriptions highlight that the depiction of the vampire via the perspective of another, generally human figure is the substantial narrative technique which contributes to the evocation of the phantastic effect[4]. Third, the catalogue functions as a constitutive element in the depiction of Edward. It contains several common traits of the prototypical vampire, such as speed, strength, beauty, and immortality (TL 117). Most of these characteristics, which have become signifiers of the 'typical' vampire, stand in direct opposition to Bella's perception of Edward, who both deviates from and corresponds to the features listed in the catalogue. Thus, one can say that Edward is related to the prototypical vampire. But as a consequence of this relation, the image of the prototypical vampire is not only 'revived' but also supplemented by Bella's perception of Edward's new features.

Edward's characterization as a new or modified representation of the prototypical vampire can be explained with the help of Roland Barthes' model of a so-

---

[4] Via the perception of the first person narrator, the reader is able to share the hesitation and doubt implied in the observations which the narrator makes of the vampire whose abilities seem to be supernatural and therefore a threat to 'normality' (cf. footnote 2). In *Dracula* the phantastic effect is narratologically intensified since the third-person narrator describes the vampire by presenting the subjective perspectives of different figures, e.g. van Helsing, Mina Murray or Jonathan Harker, in the form of their journals, diaries or records.

called 'secondary semiotic system'. Barthes operates with two levels in his model. Each level consists of the two elements of the linguistic sign according to Ferdinand de Saussure: the signifier and the signified. The two levels are connected to each other, since the first level as a whole becomes the signifier of the second level (Barthes 93). The idea behind this two-tiered semiotic system is just as simple as it is clever: The meaning, which is constituted via the connection between signifier and signified on the first level, is 'enriched' on the second level. This is the case in the depiction of the vampire in *Twilight*: The prototypical image of the vampire is evoked in the text and simultaneously contrasted with Edward or with Bella's perception of Edward. Since some of Edward's features deviate from those of a prototypical vampire, the latter's image and Bella's perception of Edward are not congruent. Thus, the old meaning of the signifier 'vampire' is enriched in order to construct a new or supplemented meaning on the second level, whereby the meaning of the first level (being a correlation of signifier and signified) becomes the signifier of the semiotic system on the second level.

Since Edward's depiction deviates from *and* coincides with the prototypical image of the vampire represented by Bella's catalogue, some aspects of the image's meaning decline while other aspects are enriched. In other words, the image of the prototypical vampire is evoked and simultaneously deconstructed by the image of a new kind of vampire. While Edward shares some of the prototypical vampire features, such as strength, with Dracula, he is equipped with new ones, such as glistening when being exposed to broad daylight.

Deconstructing the Vampire

As previously discussed, two major discourses are established via Bella's perception of Edward: the one characterizing Edward's otherworldliness, and the other his relation to art. Generally, both discourses underline Edward's artificiality due to Bella's use of exaggerated comparisons. When Bella says that Edward has an "angel's face" (TL 152), she expresses that Edward's face is as beautiful as an angel's. Although it seems almost impossible, this comparison is exaggerated even more because Bella wonders whether "an angel could be any more glorious" (TL 212) than Edward. Interestingly, in this case the text becomes contradictory in a performative way by having Bella questioning her own comparison. Thus, the text deconstructs itself. This pattern of contradiction is used frequently. Bella says that Edward looks "*like* a Greek god" (TL 18; my italics), in order to state later that "this godlike creature" is simply "*too* perfect" (TL 224; my italics).

The last two examples concern the discourse of Edward's 'celestial origin'; in the discourse of his relation to art a further strategy of augmentation is used. This augmentation changes again into exaggeration which deconstructs itself. When

Edward takes Bella into the forest in order to reveal his vampire existence to her in the broad sunlight[5], Bella remarks in her thoughts that Edward looks like a "perfect statue," since he seems "smooth like marble" and glitters "like crystal" (TL 228). As opposed to Edward, the impressive surrounding scenery of the glade in the forest loses its beauty: "The meadow, so spectacular to me at first," Bella says, "paled next to his magnificence" (TL 229). Edward's beauty defeats nature. This struggle is metapoetically interesting because the ancient topos of art competing with nature is invoked, as Edward represents the artistic field.

The isotopy of Edward's outstanding and therefore artificial beauty reoccurs later in the text when Bella uses the term 'statue' to again describe Edward. This comparison to a statue is further supplemented when Bella calls Edward "the statue of Adonis" (TL 277) – a further exaggeration because in ancient Greek myth Adonis is said to be one of the most beautiful men in the world (Becker 11). By looking at the scene in which the reference to Adonis is used, the deconstructive dimension of the text can be analyzed. Bella describes the scene as follows: "[Edward] stood in the middle of the kitchen, the statue of Adonis again, staring abstractedly out the back windows" (TL 277). Adonis is not only a figure in ancient Greek mythology, but also a famous *sujet* in the fine arts. *Twilight* presents this 'artifact' (embodied by Edward) in the setting of a simple American middle-class kitchen. Apart from being a strange juxtaposition, it is further proof for the underlying topic of artificiality in *Twilight*.

Due to the narrative devices of the text, Bella seems to 'create' Edward[6] – and she also works on her own 're-creation'. Bonnie Mann interprets Bella's insistent wish to become a vampire as her feminist concern. Bella wants to be like Edward "because in the vampire world, all bets are off when it comes to gender. Vampire women show no particular deference to men. They are endowed with superpowers just like the guys" (141). Certainly, Bonnie Mann is correct so far, but in her final summary she misses an important point when she criticizes the "reinstatement" (143) of old-fashioned, anti-feminist thinking as the 'message' of *Twilight*. By addressing female readers, *Twilight* proclaims: "[A]ssume your status as prey, as object, and you will gain your freedom as subject, as the center of action and

---

[5] This is a highly symbolical scene, since the sun is the symbol of awareness (Becker 279).
[6] Apart from all the negative criticism on *Twilight*, some of which comes from a feminist perspective, this could be a possible "feminist subtext" (Mann 139) of the novel because it is no longer the *man* who creates, but a woman. As Melissa Ames points out in her broad and differentiated overview of the current criticism on *Twilight*, "the criticism from self-proclaimed feminists has been the most regular, and often the most negative in terms of gender representations" (39). Since her body is "the locus of exaggerated stereotypical feminine incapacities" (133), Bella can be read "as a representative of the idealized womanhood" (132) revived from the pre-feminist era.

meaning. Seek your existence in the eyes of a sovereign masculine subject, and you will find it" (ibid.).

Undoubtedly, *Twilight* ostensibly forces this reading. But taking into account the novel's subtext concerning the aspect of construction and artificiality represented by the vampire figures, a different reading must be considered. Of course Edward represents masculinity and the male perspective, but he is not depicted as the masculine *subject* Mann talks about. On the contrary, Edward is presented as the *object* of Bella's imagination as well as desire, which contributes to the subversion of the classical gender roles. Bella is presented as the creator of Edward; she is the subject and Edward has turned into the desirable object (Köppel 244). This shift concerning the classic subject-object-relation in vampire literature is commented on by Rainer M. Köppel as follows: In the classical vampire tradition the human was the object of the vampire's desire, now the vampire becomes the object of human desire.[7] Of course, one could argue that the vampire in particular, and the monster in general, has always been the conscious and unconscious embodiment (and therefore object) of human desire, as implied in Cohen's "Seven Theses" on the monster as a cultural body. In a kind of reflected projection, the vampire in general is a subject[8] which 'subjects' its human prey – in *Twilight* the vampire is turned into a 'real' object of human, and especially female, desire.

Reflecting On the Vampire

"Rather than work to undermine the appeal of vampires by foregrounding their inhumanity, *Twilight* asserts their superiority" (McMahon 204) by stressing Edward's extraordinary appearance. As shown before, the narrative technique concerning the depiction of Edward can be read as a semiotic process modeling the image of a new kind of vampire. Apart from the *use* of this semiotic (and narrative) process of (re-)construction and deconstruction, the text's *reflections* on it are maybe one of the most interesting aspects in *Twilight*. In fact, Edward seems to be aware of his artificiality. Bella remarks on Edward's behavior during one of his regular visits at her home that he "*made a show* of becoming a statue on the edge of my bed" (TL 260; my italics).

Edward is set in opposition to Bella; her perspective is often used to depict the vampire and to express his artificiality, whereas in other scenes Edward's behavior and remarks are used to reflect on narrative technique. Thus, Edward's reflections can be read as metapoetical comments. Furthermore, by the use of the figures

---

[7] Originally: "In der klassischen Vampirtradition war der Mensch das Objekt der Begierde der Vampire, jetzt wird der Vampir zum Objekt der Begierde des Menschen" (Köppel 247).

[8] Due to the difficulties of allocating subject or object status to the monster, Julia Kristeva's concept of the so-called 'abject' could be a useful alternative.

Edward and Bella as literary devices the text seems to deconstruct itself as it plays off contrasts Edward's behavior and his comments with Bella's perception and perspective. During Bella's visit to Edward's home, he comments on her possible expectations about the vampires' residence: "No coffins, no piled skulls in the corners; I don't even think we have cobwebs … what a disappointment this must be for you" (TL 287). With this comment, Edward completes Bella's catalogue. At the same time, he refers to the process of deconstructing the image of the prototypical vampire. He assumes that Bella has particular expectations about the typical furnishings of a vampire residence, such as coffins, skulls, and cobwebs. By mentioning these props (in this case, Edward anticipates Bella's perspective), the image of the prototypical vampire is again invoked. Simultaneously, this image is deconstructed, since Edward denies the existence of those props in his home. Furthermore, Edward ironically comments on the effect of this deconstruction by anticipating Bella's "disappointment" (TL 287).

In the following scene, Edward points out the vampires' relation to art while he and Bella are looking at a picture in his vampire-father's office: "Solimena was greatly inspired by Carlisle's friends. He often painted them as Gods," Edward chuckled. "Aro, Marcus, Caius," he said [...]. "Nighttime patrons of the arts." (TL 297) Carlisle's friends are vampires, of course, and not surprisingly they are depicted as Gods – exactly like Edward, whose "godlike" (TL 224) appearance is insistently pointed out by Bella. Edward's amusement (he chuckles) about the fact that Solimena, a real Italian painter of the 17th century[9], painted the vampires as Gods, could be interpreted as a self-referential moment in the text, since Solimena depicted the vampires in exactly the same way as the text does.

As shown before, the figure of the vampire is a (literary) construct, since artificiality is an inherent characteristic of every monster. With reference to René Girard's *The Scapegoat* from 1986, Cohen points to this fact: "Monsters are never created *ex nihilo*, but through a process of fragmentation and recombination in which elements are extracted 'from various forms' [...], and then assembled as the monster, 'which can then claim an independent identity'" (Cohen 11). The terms 'fragmentation' and 'recombination' used by Cohen describe nothing less than the semiotic process. Interestingly, the artistic technique of fragmentation and recombination brings the genre of the collage to mind, which is described as the recombination of different elements to create a 'spark of poetry' as Max Ernst says in his famous definition[10]. Thus, the figure of the vampire could be read as a literary collage.

---

[9] Francesco Solimena, also known as l'Abbate Ciccio, lived from 1657 to 1747 and worked in Naples (*Brockhaus* 375).

[10] The collage as a literary and artistic technique and as a genre is an invention of the historic avant-garde art movements at the beginning of the 20th century (Vowinckel 1989).

Jennifer L. McMahon argues that "the appeal of vampires lies not only in their immortality, but also in their eternal youth" (196). Additionally, one can observe that these two features also fit the vampire's use as a literary figure. The motif of vampirism and the figure of the vampire have been integral to western literature since the 18th century. Today, the vampire owes his 'longevity' to the possibility of his intermedia use (Pütz 29), which is implied in the vampire's inherent potential of being (re)combinable. As a semiotic body the vampire is an immortal body because he owns the potential to return – recombined in a newly textual form. Maybe this is the real threat of the vampire in particular, and of the monster in general: On the object level the monster's body is "corporal", but on the metalevel it is "incorporeal" (Cohen 5). This last aspect implies the threat of the monster's body, "its propensity to shift" (5) and return. Thus Cohen is right by saying that the monster always escapes (4) because the escape directly implies the monster's potential return. Eternal recurrence is the vampire's fate and it is also implied in one of his pseudonyms: The revenant has to come back, since returning is implicit in his name.

(Textual) Monstrosity

Apart from parodies and other such transformations, the motif of vampirism and the figure of the vampire are being combined with other genres today more than ever. *Twilight* is a quintessential example, since it is a genre hybrid between love story and horror story. Although *Twilight* is about vampires, it is not a typical horror story because it subverts the classical role of the vampire as a monster.[11] "With its captivating tale of star-crossed lovers, [*Twilight*] seduces us into loving vampires [...]. It casts Edward as the innocent and self-scarifying Romeo, rather than as a compelling, but vicious monster" (McMahon 3).

Furthermore, *Twilight* is certainly a love story and it would not be a misreading to allocate the novel to the genre of trivial love stories. The different narrative techniques applied in *Twilight* underline this hypothesis: 1) The linguistic style is verbose. As Monica Hesse points out, Stephenie Meyer "never uses one adjective when she could use three" (par. 14). 2) The structure of the story is "less plot than endless yearning" (Hesse par. 2). 3) The addressed audience of *Twilight* are mainly "teenage girls and young women" (Sax par. 2). 4) Bella is "the locus of exaggerated stereotypically feminine incapacities" (Mann 133) and therefore the prototypical protagonist for every trivial love story. 5) The use of the romanticized myth of love at first sight is used in *Twilight*. According to this myth, "the

---

[11] Although Edward is presented as a sympathetic vampire, there are still monstrous vampires in *Twilight*. Victoria and James, the wandering vampires who hunt Bella, take over the roles of the evil monsters.

Twilight series downplays conflict in relationships" (Clasen 125). This is a typical characteristic of trivial love stories, which represent 'reality' in a simplified way.

Twilight's relation to the genre of the trivial love story cannot be the only explanation for its worldwide impact.[12] The hybrid combination of both the horror and the trivial romance genre is a further important reason for *Twilight*'s success. But hybridity is also a monstrous attribute, and, in fact, it is a basic topic in *Twilight* where Edward is presented as a hybrid since he is still related to the prototypical image of the threatening vampire. Who is the monster in *Twilight*? Edward says, "I don't want to be a monster" (TL 54), and, in fact, it is Bella who takes up a monstrous role – at least from Edward's perspective: "To me, it was like you were some kind of daemon, summoned straight from my own personal hell to ruin me" (TL 236). Thus, the classical roles can be and are at times reversed. The idea of fixed categories is rendered problematic. And thus, perspective is as relative as the allocation of the term 'monster'. Cohen is right when he says that the monster is the "harbinger of category crisis" (6). Like the monsters depicted in the form of the vampires in *Twilight*, the novel resists being "encapsulated in any conceptual system" (Cohen 7), since it is both a love story and a horror story. Indeed, the text itself might be the actual 'monster' of *Twilight*.

Bibliography

Ames, Melissa. "Twilight Follows Tradition. Analyzing 'Biting' Critiques of Vampire Narratives for Their Portrayals of Gender and Sexuality." Click et al. 2010. 37-53.
Barthes, Roland. Mythen des Alltags. Trans. Helmut Scheffel. Frankfurt a.M.: Suhrkamp, 1964.
Becker, Udo. Lexikon der Symbole. 7th ed. Freiburg et al.: Herder, 2006.
Brockhaus – Die Enzyklopädie. 19th ed. Vol. 20. Leipzig et al.: Brockhaus, 1998.
Claes, Oliver. Fremde. Vampire. Sexualität, Tod und Kunst bei Elfriede Jelinek und Adolf Muschg. Bielefeld: Aisthesis, 1994.
Clasen, Tricia. "Taking a Bite Out of Love: The Myth of Romantic Love in the Twilight Series." Click et al. 2010. 119-134.
Click, Melissa A., Jennifer Stevens Aubrey, and Elizabeth Behm-Morawitz. Bitten by Twilight. Youth Culture, Media, & the Vampire Franchise. New York: Lang, 2010.
Cohen, Jeffrey Jerome. "Monster Culture (Seven Thesis)." Cohen, Jeffrey Jerome. Monster Theory. Reading Culture. Minneapolis: University of Minneapolis Press, 1996. 3-25.
Eco, Umberto. Die unendliche Liste. Trans. Barbara Kleiner. München: Hanser, 2009.
Hesse, Monica. "'Twilight,' the love that dare not speak its shame." Washington Post 19 Nov. 2009. http://www.washingtonpost.com/wp-dyn/content/story/2009/11/18/ST2009111804551.html?sid=ST2009111804551 (04/30/2014).

---

[12] After its first publication in 2005 the novel was translated into 30 languages and has been sold more than 100 million times (Köppel 243).

Housel, Rebecca, and Jeremy Wisnewski. Twilight and Philosophy. Vampires, Vegetarians, and the Pursuit of Immortality. Hoboken: John Wiley & Sons, 2009.

Knepp, Dennis. "Bella's Vampire Semiotics." Housel and Wisnewski 2009. 209-271.

Köppel, Rainer Maria. Der Vampir sind wir. Der unsterbliche Mythos von Dracula biss Twilight. St. Pölten et al: Residenz, 2010.

Kristeva, Julia. Powers of Horror. An Essay on Abjection. Trans. Leon S. Roudiez. New York: Columbia University Press, 1982.

Mann, Bonnie. "Vampire Love: The Second Sex Negotiates the Twenty-first Century." Housel and Wisnewski 2009. 131-145.

McGeough, Danielle Dick. "Twilight and Transformations of Flesh: Reading the Body in Contemporary Youth Culture." Click et al. 2010. 87-102.

McMahon, Jennifer L.: "Twilight of an Idol: Our Fatal Attraction to Vampires". Housel and Wisnewski 2009. 193-208.

Meyer, Stephenie. Twilight [FE 2005]. London: Atom, 2010.

Russell, David John. "Monster Roundup. Reintegrating the Horror Genre." Browne, Nick. Refiguring American Film Genres. Theory and History. Berkeley: University of California Press, 1998. 233-254.

Pütz, Susanne. Vampire und ihre Opfer: Der Blutsauger als literarische Figur. Bielefeld: Aisthesis, 1992.

Sax, Leonard: "'Twilight' Sinks Its Teeth Into Feminism." Washington Post 17 Aug. 2008. http://www.washingtonpost.com/wp-dyn/content/article/2008/08/15/AR2008081503099.html (04/30/2014).

Stevens Aubrey, Jennifer, Scott Walus, and Melissa A. Click. "Twilight and the Production of the 21st Century Teen Idol." Click et al. 2010. 225-241.

Stoker, Bram: Dracula [FE 1897]. London: Penguin, 2003.

Todorov, Tzvetan. Einführung in die fantastische Literatur. Trans. Karin Kersten et al. München: Hanser, 1972.

Vowinckel, Andreas. Surrealismus und Kunst. 1919 bis 1925. Hildesheim et al.: Olms, 1989.

Life Writing Projects in Posthuman Science Fiction

Sarah Herbe

"I was born in 2520, an unexceptional child of the twenty-sixth century. [...] By comparison with the children of previous centuries, however – excepting a minority of those born in the latter decades of the twenty-fifth century – I and all my kind were new. We were the first true emortals, immune to all disease and further aging." (Stableford *Fountains*, 15) This is how Brian Stableford's science fiction novel *The Fountains of Youth*, cast as the autobiography of the historian Mortimer Gray, starts. Reminiscent of conventional autobiographies, the reader is introduced right at the beginning to an utterly changed world, in which immortality presents the norm and in which the first person narrator refers to himself as 'emortal' as opposed to 'human'. Stableford was not the first science fiction author who reverted to formal strategies of life writing in order to depict strange worlds and transformed humans. In a special issue of the journal *Biography* on "Life Writing and Science Fiction", published in 2007, John Rieder argues that already the classics of science fiction "constantly employ the tropes and strategies of life writing" (v) and gives the first-person account in H. G. Wells' *The Time Machine* or the autobiographical letters in Mary Shelley's *Frankenstein* as examples. 'Life writing', however, does not just refer to autobiographical writing: it "encompasses the writing of one's own or another's life" (Jolly ix) and can thus be also "biographical, novelistic [or] historical" (Smith and Watson 4) and it is not necessarily restricted to written work. In this essay, I shall examine examples of autobiographical, novelistic, historical and biographical life writing projects carried out in five science fiction novels published in the first decade of the twenty-first century, namely Brian Stableford's *The Fountains of Youth* (2000) and *The Omega Expedition* (2002), Charles Stross' *Accelerando* (2005), Ken Macleod's *Learning the World* (2005) and Alastair Reynolds' *Revelation Space* (2000). In these novels, it is taken for granted that a transformation of humans into posthumans will take place at some point in the future, i.e., that humans will ultimately modify "themselves so extensively by cyborgisation and genetic engineering as to liberate themselves from the traditionally recognized 'human condition'" (Stableford *Science Fact*, 401) and, conspicuously, life writing projects are employed in attempts to record the transition from humanity to posthumanity.

Reflections on Autobiography

The two final instalments of Brian Stableford's *Emortality Series*, in which humanity gradually attains near-immortality with the help of genetic engineering and cyborgisation, are the fictional autobiographies of their protagonists. In *The Fountains of Youth*, the transition from humanity to posthumanity is outlined from the vantage point of the historian Mortimer Gray, who writes his life when he is 505 years old. Apart from the fact that Mortimer Gray is not a real historical person, Gray's life writing project corresponds to the idea of the conventional autobiography as defined by Philippe Lejeune in *The Autobiographical Pact* (1975) as "*[r]etrospective prose narrative written by a real person concerning his own existence, where the focus is his individual life, in particular the story of his personality*" (4; italics in the original). Gray's autobiography formally starts like a conventional autobiography ("I was born in 2520 . . ." [15]), but the narrator points out that the genre is no longer familiar to all his contemporary readers (while it of course is to the actual readers of Stableford's novel), since he explains that he is "*resurrect[ing]* the dubious genre of spiritual autobiography" (19; my italics). Gray reflects on the idea that one has to be in some way "exceptional" in order to write one's autobiography, and gives as reasons for his exceptionality that he "has tried as hard as [he] can these last five hundred years to make his fellow human beings conscious of the privileges and responsibilities of the emortal condition." (15) Being "emortal" means that people no longer die a natural death, but are still susceptible to violent deaths. His autobiography is intended to remind his fellow emortals of humanity's past so that they can duly esteem their own condition and do not forget the advantages emortality has brought them. The novelty of the emortal race can only be maintained as long as it is seen in opposition to the 'old humans'.

Since Gray's life writing project relies on the conventional, reflective form of the spiritual biography it represents in itself a form of the past; it does not only remember pre-emortal times and people, but also strives to keep alive the tradition of autobiography as such as a form of self-expression and identity formation. Moreover, it continues reflections about autobiography which were central to twentieth century life writing criticism. Even though Gray, at the beginning of the third millennium, has at his disposal digital sources on almost every event of his life (since everything is witnessed by multiple recording devices and then stored) he still adheres to the idea that writing one's life always includes construction, selection and interpretation, which critics and practitioners of life writing basically agree upon, and can never result in the one ultimate or objective life of its subject:

"Like history, autobiography is a kind of fantasy, but each and every one of us is permanently involved in constructing the story of his or her own life, and even those of us who are perfectly content to act without recording remain creatures of fantasy. Those of us who record as well as acting [sic] are attempting to grasp the substance of our personal fantasies and to be as precise as possible in the construction as well as their interpretation." (95–6)

The beginning of Stableford's *The Omega Expedition* equally recalls conventional openings of autobiographies on the level of form, though the content already points toward crucial changes in the lives of humans: "Like many a man born in 2163, I know nothing at all of my biological ancestry." (51) Due to a sterility plague people are no longer conceived and born, but hatched from artificial wombs before they are raised by a group of foster parents. After more than a thousand years, the first-person narrator Madoc Tamlin awakes from a cryogenic sleep to a world which offers a variety of posthuman alternatives for him to choose from, and after a near-fatal encounter with a hostile artificial intelligence, which tried to convince him of the advantages of becoming transferred into a machine, he writes down his experiences and reflects on the writing of stories, histories and autobiographies. He concludes that reading stories has played a decisive role in creating humanness and, drawing attention to the materiality of the written text, explains that

"[i]t really was inevitable that we'd have to write our accounts, because text retains certain qualities that even the very best VE [virtual environment] scripts will never be able to emulate. [...] when you read you switch off your other senses and turn your eyes into code readers, retreating into a world of pure thought and true abstraction. It was that world of abstraction that had shaped and organized our ancestors' inner lives during the early phases of the technological revolution; it was there that they learned to be the complex kind of being we now call human. It is there that true humanity still resides, even after all this time." (516)

Writing down one's experiences is thus here not only done to create a reminder of past events, but producing a written artefact that can then be read by posterity in itself is presented as an inherent feature of the 'human condition' which Madoc Tamlin is loath to leave behind entirely. He further believes that "if we want to recollect what it was like to be human, we have to start doing it now" (517) in order to make sure that the remaining old humans document their past before they forget it or no longer care about it as soon as they choose to make a transition from a human to a posthuman form which will ultimately influence their states of mind and their concerns. So putting one's life into the form of a story is presented as a means of documenting what it was like to be human, not just for posterity, but also for the posthumans themselves if they choose to live forever or to become part of a machine. It does not become clear, however, just why it is so important to remember one's past.

Family Histories

In Ken Macleod's *Learning the World*, set in the year 14,364 on a remote 'ship-world', a character called Grant Cornforth Dialectic intends to write a novel dealing with the lives of the generation of his parents, who, due to longevity techniques, were young about half a millennium ago and are still alive today. When Grant's friend Atomic Discourse Gale wonders about who would ever want to read such a book, the prospective author says: "'[...T]here must be stories to tell. Think about it, four hundred years! [...] Their past before they took ship!' 'Yes, [...] but who would read it?' 'The next generation, [...]. The one after us.'" (79–80) By writing the novel, Grant wishes to familiarise himself with the lives of his ancestors and tries to define himself and his own generation by way of contrast. Further, he once more wishes to preserve the past lives of his parent generation for posterity. He sees himself as a link between past and future generations and tries to secure a certain kind of continuity from generation to generation.

In Charles Stross' *Accelerando*, Sirhan voices his idea to write a family history in an argument he has with his grandmother about immortality: his grandmother believes that growing old is natural and that "wanting to live forever is immoral", while Sirhan firmly supports the posthuman project which makes immortality an option. The attempt to write his family history is made at a point when specimens of the 'original' humans are still alive, and it would thus be another record of the transition from human to posthuman. Sirhan envisages it as "[a]n old-fashioned book covering three generations, living through interesting times", but at the same time makes clear that it would be "a work of postmodern history – the incoherent school at that" (279). Since in the world of *Accelerando* it has become possible to live multiple and serial lives[1] due to downloadable minds and cloned bodies, new strategies would have to be found to document such new life courses. However, just like in *Learning the World*, the reader does not get to see the result of the life writing project, i.e., the family history is only talked about but not included on the diegetic level of the story. The novel *Accelerando* itself, of course, documents the transition but since the narrative basically concentrates on only one incarnation of a character and mentions the life courses of the other copies only in passing, it fails to convey the complexity of these posthuman lives convincingly.

---

[1] For a more detailed discussion of these new life courses see Herbe 2011.

The Art of Biography

In the central example of this essay, the life writing project is not shown either: it makes use of advanced technologies and exists in a virtual reality. Still, the biography of Dan Sylveste in Alastair Reynolds' *Revelation Space* is described in more detail and readers get an idea of its structure and the way it works.

The biography is commissioned by Dan Sylveste's opponent, Nils Girardieau, who wants to bring to public attention Dan's role in his father Cal's notoriously failed project of scanning the brains of eighty people into a computer, so this biography deals centrally with the failed transition from a human, embodied state to a disembodied existence in a machine, a mind-upload. The description of Dan Sylveste's biography addresses issues central to biography criticism of the twentieth and twenty-first centuries: questions of power and truth, the availability and selection of material, the reception and popularity of biographies, and the form and nature of biography.

Dan Sylveste, who is Nils Girardieau's prisoner at the time the biography is commissioned, is wondering about why his opponent would want to engage in such a project, but it soon becomes clear that it is a question of power: Nils Girardieau wishes to create a version of Dan Sylveste's past that is in his control and that he can use for his own ends. Girardieau has realised that Sylveste is, despite the dubious role he played in his father's undertakings, "still a figure of fascination to the populace" (65) and he knows that biographies can crucially influence the image of a figure of public interest. By taking the project into his hands, Sylveste's opponent taps into the power potentials of biographical writings discussed by theorists such as William H. Epstein: "The entrance of a biographical subject into written discourse is [...] a momentous occasion, an event that can, among other things, reaffirm cultural eminence, contextualize social action, alter literary opinion, deputize political influence, or instruct economic conduct" (222). The fact that Girardieau wishes to employ the biography for his own ends further illustrates the fact that biographical presentation is always subjective to some extent and coloured by its author's attitude towards its subject. Written by Girardieau's daughter Pascale, the biography is ultimately shaped by Girardieau's intentions:

"For all its technical accuracy [...] it remained what Girardieau had always planned: a cunningly engineered weapon of precision propaganda. Through the biography's subtle filter, there was no way to view any aspect of his past in a light which was not damaging to him; no way to avoid his depiction as an egomaniacal, single-minded tyrant: capacious of intellect, but utterly heartless in the way he used people around him. In this, Pascale had been undoubtedly clever. If Sylveste had not known the facts himself, he would have accepted the biography's slant uncritically. It had the stamp of truth." (116-17) by postmodern criticism, many critics agree that since there is no such a thing as the ultimate 'truth' about someone's life, it cannot be told either. Sylveste, however, believes in the facts of his life, but even he has to admit that this is not true of all his experiences: "All that was known [about his expedition to the Shrouds, an unknown alien territory] was what Sylveste himself remembered – and as Sylveste, by his own admission, underwent periods of altered or diminished consciousness in the vicinity of the Shrouds, his memories could not be taken as the literary truth of events." (110) In this case, his fragmentary memories cannot be substantiated by other records, because "most of the information gleaned [...] was lost, including the data transmitted back to the station", which makes "the timescales uncertain" (109) and the "precise order of events [...] questionable" (110).

That the way a person's life is presented is crucially influenced by the material that is accessible to the biographer in the first place and then by the material the biographer chooses to include becomes apparent from the passage quoted above. Since Dan Sylveste is still alive when Pascale writes his biography, she has the chance to elicit first-hand information in interviews. Since he is a prisoner, he does not have the freedom to deny Pascale and her father access to all the other data that exists on his life. Girardieau explains, "we [...] own all your records and archival material. [...] We have access to the documents from the Yellowstone years which no one beyond your immediate family even know exist. We'd exercise a certain discretion in using them of course – but we'd be fools to ignore them." (65) Further, the "harming portrait" of Dan Sylveste is also "shaped by the testimonials of people who had known him" (117), among them also the beta-level, digital version of his own father, Cal. The mis-use of this information makes Dan suspicious of digital material, and he finally reverts to making old-fashioned, hand-written notes: "These days, he favoured pen and paper over modern recording devices where possible. Digital media were too susceptible to later manipulation by his enemies. At least if his notes would be pulped they would be lost for ever, rather than returning to him in a guise warped to suit somebody else's ideology." (147)

Sylveste thus wishes to retain a certain integrity and protect his identity with the help of old-fashioned recording techniques.

Pascale's biography of Dan Sylveste is not the first biography written about him. There were earlier ones, written immediately after the failure of mind uploads, but, as Girardieau explains, "The problem was [...] your previous biographers were too close to the events – too much part of the societal milieu they were attempting to analyse. Everyone was in thrall to either Cal or yourself, and [...] there was no room to step back and see the wider perspective." (64) Girardieau thus addresses a question that surfaces repeatedly in critical discussions of biography, namely that of the distance between biographers and their subjects (see e.g.

Tekcan). He further draws attention to a phenomenon well-known from the actual world of the reader, namely that there is usually not just one biography of a famous or infamous figure, but that more biographies of the same subject are available. This phenomenon once again illustrates the impossibility of telling 'the' ultimate life of a person. Further, it testifies to the popularity of the genre which acts as incentive for ever new biographies to be written. According to Richard Holmes, the (literary) biography "is arguably the most successful [...] literary form which has held a general readership in Britain since the 1960s" (20), and Paula Backscheider makes a similar point for the United States in *Reflections on Biography* (xiii). That the genre is imagined to be still popular in the twenty-sixth century when Dan Sylveste's biography becomes a success, might be extrapolated from the idea that the biography, perceived as an art form that has the ability to confirm and support received values and norms, flourishes in times of crisis and transformation, as has been argued for example by Siegfried Kracauer (78–9).

Pascale's biography, however, is different from earlier biographies of Dan Sylveste, both in scope and in form. Contemporary critics of biography sometimes lament that there is too little innovation concerning the form of biography: In a Guardian books podcast on biography broadcast in 2012, Sarah Crown points out that what we mostly still get today are biographies following the chronological cradle-to-the grave model and she believes that there are too few experimental biographies. Pascale's life writing project is definitely more experimental than the examples found in Stableford's, Stross' and Macleod's novels; and in contrast to the histories envisioned by Grant and Sirhan, the reader is allowed a glimpse of the biography. Its conception is described as follows: "The biography [...] would be capable of being accessed in many ways, from many different viewpoints, and with varying degrees of interactivity. It would be an intricately faceted thing, detailed enough that one could easily spend more than a lifetime exploring only a segment of his past." (91) Since it is not a traditionally written biography but is accessible in virtual reality, it extrapolates from already existing digital biographies and moves beyond the virtual biographies proposed by the Ludwig Boltzmann Institute for the History and Theory of Biography in Vienna as a new form of non-linear, multiperspectival biography:

"In contrast to traditional forms of biography, 'net-biographies' facilitate multiperspectival, non-linear approaches to the subject's life. Here the individual components – text, image, audio recordings, videos etc. – are linked together through a multi-branching categorization and reference system, allowing new and compelling pathways through the biography of the person concerned to be followed each visit." ("Virtual Biography")

Sylveste's biography does not follow a linear, chronological structure and it offers multiple perspectives:

"Pascale's flashbacks were nonsequential; the biography was constructed with no regard for the niceties of linear time. At first [Dan] was disoriented, even though he was the one person in the universe who ought not to have been adrift in his own history. But the confusion slowly gave way to the realisation that [it...] was right to treat his past as shattered mosaic of interchangeable events; an acrostic embedded within numerous equally legitimate interpretations." (95)

When Dan Sylveste immerses himself in the virtual experience of the biography for the first time he has to remind himself that "none of this is real [...] just a narrative strand from his biography" and admits that "[t]hat's how it was [...] How it felt" back then (91), so this form of virtual biography seems to be effective for the recipient. It is a prototypical example of the postmodern biography as outlined by Cornelia Nalepka in 2009: Such a biography, of which there are still not too many examples in the 'real world', would be based on a decentred conception of the subject, blur the boundaries between author and reader and fact and fiction, question the objectivity of the source material and the coherence of life, would be fragmentary and offer not just one but multiple perspectives, feature discontinuous and non-chronological narratives structure as well as reflections on the meta-level (394). Pascale's biography further comes close to the ideal of an 'open biography' proposed by Tobias Heinrich (368), which aims at a multi-layered and fragmentary presentation of a subject that is no longer perceived as unified. The biography devised inside *Revelation Space* thus illustrates that the "juxtaposition of life writing and science fiction [does not only afford] a striking opportunity for posing questions about genre" (Rieder xi), but that life writing projects attempted on the diegetic level of science fiction novels can, since they can rely on improved access to source material and new technological possibilities, be path breaking and inspiring for future biographies in the real world.

On the level of narrative mediation, the characters' comments on the difficulty of compiling the biography and the comments on its truthfulness are, without warning and without any difference in font or layout, interspersed with the experiences and memories recorded in the biography, so that the reader gets an idea of the immersive nature of this new kind of virtual life writing. As the readers re-live part of Dan Sylveste's life along with him, parts of the character's back-story are established. Apart from reminding the population of Dan's past on the diegetic level, the biography thus serves an expository function.

By referring to the biography as "the first major work of indigenous art produced on Resurgam" (123), Pascale answers the question whether biography is an art or a craft, posed for example by Virginia Woolf in 1939, and thus continues a critical discussion on the one hand and an artistic tradition on the other. The biography is presented as a foundational artwork of a newly established civilisation on a planet distant from Earth. Further, the role of the biographer as an artist and not just as a collector and compiler of material is emphasised ("Pascale's narrative", "Pascale's flashbacks" etc.), and thus the biography becomes a means of self-expression as well. The biography is more than just a reminder of the past and a tool of propaganda in a power struggle: it serves to strengthen the present state of a newly-formed society because it manifests its creative potential and establishes an artistic practice. This new art produced on Resurgam, however innovative, experimental and virtual it might be, though, still harks back to monumental biographies such as Boswell's *Life of Johnson* (1791) or Richard Ellmann's *James Joyce* (1959) in its attempt to present a picture of an historical figure supported by an abundance of detail, and thus joins a century-old cultural tradition. The basic impulse to write someone's life and present it to the public is retained and continued.

Conclusion

The life writing projects attempted or discussed by characters in posthuman science fiction novels are not necessarily central to the plots of the novels, but they point towards central issues in the lives of the depicted posthumans. The projects vary in complexity and means of production and mediation, but they all clearly, if self-consciously, inscribe themselves in a tradition of life writing contemporary readers will be familiar with; they even continue discussions central to life writing criticism. They introduce readers to strange aspects of posthuman societies with the help of familiar forms, and are as such an elegant means of exposition. It seems indeed plausible that in times of fundamental change and transition characters should revert to forms that are centrally concerned with questions of identity and which, like autobiography, "inevitably reflect [...] upon what it means to be human" (Bould and Vint 87). The life writing projects discussed here record characters' attempts to grasp and emphasise differences from their ancestors and to create identities of their own. They combine the almost nostalgic desire not to lose all links with the past and the wish to preserve the present moment for future generations of posthumans. However, these impulses, expressed with the help of familiar conventions borrowed from life writing, betray the underlying assumption that (post)humans will still have the urge to record and make their lives into stories in the future, and that posthumans will still have an interest in their past. The assumption that such essential features exist in the first place, and that they will not be lost in a transition from human to posthuman, makes it difficult, if not impossible, to imagine future humans – or posthumans – as truly different. So borrowing from life writing might be an apt means for illustrating the anxieties of those who find themselves in transition since it emphasises continuities rather than discontinuities, but it is not conducive to "imagining what human beings might become in a future of unimaginable difference" (Hollinger 271).

Bibliography

Armitstead, Claire. "Books podcast: Biography lives on – from David Foster Wallace to Dumas." Guardian Online 26 Oct. 2012; http://www.guardian.co.uk/books/audio/2012/oct/26/biography-david-foster-wallace-alexandre-dumas-podcast; 29 March 2013.

Backscheider, Paula. Reflections on Biography. Oxford: Oxford University Press, 1999.

Bould, Mark and Sherry Vint. "Of Neural Nets and Brains in Vats: Model Subjects in Galatea 2.2 and Plus." Biography 30.1 (Winter 2007): 84-104.

Epstein, William H. "(Post)Modern Lives: Abducting the Biographical Subject." Contesting the Subject: Essays in the Postmodern Theory and Practice of Biography and Biographical Criticism. Ed. William H. Epstein. West Lafayette, Ind.: Purdue University Press, 1991. 217-36.

Halpern, Jeanne W. "Biographical Images: Effects of Formal Features on the Ways We See a Life." Biography 1.4 (Fall 1978): 1-14.

Heinrich, Tobias. "Die montierte Biographie: Alexander Kluges Lebensläufe als Modell 'offener' Biographik." Die Biographie – Beiträge zu ihrer Geschichte. Ed. Wilhelm Hemecker. Berlin et al.: De Gruyter, 2009. 367–92.

Herbe, Sarah. "Living in a Cartesian Theatre: Parallel and Serial Lives in Charles Stross's Accelerando and Glasshouse." From the Cradle to the Grave: Life-Course Models in Literary Genres. Eds. Sabine Coelsch-Foisner and Sarah Herbe. Wissenschaft und Kunst. Heidelberg: Winter, 2011. 217-28.

Hollinger, Veronica. "Posthumanism and Cyborg Theory." The Routledge Companion to Science Fiction. Eds. Mark Bould et al. London and New York: Routledge, 2009. 267-278.

Holmes, Richard. "Biography: Inventing the Truth." The Art of Literary Biography. Ed. John Batchelor. Oxford et al.: Clarendon Press, 1995. 15-25.

Jolly, Margaretta. Editor's Note. Encyclopedia of Life Writing: Autobiographical and Biographical Forms. Ed. Margaretta Jolly. 2 vols. London et al.: Fitzroy Dearborn, 2001. 1: ix-xii.

Kracauer, Siegfried. "Die Biographie als neubürgerliche Kunstform." Das Ornament der Masse. Frankfurt a.M.: Suhrkamp, 1977. 75-80.

Lejeune, Philippe. "The Autobiographical Pact." On Autobiography. Ed. Paul John Eakin. Trans. Katherine Leary. Minneapolis: University of Minnesota Press, 1989. 3-30.

MacLeod, Ken. Learning the World: A Novel of First Contact. London: Orbit, 2005.

Nalepka, Cornelia. "Postmoderne Biographik: Dieter Kühns N und Hans Magnus Enzensbergers Der kurze Sommer der Anarchie." Die Biographie – Beiträge zu ihrer Geschichte. Ed. Wilhelm Hemecker. Berlin et al.: De Gruyter, 2009. 393-421.

Reynolds, Alastair. Revelation Space. New York: Ace Books, 2002.

Rieder, John. "Life Writing and Science Fiction: Constructing Identities and Constructing Genres." Biography 30.1 (Winter 2007): v-xvii.

Smith, Sidonie and Julia Watson. Reading Autobiography: Interpreting Life Narratives. Minneapolis and London: University of Minnesota Press, 2010.
Stableford, Brian. The Fountains of Youth. New York: Tor, 2000.
— The Omega Expedition. New York: Tor, 2002.
— Science Fact and Science Fiction: An Encyclopedia. New York and London: Routledge, 2006.
Stross, Charles. Accelerando. 2005. New York: Ace, 2006.
Tekcan, Rana. The Biographer and the Subject: A Study on Biographical Distance. Stuttgart: Ibidem-Verlag, 2010.
"Virtual Biography." Homepage of the Ludwig Boltzmann Institut für Geschichte und Theorie der Biographie. http://gtb.lbg.ac.at/en/en4/2; 25 March 2013.
Woolf, Virginia. "The Art of Biography." The Death of the Moth and Other Essays. London: The Hogarth Press, 1947. 119-26.

The Omega Legend: Or, How the Cyberpunk Discourse Infested the Zombie Genre

Alexander Knorr

Anthropology and the Fantastic

Not long ago the anthropologist Gordon Gray remarked: "For many people the words 'anthropology' and 'cinema' go together like bread and gasoline. This is unfortunate as they have a substantial amount to offer one another." (Gray, x) It may appear even stranger when an anthropologist is not only occupied with film, but with computer games, with science fiction, cyberpunk, horror, and the fantastic. But all these offer a substantial amount to anthropology, too. I even maintain that a contemporary anthropology has no choice but to deal with these genres and forms of media. Anthropology is about trying to understand how people are living, what they do, think, and feel. Anthropologists are interested in cultural meanings, in social processes and structures. Nowadays virtually every design of leading, managing, and coping with life created by human beings is or can be subject of anthropological work. Anthropologists do not cease to stress that they strive to grasp societies and cultures in a holistic way. Nevertheless, when approaching a human collective you need a cardinal point of access, a focus. In order to break through into a sociocultural realm apart from your own, you need a vehicle of access. Universal phenomena which seem to have substantial importance almost everywhere are predestined for this role. For a long time in anthropology said role was fulfilled by kinship or religion, magic and mythology – thus, in anthropology there already is a substantial tradition in dealing with the fantastic.

But with the still accelerating global proliferation of technology another privileged vehicle of access has become obvious. In my view, scrutinizing the interrelationships between human beings and technology is the starting point of choice for anthropological inquiry today. If we do that, we have to understand how people envision technology and by what their dealing with technology is informed. It is my conviction that cyberpunk is crucial in this. Commonly 'cyberpunk' denotes a literary sub-genre of science fiction which emerged during the late 1970s and early 1980s in the USA. At first glance this makes it a case for literary criticism.

But there indeed is a rationale why anthropologists should be interested in such things: "Like the myths of small-scale society as rendered in the anthropological classics of the past, contemporary literary fantasies tell us something about displacement, disorientation, and agency in the contemporary world." (Appadurai 58) As Appadurai explains further: "[M]any lives are now inextricably linked with representations, and thus we need to incorporate the complexities of expressive representation (film, novels, travel accounts) into our ethnographies, not only as technical adjuncts but as primary material with which to construct and interrogate our own representations." (63-64) The fictional needs to be used as primary material for ethnographies because it not just reflects culture and society but also inspires and informs ways of living. It serves both as a model of and a model for, as Clifford Geertz would have it. (Geertz 9, 34, 40)

In Appadurai's thinking the imaginary of these fantasies are haunting the earth in global cultural flows. These flows in turn are situated in abstract landscapes: ethnoscapes, mediascapes, technoscapes, financescapes, and ideoscapes. (33-43) This is a fine idea, no doubt about it, but it provides us with no tools. Appadurai's -scapes are not quite palpable, rather an abstract concept. Foucault's notion of discourse comes in handy here: a system of propositions or statements. A pool or portfolio not unlike its legal-economic analogon, the intellectual property franchise. One set of transitions mentioned in the conference abstract – *inter-media adaptations* and *transpositions into new media* – are easier grasped and dealt with, when we look at them the other way round. Instead of proposing rather linear itineraries followed by fictional material, identifying discourses seems more appropriate.

This view does not focus on, for example: A and B are comic book and computer game adaptations of C, a movie. Rather: A, B, and C are drawing from the same pool of statements, are manifestations and elements of a discourse. This perspective also more properly reflects the actual practices within the industry. For example, within the corporate jungle of *Star Wars* (formerly owned by George Lucas, nowadays by Disney), one of the biggest and most diversified multimedia franchises in existence, there is a vast archive where every single artefact based on the *Star Wars* universe is collected and curated. There even is a full-time employee who sorts the material (not just narrative content, but also visuals, etc.) into six categories defining how close it is to the *Star Wars* canon. This systematics in turn defines what can and what cannot be done with a purchased *Star Wars* licence. Just like the formation rules of a Foucaultian discourse define what can and cannot be stated.

The Cyberpunk Discourse

In my view the mightiest river currently flowing through Appadurai's global mediascapes is what I like to call, conceptually following Foucault, 'the cyberpunk discourse.' 'Cyberpunk' most commonly denotes a subgenre of science fiction, or even 'a variety of Postmodernist fiction' (Nichols), which emerged during the 1980s in the USA. Usually it is linked to a comparatively small group of writers – who called themselves 'The Movement' – comprising William Gibson, Bruce Sterling, Rudy Rucker, Lewis Shiner, and John Shirley. But cyberpunk is not only fixedly associated with Gibson's novel *Neuromancer*, but also with the motion picture *Blade Runner*. Furthermore it is connected with the 1960s New Wave Science Fiction. And just recently Bruce Sterling remarked in an interview: "There are plenty of critics who see 'cyberpunk' as a distant belated echo of London New Wave SF. Maybe it was ever thus."

A discourse in Foucault's sense does not have a beginning in the strict sense of the term. But there are historical thresholds. At the transition from the 1970s to the 80s the cyberpunk discourse reached critical mass, became manifest as a literary genre, and was given a name. My central point here will be that this discourse gathers ever more momentum, is more influential on a global scale than ever, and hence must be considered if we strive to understand our contemporary world. But before this can be shown it needs to be made clear, at least heuristically, what the cyberpunk discourse consists of. What is the pool filled with? What themes, subjects, topoi, plots, scripts, settings, ideas, notions, values, norms, artefacts, signs, symbols, aesthetics, expressive and representational conventions and strategies are within the portfolio?

At the thematic core are the reciprocal effects or dialectics between state-of-the-art science and technology on the one hand, and culture, society, the individual, and even humanity in general on the other hand. The focus may be on digital electronics in all its guises and fictional interpolations, more often than not computer and network technology, but also on bio- and genetic technologies, and nanotechnology. It hardly occurs that technologies are rendered downright negative; rather, their depiction often is fundamentally ambivalent.

In respect to the individual the motif of invasive technologies, up to human-machine fusion, is central. No matter whether these technologies are mechanical, electromechanical, electronic, chemical, psychological, or consisting of combinations of these. From artificial intelligence up to sentient systems, and synthetic humans, both genetically engineered ones and robotic androids. The motifs inevitably culminate to the basic anthropological question: What is human?

In the same context the portrayal of omnipresent information technologies, up to fully immersive virtual realities and the cybernetic vision of uploading human minds into computer systems, powerfully poses one of the most basic philosophical questions possible: What is real?

In respect to society the topos of totalitarian regimes is a prominent one. Those may be nation states, but oftentimes are transnational, megalomaniacal corporations. The latter oftentimes are dubbed 'evil corporations,' in some respects 'mad scientists' as a collective. They may exert societal and social control by heavily relying on ubiquitous and networked surveillance technology – thereby impairing civic rights. Results are dramatically stratified societies with embedded gated communities where the elites live highly privileged. Thus a whole array of contemporary and relevant ethical and political questions is addressed. The core themes are reflected in or transported by specific settings, protagonists, aesthetics, and strategies of representation and narration. The stories are often set within gigantomaniacal metropolitan landscapes. Both on the levels of the street and the cityscape legacy to Fritz Lang's *Metropolis* and Ridley Scott's *Blade Runner*. Sceneries of urban decay on the one hand, and high-tech glitz interiors and exteriors on the other hand are tropes illustrating the two-tier society. The visual appearance of architectural and other artefacts depict retrofitted futures, blending downright futuristic designs with neo-gothic, 19th century, Victorian, or even Baroque styles. In the case of movies and computer games the visuals are complemented by industrial music or soundscapes à la Vangelis. Fittingly the time frames are recognizable near futures, maybe dystopian or even post-apocalyptic (after the nuclear holocaust, ecological collapse, pandemic, rise of the machines ...), and alternate histories.

The protagonists usually are outsiders, outcasts, underdogs, loners, and anti-heroes. Here the influence of hardboiled detective fiction and film noir is very clear-cut. This influence also is manifest in conventions and strategies of representation and narration. The perspective often is one 'from below,' from the fringe of society, or even the underground. Hence resistance and subversion are prominent themes. The anti-heroes, subalterns, and outcasts may be empowered by science and technology, which again points to their ambivalence. (Knorr 64-102)

To me it seems that the discourse sketched above has become so dominant that it doesn't even stop in front of the supernatural and the occult. Which at first glance appears odd for stories firmly bound to 'hard science fiction,' meaning the principle of plausible interpolation of existing science and technology. In order to illustrate my argument allow me to relate how the cyberpunk discourse infested the zombie genre.

The Omega Legend

It may well be a truism, but Stephen King is fond of zombie movies (King, 134), of Romero's classics in particular. Cyberpunk writers and fans are, too. But in George A. Romero's debut *Night of the Living Dead* (1968) none of the canonical elements outlining cyberpunk as a genre can be found – with the exception of the postapocalyptic setting. Ten years later, during the cyberpunk discourse's historical threshold, the picture had changed. Richard Kadrey and Larry McCaffery sum it up:

"'Dawn of the Dead' (George Romero, 1978, Media). The mindless zombies who can eagerly (but placidly) rip-and-devour the flesh of gug-toting bikers (when they're not riding the escalators or being drawn to Blue Lite Specials) and prowl the shopping mall scene of this classic, horrifically funny film are, of course, the same folks we've hurried past on our way to the Cineplex 12. The nightmarish, punk extremities of surreal violence, the relentless exposure of capitalism's banalizing effect on individuals, the insistence on visceral, bodily reality that our airbrushed, roboticized exteriors deny – all would find their way, in transmuted form, into cyberpunk's own brand of dark humor, aesthetic extremity, and notions of guerilla-tactics survival." (Kadrey/McCaffery 1991, 23)

But there is yet more to it, because a discursive link developed. James Kakalios noted that the narrative snippets relating to the mythical origins of superheroes get updated, and at intervals are synchronized with the elements of the empirical world, with what happens in history and technoscience. In 1962 the spider that bit Peter Parker, gave him his superpowers and transformed him into Spider-Man was affected by radioactivity. In the 2000s it was tinkered with by genetical engineering. (33) With the armoured knight it's a similar story. In 1963 Tony Stark had his traumatic experiences, which led to him becoming Iron Man, in Vietnam. In the 2000s he lived through them in Afghanistan. These changes are necessary, I guess – the adaptations allow the superhero-tales to fulfill their mythical functions. (Schechter 1980) What is true for superheroes in a similar way is true for zombie movies. They keep pace with the world. From my perspective, they increasingly become subject to the cyberpunk discourse.

I will make my argument plausible by focusing on the remakes of one and the same subject matter.

It was Mary Shelley who forcefully drove the idea of artificial life and the synthetic human being deep into our global cultural legacy. Her 1818 novel *Frankenstein; or, The Modern Prometheus* accomplished this much more effectively than the lore of the Golem could. Thus, not only science fiction in general, but cyberpunk in particular owes her quite something. What is lesser known is the fact that she also gave us the topos of a world which is emptied by a pandemic of infectious disease until only one single human being is left: *The Last Man*. We don't know for sure, but it is quite plausible that Richard Matheson was inspired by Shelley's novel – or maybe even its 1924 satirical motion picture interpretation directed by Richard Blystone – when he wrote *I am Legend* (1954). In the novel, the whole human race is turned into vampires. Although those vampires have to be killed by driving a stake through their hearts, and garlic is the repellant of choice, Matheson turned considerably away from the supernatural vampire lore. In *I am Legend* the reason why humans turn into vampires is not to be found beyond the grave, but under the microscope – it's a germ. Both George A. Romero and Stephen King have praise for Matheson's book and openly admit that it inspired them a lot. The very first published review of *I am Legend* already gives ample testimony of its belonging to the cyberpunk discourse:

"Most rewarding of 1954's new novels this month is Richard Matheson's I Am Legend (Gold Medal, 25 ¢), an extraordinary book which manages to do for vampirism what Jack Williamson's Darker Than You Think [1948] did for lycanthropy: investigate *an ancient legend in terms of modern knowledge of psychology and physiology,* and *turn the stuff of supernatural terror into strict (and still terrifying!) science fiction.* Matheson has added a new variant on the Last Man theme, too, in this tale of the last normal human survivor in a world of bloodsucking nightmares, and has given striking vigor to his invention by a forceful *style of storytelling which derives from the best hard-boiled crime novels.* As a hard-hitting thriller or as fresh imaginative speculation, this is a book you can't miss." (Boucher 1954, 98 [emphasis mine])

Ten years after publication, Matheson's novel for the first time is adapted to the silver screen as *The Last Man on Earth,* starring Vincent Price – an actor, together with Boris Karloff and Christopher Lee, almost synonymous to cinematic horror. Matheson wrote parts of the screenplay (but was not satisfied with the final outcome), and the movie differs in some respects from the novel. The infected, for example, now very much live up – no pun intended – to the standard vision of a zombie as later established by Romero's movies. The novel's vampires are fast and agile in contrast. As in the novel the reason for the zombification is a pandemic of disease, the origin of which is not explained. Fittingly enough the movie's main protagonist is a scientist, in the novel he was a plant worker.

In 1971 the next movie version of Matheson's *I am Legend* came to the cinemas. *The Omega Man* directed by Boris Sagal, and starring Charlton Heston – in the movie the latter pries quite some guns from dead cold hands. Meanwhile, in the form of New Wave Science Fiction, the cyberpunk discourse has reached significant mass and density. Most notable for our context here is Harlan Ellison's *A Boy and His Dog* and everything that sprouted from it, which I won't follow here and now. Instead, let's return to *The Omega Man*. The story's backdrop having been changed, now the reason for the disease is man-made biological warfare. Every trace of vampire lore is removed. Only the infected's sensitivity to light remained. Although staying well within the Cold War scenario, the movie does not blame the USA, rather the biological war which killed almost all mankind was led between the Soviet Union and the People's Republic of China – another connection to Ellison's *A Boy and His Dog*.

For the 2007 movie version of *I am Legend,* starring Will Smith, the Cold War background was no more interesting. Instead another core element of the cyberpunk discourse was placed at the heart of the story – the ambiguity of technoscience. Now the reason for the disease is a virus which originally was genetically engineered to fight cancer. In the same year a B-picture variant was released: *I Am Omega,* starring Mark Dacascos. Here also a genetically engineered virus has caused everything.

So much on the movies directly based upon Matheson's novel. But there are more recent examples which successfully combine the zombie motif with cyberpunk aspects. *28 Days Later,* starring Cillian Murphy, its sequel *28 Weeks Later,* and of course the *Resident Evil* series, which to date comprises five movies released in 2002, 2004, 2007, 2010, and 2012 repectively. The star of the series, Milla Jovovich, has already become a globally recognized cinematic cyberpunk icon by means of Luc Besson's *The Fifth Element* and Kurt Wimmer's *Ultraviolet.* The Resident Evil franchise is especially interesting, because besides the genetically engineered virus we have an evil corporation and all kinds of cyberpunk aesthetics, from urban decay scenarios via the architecture of the Umbrella Corporation's underground facilities, to Ms Jovovich's costumes and choreography of movement. Little wonder, as the movies are based on the computer game series of the same name, comprising, from 1996 to 2012, 23 games all in all. And computer games, especially the action- and first-person genre, are even more subject to the cyberpunk discourse than motion pictures ever were.

Now you may ask 'What with that immense revival of the Vampire in the wake of Anne Rice?' Well, have you seen *Daybreakers* . . . ? But now that we have reached computer games, let's not go back to the movies, but from the last man on Earth to the last man on Mars.

If we were to do a review of those computer games from the first-person and action genre which have become international hits during recent years, we would find that the majority of them – even when they are not downright cyberpunk like for example *Deus Ex: Human Revolution* – are choke full of elements from the cyberpunk discourse. Even franchises like *Assassin's Creed* bow down to it. Although the main plots have historical settings – the first game during the Third Crusade, the second during the Renaissance, and the third during the American Revolution – the story which forms the framework is pure cyberpunk. The evil corporation 'Abstergo' dissolves the boundaries of time and space by cyberpunkish technology, the 'Animus,' a computer revoking 'genetic memory' and projecting the test person into a virtual reality resurrecting times gone by.

The whole immersive-3D first-person genre, and with it computer games as we know them today, more or less began with the release of id Software's *Doom* in 1993. The innovations, in respect to technology and game design, were groundbreaking. Above all that the story of *Doom* achieved a remarkable feat. The player takes the role of an unnamed space marine sent to Mars. There he is working for the security detail of an evil corporation, the Union Aerospace Corporation (UAC). The UAC also has research facilities on the Martian moons Phobos and Deimos. Secret teleportation experiments are undertaken, opening gateways between the two moons. Then something goes wrong. The systems on Phobos malfunction and Deimos completely disappears. The space marine witnesses how a scientist is turned into a Zombie when the malfunction occurs. During his lonely fight through Phobos station he encounters the rest of the personnel, either slaughtered or zombified. But there are even more dangerous adversaries: monster demons!

After much fighting and gore our hero reaches the teleportation gate and beams over to the station on Deimos. The same picture here, only more gruesome. Parts of the station's architecture now are strangely altered and warped – pictures from H. P. Lovecraft's brain. Having fought his way through Deimos station the lonesome space marine realizes that the moon is no longer part of our known universe – it now floats above Hell itself. Within *Doom* environments like straight out of Doré's visual interpretations of Dante's *Inferno* seamlessly go together with high-tech environments of the cyberpunkish kind, dirty and lived-in. The same is true for the protagonists. The undead and demonic monsters act along a soldier in high-tech armoury. In the 2004 remake, *Doom 3,* robots join the cast.

Visually we of course had this juxtaposition before, such as in Ridley Scott's 1979 *Alien*. There, on the one hand we have the xenomorph, swiss artist H. R. Giger's creature, and on the other hand the high technology furnished by the evil corporation Weyland-Yutani. This contrast becomes especially visible during the showdown when Lt. Ripley defeats the alien by means of a power loader exoskeleton. But *Doom* goes a step further. *Doom* fuses cyberpunk science fiction with the supernatural. Best illustrated by Pinky from *Doom 3* who is half demonic monster, half robot. The realms of the occult and high-tech now are compatible.

In the introduction to Charles Stross' 2003 novel *The Atrocity Archives,* which achieves a similar fusion, I found the following beautiful passage:

"Imagine a world where speaking or writing words can literally and directly make things happen, where getting one of those words wrong can wreak havoc, but where with the right spell you can summon immensely powerful agencies to work your will. Imagine further that this world is administered: there is an extensive division of labour, among the magicians themselves and between the magicians and those who coordinate their activity. It's bureaucratic and also (therefore) chaotic, and it's full of people at desks muttering curses and writing invocations, all beavering away at a small part of the big picture. The coordinators, because they don't understand what's going on, are easy prey for smooth-talking preachers of bizarre cults that demand arbitrary sacrifices and vanish with large amounts of money. Welcome to the IT department." (MacLeod 2003, xii)

Kenneth MacLeod's analogy textually achieves the same as the design of Pinky does visually. Both are renditions of what Arthur C. Clarke said in one sentence: "Any sufficiently advanced technology is indistinguishable from magic." (Clarke, 36) In this respect my coinage of anthropology is very much in line with the more than a hundred years old anthropological tradition of dealing with the fantastic.

Bibliography

Primary Works

28 Days Later. Dir. Danny Boyle. 20th Century Fox, 2002.
28 Weeks Later. Dir. Juan Carlos Fresnadillo. 20th Century Fox, 2007...
Alien. Dir. Ridley Scott. 20th Century Fox, 1979.
Dawn of the Dead. Dir. George Andrew Romero. United Film Distribution Company, 1978.
Daybreakers. Dir. Michael Spierig and Peter Spierig. Lions Gate Entertainment, 2009.
Eidos Montreal and Nixxes Software. Deus Ex: Human Revolution. Computer Game. Shibuya: Square Enix, 2011. DVD-ROM.
Ellison, Harlan Jay. A Boy and His Dog. New Worlds 189 (1969): 4-16.
– "A Boy and His Dog." The Beast That Shouted Love at the Heart of the World. Ed. Harlan Ellison. New York: Avon, Harper-Collins, 217-254.
Gibson, William. Neuromancer. New York: Ace, 1984.
I Am Legend. Dir. Francis Lawrence. Warner Bros., 2007.
I Am Omega. Dir. Griff Furst. The Asylum, 2007.
Id Software. Doom. Computer Game. Mesquite et al.: id Software et al., 1993. Floppy Disk.
Id Software. Doom 3. Computer Game. Santa Monica: Activison, 2004. CD-ROM.
Matheson, Richard. I Am Legend. Robbinsdale: Gold Medal Books, 1954.
Metropolis. Dir. Fritz Lang. Berlin: Ufa, 1927.
Night of the Living Dead. Dir. George Andrew Romero. The Walter Reade Organization, 1968.
Resident Evil. Dir. Paul Anderson. Screen Gems, 2002.
Resident Evil: Apocalypse. Dir. Alexander Witt. Screen Gems, 2004.
Resident Evil: Extinction. Dir. Russell Mulcahy. Screen Gems, 2007.
Resident Evil: Afterlife. Dir. Paul Anderson. Screen Gems, 2010. Film
Resident Evil: Retribution. Dir. Paul Anderson. Screen Gems, 2012.
Shelley, Mary. *Frankenstein; or, the Modern Prometheus.* London: Lackington, Hughes, Harding, Mavor & Jones, 1818.

— The Last Man. London: Henry Colburn, 1826.
Stross, Charles. The Atrocity Archives. London: Orbit, 2003.
The Fifth Element. Dir. Luc Besson. Gaumont Film Company, 1997.
The Last Man on Earth. Dir. John G. Blystone. The Fox Film Corporation, 1924.
The Last Man on Earth. Dir. Ubaldo Ragona and Sidney Salkow. American International Pictures, 1964.
The Omega Man. Dir. Boris Sagal. Warner Bros., 1971.
Ubisoft Montreal. Assassin's Creed. Computer Game. Montreuil: Ubisoft, 2007. CD-ROM.
Ubisoft Montreal. Assassin's Creed II. Computer Game. Montreuil: Ubisoft, 2009. CD-ROM.
Ubisoft Montreal. Assassin's Creed III. Computer Game. Montreuil: Ubisoft, 2012. DVD-ROM.
Ultraviolet. Dir. Kurt Wimmer. Screen Gems, 2006.

Secondary Works

Appadurai, Arjun. Modernity at Large: Cultural Dimensions of Globalization. London: University of Minnesota Press, 1996.
Boucher, Anthony. "I am Legend by Richard Matheson." Rev. of I am Legend by Richard Matheson. Magazine of Fantasy and Science Fiction 7.5 (1954): 98.
Clarke, Arthur C. Profiles of the Future: An Inquiry into the Limits of the Possible. London: Macmillan, 1973 [1962].
Foucault, Michel. L'archéologie du savoir. Paris: Gallimard, 1969.
Geertz, Clifford James. "Religion as a Cultural System." Anthropological Approaches to the Study of Religion. Ed. Michael Banton. London: Tavistock, 1966. 1–46.
Gray, Gordon. Cinema: A Visual Anthropology. Oxford, New York: Berg, 2010.
Kadrey, Richard, and Larry McCaffery. "Cyberpunk 101: A schematic guide." *Storming the Reality Studio: A Casebook of Cyberpunk and Postmodern Science Fiction.* Ed. Larry McCaffery. Durham, London: Duke University Press, 1991. 17–29.
Kakalios, James. The Physics of Superheroes. New York: Gotham Books, 2005.
King, Stephen Edwin. Danse Macabre. New York: Everest House, 1981.
MacLeod, Kenneth. "Introduction: Charlie's Demons." The Atrocity Archives. Ed. Charles Stross. London: Orbit, 2003. xi–xv.
Nichols, Peter Douglas. "Cyberpunk." The Encyclopedia of Science Fiction. http://www.sf-encyclopedia.com/entry/cyberpunk 2013 31 March 2013.
Schechter, Harold. New Gods: Psyche and Symbol in Popular Art. Wisconsin: University of Wisconsin Press, 1980.
Sterling, Bruce. Interview by Gunhead. Cyberpunkreview.com. 3 Mar. 2011. 31 March 2013.

Contributors

AMOS BIANCHI is head of program development at NABA (Nuova Accademia di Belle Arti Milano, (www.naba.it) and Domus Academy (www.domusacademy.it). At the same institution, he has been Assistant Professor of Theory and Method of Mass Media, and he is currently Lecturer of Research Methods and History of Cinema. He is a Ph.D. researcher of the University of Plymouth, Planetary Collegium.

GRACIELA SUSANA BORUSZKO, Dr., is an associate professor at the International Studies and Languages Division at Pepperdine University. For much of her career, she focused on teaching and researching in the areas of Hispanic Philology, Comparative Literature and Linguistics, French Studies, French Philology, Hispanic Studies, Literatures and Cultures. Her multicultural background forged in her a passion for Cultural, Linguistic and Literary Studies in its multiple representations. Her research topics include: the transnational, identity, ethnicity, multiculturalism, migration, languages and its linguistic and literary spaces. As a result she counts with many publications, nationally and internationally. Her latest book: *A Literary Map of Spain in the 21st Century*.

DANA FREI has earned a doctoral degree with her work on television series focusing on LGBTQ issues: *Challenging Heterosexism from the* Other *Point of View – Representations of Homosexuality in Queer as Folk and The L Word* (2012). She has further shown a special interest in superhero fiction in her research as well as her lecturing in the field of popular literature and media studies. Further interests include autobiographical comic books, stardom and star image, as well as utopian and dystopian literature. She currently teaches English to adolescents at a business school, lectures on young adult future fiction at a teacher training college and functions as co-editor of the online journal of youth media research *kids+media*. Further information: www.ipk.uzh.ch/aboutus/people/frei.html

INKEN FROST obtained her diploma in cultural studies at the European University Viadrina Frankfurt (Oder) in 2009. She is currently a PhD student with Prof. Christa Ebert. Her doctoral thesis focuses on the semantics of the topos of the forest in the European fairy-tale. On this subject she has also published several articles. Her research interests include roleplaying as collaborative narrative, the validity of romantic dream theory for Dostoevsky's work, the *Doppelgänger* and the uncanny.

GABRIELA GALATI is a researcher, editor and art historian specialised in contemporary art and new media. She is Professor in Theory and Methodology of the Mass Media at NABA, Nuova Accademia di Belle Arti Milano; and was Adjunct Professor in Semio-Epistemology in Social Science at the Universidad de Buenos Aires and at the Universidad del Museo Social Argentino. She is also Director at FL Gallery, and is currently pursuing a PhD at Plymouth University/Planetary Collegium, where her study focuses on how new technologies, especially the Internet, affect the contemporary artistic field.

MICHAEL HEITKEMPER-YATES, Ph.D., is currently engaged as an associate professor of British and American literature within the Graduate School of Humanities faculty of letters at Kobe University. His research interests include philosophical and literary forms of irony and the narrative structure of parody. At present, he is working on a study of postmodern metafictional praxis in American literature during the 1960s and 1970s (with special attention to the subversive poetics of writers such as Donald Barthelme, Robert Coover, Ishmael Reed, John Barth, and Thomas Pynchon).

SARAH HERBE is Assistant Professor at the Department of English and American Studies, University of Salzburg. Her research interests include life writing, paratexts, seventeenth- and eighteenth-century poetry, British science fiction and relationships between poetry and popular culture. Her PhD thesis on Characters in New British Hard Science Fiction with a Focus on Genetic Engineering in Paul McAuley, Alastair Reynolds and Brian Stableford was published in 2012 (Winter). She is the editor of *From the Cradle to the Grave: Life Course Models in Literary Genres* (2011) and *New Developments in the European Fantastic* (2012). www.uni-salzburg.at/ang/herbe

MINWEN HUANG is currently a Ph.D. graduate in the Department of English at the University of Leipzig in Germany. She studies the genre of Fantastic Literature in the light of literary imaginary and cognitive poetics, and is investigating the writings on artificial human for her doctoral thesis. Her master's thesis, *The Matrix Trilogy as a Postmodern Myth*, was published in 2008.

DANIEL ILLGER, Dr., since 2007: member of the Collaborative Research Centre 626 "Aesthetic Experience and the Dissolution of Artistic Limits" at Freie Universität Berlin; PhD completed in 2009; since 2011: Research associate at the Cluster of Excellence "Languages of Emotion" at Freie Universität Berlin. Publications include: *Heim-Suchungen. Stadt und Geschichtlichkeit im italienischen Nachkriegskino* (Berlin 2009), *Pedro Almodóvar* (Co-Editor with Hermann Kappelhoff, Munich 2008), *Zeitschrift für Fantastikforschung* (Co-Editor with Jacek Rzeszotnik und Lars Schmeink, since 2011). www.loe.fu-berlin.de/zentrum/personen/wimi/daniel_illger/index.html

NILS JABLONSKI, M.A., born in 1985, studied German literature and visual arts as well as applied literary and cultural studies in Dortmund and Zurich. Works as a research associate at the Institute for German Language and Literature of the Faculty for Cultural Studies at TU Dortmund University. PhD project on literary Kitsch. Additionally: Curatorial work. Further scientific interests: experimental literature and poetry, avant-garde, film and media studies, humor research as well as popular culture. www.studiger.tu-dortmund.de/index.php?title=Nils_Jablonski

ALEXANDER KNORR, PD Dr., has studied social and cultural anthropology with psychology and theatre studies as minors. In 2002 he got his doctoral degree and in 2009 his Habilitation at the Ludwig-Maximilians-Universität München. At the moment he is *Privatdozent* there. Since more than a decade his research work constitutes an amalgam out of technology- and media-anthropology, popular culture, science and technology studies, and epistemology. This forced his regional interest, Asia's great mountains, and his former systematic focus (religion, mythology, and magic) somewhat into the background. Currently he strives towards a re-fusion between sociocultural anthropology and science and technology studies, hoping that a multiply symmetric anthropology will result. www.ethnologie.uni-muenchen.de/personen/privdoz/knorr/index.html

THOMAS KULLMANN, Prof. Dr., is Professor of English Literature at the University of Osnabrück. Currently, his main research interests are Shakespeare and Renaissance Culture; English Children's Fiction and Images of India in 19th-century Britain. His publications include two books on Shakespeare, one on landscape and weather in the nineteenth-century English novel and one on English children's and young adults' fiction as well as numerous articles on English Renaissance Literature, Victorian and twentieth-century literature and culture, and children's literature. He also edited two volumes of essays on aspects of English children's fiction. www.ifaa.uni-osnabrueck.de/mitarbeiter/tkullman

CHRISTINE LÖTSCHER is a research associate at the Institute of Social Anthropology and Cultural Studies at Zurich University. Her current research focuses on theories of nonsense and materiality. Her doctoral thesis on magic books in fantasy, *Das Zauberbuch als Denkfigur*, is part of the SNF-project "Transitions and Dissolving Boundaries. World, Knowledge and Identity in Fantastic (Children's and Youth) Literature and Media". Moreover, she works as a literary- and film critic.

DIETER PETZOLD (b. 1945) studied English and German at the Universities of Würzburg and Erlangen, and at Amherst College (U.S.A.). He has taught English literature at the University of Erlangen-Nuremberg and, as a guest professor, also at the University of North Carolina at Chapel Hill (1983-84) und at the University of British Columbia at Vancouver (1992-93). He is the author of books on 19th-century nonsense literature (1972), on 19th-century English literary fairy tales (1981), on *Robinson Crusoe* (1982) and on J.R.R. Tolkien (1980 and 2003), has (co-)edited several books of scholarly essays, and published numerous articles on English, American, Canadian and German literature, in particular on various genres of the fantastic and on children's literature. Since 1996 he has been the editor of *Inklings – Jahrbuch für Literatur und Ästhetik* (www.inklings-gesellschaft.de/en/?Yearbooks).

ALESYA RASKURATOVA (Freie Universität Berlin) studied in Osnabrück and Berlin, where she received her B. A. in 2012 with a thesis on hybridity in H. P. Lovecraft's works. Currently, she is finishing her Master in English Studies, with a focus on Medieval English literature. To her special research interests belong late medieval literature (Chaucer and the Pearl poet), as well as psychoanalysis, gender studies and fantastic literature. https://fu-berlin.academia.edu/AlesyaRaskuratova

LARS SCHMEINK, Lecturer of Literature and Media; teaches at the University of Hamburg and the HarborCity University. PhD candidate (2014) at the Humboldt University Berlin, Thesis: Biopunk Dystopias: Genetic Engineering, Society and Science Fiction. President of the Gesellschaft für Fantastikforschung (Association for Research in the Fantastic); Co-Editor of the *Zeitschrift für Fantastikforschung*; Managing Editor of the *SFRA Review*. Selected Publications: *Fremde Welten: Wege und Räume der Fantastik im 21. Jahrhundert*. Ed. with H.-H. Müller (2012, De Gruyter, Berlin); *Collision of Realities: Estab-*

lishing Research on the Fantastic in Europe. Ed. with A. Böger (2012, De Gruyter, Berlin). www.larsschmeink.de.

PETRA SCHRACKMANN, MA, studied German Literature and Linguistics, European Folk Literature and English Literature at the University of Zurich, Switzerland. 2008–13 she worked as a research assistant at the Institute of Popular Culture Studies at the University of Zurich, where she still teaches. Her master's thesis on Peter Pan adaptations was published in 2009. Her doctoral thesis on the fantastic in recent film adaptations of literature for children and young adults is part of the research project "Transitions and Dissolving Boundaries. World, Knowledge and Identity in Fantastic (Children's and Youth) Literature and Media", supported by the Swiss National Science Foundation. Research interests: the fantastic, adaptation, gods, vampires, werewolves, zombies, fan fiction and fandom, comics. www.isek.uzh.ch

SARA TAGLIALAGAMBA holds a fellowship at the Istituto Nazionale di Studi sul Rinascimento (Firenze, Palazzo Strozzi) and is a Post-PhD scholar at the École Pratiques Hautes Études (Paris, Sorbonne). She got her PhD in 2010 at the University of Siena and has dedicated herself to the study of Leonardo working on surprisingly less known subjects such as the grotesques, fantastic animals, automations, robotics, clock making, architecture and hydraulics and has written several books on his artistic and technological production. With Carlo Pedretti, she recently published the National Editions of the drawings and manuscripts of Leonardo da Vinci for Giunti and Treccani (Firenze 2014).

INGRID TOMKOWIAK, Prof. Dr., teaches Popular Literature und Media at the Institute of Social Anthropology and Cultural Studies at Zurich University and is head of research at the Swiss Institute for Children's and Youth's Media SIKJM, Associated Institute of Zurich University. She concentrates on cultural analysis of popular literature and media for all ages. Scientific lead of the research project "Transitions and Dissolving Boundaries. World, Knowledge and Identity in Fantastic (Children's and Youth) Literature and Media", supported by the Swiss National Science Foundation. Co-editor of *Kinder und Jugendliteratur in Medienkontexten* (2014) and *Kinderliterarische Mythen-Translation. Zur Konstruktion phantastischer Welten bei Tove Jansson, C.S. Lewis und J.R.R. Tolkien* (2013). www.isek.uzh.ch, and www.sikjm.ch/forschung/

MARIA-ANA TUPAN, Prof. Dr., is Habilitated Professor of the English Department of Bucharest University, where she teaches courses in British literature and in applied literary theory. She was affiliated with Penn State University as Senior Fulbright Grantee in 1994-95. She is a member of the Romanian Writers' Union and of several academic societies (EFACIS, Gesellschaft fur Fantastikforschung, Flann O'Brien Society). She has published 17 books, and a considerable number of book chapters and articles in the fields of literary history and theory, comparative literature, genre theory, discourse analysis, and cultural studies. The list of her publishers include Cambridge Scholars Publishing, Publishing House of the Romanian Academy, Universitätsverlag Winter (Heidelberg), Bucharest University Press.

ALETA-AMIRÉE VON HOLZEN studied German literature and language, European folk literature (popular literature and media) and Old Norse literature. 2008–2013 she was employed as a research assistant at the Institute for Popular Culture Studies, Dpt. Popular Literature and Media (now: Institute for Social Anthropology and Cultural Studies), at the University of Zurich, Switzerland, where she is still lecturing. Her doctoral thesis focuses on the double identities of masked heroes and is part of the SNF-project "Transitions and Dissolving Boundaries. World, Knowledge and Identity in Fantastic (Children's and Youth) Literature and Media". www.isek.uzh.ch

Fantastikforschung / Research in the Fantastic

Christine Lötscher; Petra Schrackmann; Ingrid Tomkowiak; Aleta-Amirée von Holzen (Hg.)
Übergänge und Entgrenzungen in der Fantastik
Fantastik verhandelt virulente kulturelle und gesellschaftliche Entwicklungen und hinterfragt bestehende Grenzziehungen. Dabei werden hybride Zonen der Autonomie entworfen, die als Gegenentwürfe zum herkömmlich vermittelten Verständnis von Welt, Wissen oder Identität gelesen werden können.
Untersucht werden fantastische Erzählungen in all ihren historischen und gegenwärtigen sowie sämtlichen medialen Erscheinungsformen, vom Roman über den Film bis zum Computerspiel. Weltenwechsel, Zeitreisen, Verwandlungen, Mischwesen sowie Grenzübertritte aller Art stehen ebenso im Fokus wie Genrehybridisierung und Intermedialität.
Bd. 1, 2014, 584 S., 54,90 €, br., ISBN-CH 978-3-643-80186-9

LIT Verlag Berlin – Münster – Wien – Zürich – London
Auslieferung Deutschland / Österreich / Schweiz: siehe Impressumsseite

Literatur: Forschung und Wissenschaft

Uwe Durst
Theorie der phantastischen Literatur
Diese strukturalistische Untersuchung entwickelt eine allgemeine Theorie der Phantastik. Im Gegensatz zu bisherigen Arbeiten wird das Wunderbare nicht als Abweichung von der Wirklichkeit, als Verstoß gegen naturwissenschaftliche Vorstellungen begriffen, sondern als Bloßlegung literarischer Verfahren, deren immanente Wunderbarkeit durch Traditionsbildung unkenntlich und heimlich geworden ist.
Fragen der Inszenierung und literaturgeschichtlichen Entstehung des Phantastischen werden beantwortet. Themenlisten und psychologistische Spekulationen werden durch eine Theorie des wunderbaren thematischen Materials ersetzt. Ausführlich wird auf die Veränderungen des Genres im 20. Jahrhundert eingegangen und das Verhältnis zu anderen Genres, wie Kunstmärchen, Kriminalerzählung, Science Fiction usw., erörtert. Ein abschließendes Kapitel widmet sich der parodistischen Bedeutung der Phantastik.
Diese Arbeit, die mit erheblichen Korrekturen die Forschungslinie Tzvetan Todorovs fortsetzt, entwirft eine operable Systematik und stellt der Forschung ein terminologisches Instrumentarium zur Verfügung.
Bd. 9, 2. Aufl. 2010, 440 S., 29,90 €, br., ISBN 978-3-8258-9625-6

LIT Verlag Berlin – Münster – Wien – Zürich – London
Auslieferung Deutschland / Österreich / Schweiz: siehe Impressumsseite